My Remarkable Journey

LARRY KING

My Remarkable Journey

with Cal Fussman

WEINSTEIN
BOOKS

To the women in my life

My wife, Shawn Southwick-King,
who gets the civilian purple heart

and

Wendy Walker, my executive producer
and, more importantly, my friend

The reason there's nothing better than fatherhood is what it produces. In my case, it produced: Andy, Larry Jr., Chaia, Chance, and Cannon. They are my reason for being.

Memory

MEMORY IS FUNNY. You can remember something that happened to you on an afternoon fifty years ago, but you forget where you had lunch yesterday.

The problem is, the longer you live, the more there is to remember. Therefore, it makes sense that you have a better memory at thirty than you have at seventy-five. I have more than seventy-five years of memories embedded in me. Another day was added to that yesterday. Another will be added today.

Sometimes, photographs can refresh our memories. Other times, they *become* our memories. I remember talking with John F. Kennedy Jr. about the famous picture of him as a three-year-old saluting at his father's funeral. He had no memory of that moment, but he knew the picture. He'd seen the picture all his life. The picture turned into his memory.

Like photos, stories can preserve memories. But they can also touch them up. There's always going to be some embellishment when you tell a story. How can you not embellish? Maybe you forget what somebody said at a certain point and you substitute a phrase that's a little funnier. It gets a laugh, so you bring it along for the next telling. After a while, you can't remember the incident any other way.

So the memories on the following pages may not be exactly the way they happened. A lot of them have been preserved by humor. But their general essence is correct.

There are times when I get a little frustrated when I can't remember something. There's that old joke: "I just read this great book, *Ten Steps to a Perfect Memory* by, uhhhh . . ." But I never forget jokes and funny stories. Humor is the one thing I retain fully. I can remember moments that made me laugh from the time I was a kid. And I have a feeling that humor will be the last part of my memory to go.

This may surprise you if you've only seen me on my CNN show. But if I hadn't gone into broadcasting, I probably would have become a comic. Making people laugh is still my biggest kick.

Memories are all we have. Lose them, and we have nothing. But memories touched by humor, those are the best of all.

There are other memories throughout this book. These are the memories of my family, my friends, and those who know me best. They are sure to include thoughts about me that I wouldn't think about myself. They'll help you see me as a whole. I'm not going to read these other memories until the book is published. I certainly wouldn't want to be in the position to edit them or tell anybody what to say.

So the funny thing is, when I pick up this book, I may be just as surprised to learn about my life as you.

Chapter 1

What Am I Doing Here?

Y OU'D SEE ME in a different way if you were sitting at my table at Nate 'n Al Deli over breakfast every morning. First of all, I don't wear the suspenders there. Second, you'd realize that I hate eggs. And third, you'd have to imagine me in a car trunk—because sooner or later the story of the "exclusive interview of the century" would come up.

This took place a while back. There was a producer on my show—call him Bob. A good guy, but the most hyper person I've ever known. One day Bob got a call from a bigwig at CNN International.

The bigwig said, "Bob! An incredible thing is about to happen!"

"What? What? What?" Bob was already on the edge of his seat.

"We've got an exclusive with Osama bin Laden."

"Holy shit!"

You can understand Bob's reaction. The United States' armed forces had been searching for bin Laden since September 11, 2001. Television news couldn't have landed a bigger interview unless it found talking aliens.

3

"It's going to be in Pakistan."

Bob was nodding furiously.

"But here's the only way it's going to work. We're going to fly you and Larry in to a very remote area. You won't have a film crew with you. We can't bring any equipment. The film crew will be theirs. The sound crew will be theirs. The interpreter will be theirs. They'll do the taping. When the interview is finished, they'll give us the tape to bring home. That's the deal we had to make.

"Oh, and Bob, there's one other proviso. When you and Larry get to Pakistan, you're going to be driven to a special spot. Then you and Larry will get out of the car. You will wait at that spot. Larry will get in the trunk of another car so he can be driven to Osama. There's no other way to do it. They can't risk anyone knowing the slightest details about Osama's whereabouts.

"Larry will do the interview. They'll give him the tape. He'll get back in the trunk. The car will return to you. You and Larry will go back to the airplane. Then you come home."

The phone call ended and Bob went berserk. As much as he wanted the exclusive of the century, he was also worried about the ramifications. *Larry's had quintuple bypass surgery. What if he has a heart attack in the trunk? What if they kill Larry? What if they take Larry hostage? What if they take Larry and me hostage? But how can we pass this up?*

Bob called his mother. "Ma, what should I do?"

And his mother said, "Well, how long will Larry be in the trunk?"

"They didn't say. Just that he'll be in the trunk."

Bob became frantic. He was calling people left and right. He was going crazy. Couldn't contain himself. My executive producer, Wendy Walker, had to cut the April Fools' Day joke short before he went absolutely nuts.

The thing is, if Bob had stopped in for breakfast at Nate 'n Al, he would've discovered that he had no reason to worry. George, who sits in the aisle, would've set him straight. "Larry would be in the trunk before you could finish asking him if he wanted to go," George would've told him. "And I'd lay even odds that when Larry got ready to leave, Osama would get in the trunk with him so they could keep on talking."

That may be a little farfetched. But one thing I can tell you. If I had gotten into the trunk, I'd be in a very familiar place. I'd be asking myself the same question I've been asking for the last fifty years.

What am I doing here?

Those five words sum up my whole life.

I'm telling you, there are times when my life feels like an out-of-body experience. I have to pinch myself to believe that little Larry Zeiger from Brooklyn is being beamed 22,300 miles into space, bounced off a satellite so that some guy in Taipei can watch me ask questions along with people in 200 other countries and territories around the world.

Was it really me, the kid who never went to college, who set up that million-dollar scholarship at George Washington University? Who got into a traffic accident with John F. Kennedy and came to know every president since Nixon? Who had Frank Sinatra sing to me while the two of us were alone in the greenroom? Who walked with Martin Luther King Jr. and then sat down with King's murderer? Who got a phone call during dinner at Mr. Chow's in Beverly Hills from the king of Jordan? Who fathered two boys while I was in my late sixties and watched them collect candy on Halloween dressed in Larry King masks and suspenders?

Nahhhhhh. The little Larry Zeiger I remember sat at home listening to the radio broadcast of the 1949 All-Star

Game at Ebbets Field because I couldn't afford a ticket. How could I have walked on the field during batting practice at an All-Star Game forty years later and been asked to sign autographs . . . by the players?

Come-mahhhhn, as we used to say in Brooklyn. It's just not possible. The little Larry Zeiger who watched people crying in the streets of Brooklyn when Franklin Delano Roosevelt died never dreamed of getting into the Oval Office. But Larry King has been many times. Once I even sat with Hillary Clinton in the White House under a portrait of Eleanor Roosevelt. When I casually mentioned, "Oh, yeah, I interviewed Eleanor," it was Hillary who gasped.

Did Mikhail Gorbachev actually show up to meet me for dinner wearing suspenders? Did a college crowd in Florida actually chant "Lar-ry! Lar-ry! Lar-ry!" when I showed up to interview John McCain during the recent presidential election? And did a Secret Service agent really turn to me and say, "Maybe we should be protecting *you*?"

It still amazes me that my oldest friend, Herbie, and I were invited to the governor's mansion in New York. Get this. The butler actually came over to us and asked, "Would the gentlemen care for an aperitif before retiring for the evening?"

Aperitif? Who ever heard a word like that in Maltz's candy store?

Maybe Mario Cuomo, the guy who invited us, best understood what an unbelievable ride it's been. Once, before he presented me with an award honoring the children of immigrants at Ellis Island, he told this story:

Somebody gave Larry King a present—cloth to make a suit. So Larry went to the tailor in Miami and asked for a suit with two pair of pants.

"I'm sorry, Larry," the tailor said. "There's not enough material to make you two pair of pants."

So Larry went to another tailor, in Washington.

The tailor measured the cloth and shook his head. "Sorry," the tailor said, "just not enough material here for an extra pair of pants."

Larry tried Los Angeles. Same thing happened.

Finally, Larry went home to his old tailor in Brooklyn.

"Sure," the old tailor in Brooklyn said, "I'll make you a suit with two pair of pants *and* a vest."

"How can you do that?" Larry asked.

The tailor said, "Because in Brooklyn, you're not that big."

Chapter 2

Nine Books

I WAS WALKING home from the library carrying nine books. That's the way my memory sees it. I can't know for sure if it was exactly nine books. Maybe I picture nine books because I was nine years old. I'm certain that I was nine years old, because I'm sure of the date—June 9, 1943. There were a lot of books under my arm on that summer day because I loved books. I wonder what happened to those nine books . . .

There were three squad cars in front of my apartment building. Flivvers, we called them. I don't remember exactly when I started to hear my mother's screams. But as I hurried up the steps, a cop quickly came down, straight for me. He picked me up and the books went flying.

I'm not sure if I knew the cop. But I may have. For years, before the war started and my father went to work in the defense plant, he'd owned a little neighborhood bar and grill. He was friendly with all the cops. The cops loved my father the way they loved any bar owner who had a great sense of humor. I remember having my own police costume when I was very young. A badge and a little nightstick came with it. I'd make like I was walking the beat.

The cop put me in the squad car. He told me that my father had died. Heart attack.

I didn't cry. I remember that. I didn't cry. I was more befuddled than anything else. It must have been difficult for the cop. He started the car and drove. We wound through the streets of Brownsville and ended up at a movie theater.

I'll never forget the movie, *Bataan,* starring Robert Taylor as Sergeant Bill Dane. It was about a bunch of American soldiers trying to stave off the Japanese invasion of the Philippines.

Sergeant Dane and his patrol are ordered to blow up a bridge to stop the advancing enemy. They're cut down one by one until only Sergeant Dane and two others remain. The first is killed by a sniper. The second is stabbed by a Japanese soldier who'd been playing dead. The movie ends with Sergeant Dane firing his machine gun straight into the camera at the Japanese soldiers coming at him in one last act of courage and defiance.

I don't remember what it was like when I got home that day. A lot about that day I've blocked out. My younger brother Marty has blocked it out, too. He was only six at the time. But there are a few more memories attached.

I didn't go to the funeral. I'd been so close to my father— yet I refused to go. I stayed at home. There must've been somebody watching me, but I remember being alone. I remember bouncing a spaldeen—the Spalding rubber ball we used to play stickball—off the front stoop.

Two other things I can tell you for sure. I never went back to that library again, and from that day on I was nervous if I saw a squad car in my neighborhood. If one parked by my apartment building, I'd start running home, in fear that my mother had died.

Chapter 3

Momma & the Radio

WHAT'S THAT OLD JOKE? A little boy walks in on his mother and father making love.

The boy yells, "Oh my God!" and runs out of the room.

The father says to the mother, "I better go settle him."

So the father goes to look for the kid. Doesn't find him in his room. Finds him upstairs in the grandmother's room, in bed with the grandmother.

The father says, "Oh my God!"

The kid says, "Now you know what it's like to see someone sleeping with your mother."

It's hard for any kid to see his mother as a young woman. My mother was *Mom* to me, not Jennie Zeiger. While I knew how tough it was on her after my father died, it wasn't until years later that I was able to see the bigger picture. Jennie had a pretty rough life.

I remember her telling me about her earliest memory. It was fear—fear of the eye exam at Ellis Island.

I've seen photos of the packed ships coming to America at the museum on Ellis Island. But it's impossible for me to imagine what she felt when she first set eyes on the Statue of Liberty. She was seven years old, the youngest of seven sisters. Her mother was with them on the SS *Arabia*, though I'm not certain about her father. It was 1907. What could a seven-year-old have known about the eye test? Would she have even heard of the strange-sounding disease the doctors were on the lookout for? Trachoma.

Trachoma was a highly contagious eye infection often caused by overcrowded conditions and lack of sanitation. It could lead to blindness, and doctors at Ellis Island could spot it in tiny bumps under the eyelid. Maybe, in her situation, seven-year-old Sheine Gitlitz knew all she needed to know. Fail the eye test, and you got sent back to Russia.

How could I describe what she went through to my eight- and nine-year-old sons today? So many thoughts must have been running through her mind. *What if my mother and sisters pass the eye test and I don't? What will happen then?* It must have been nerve-racking for all of them. It was impossible to know what was coming. But it's clear now. Those who failed the eye test and were sent back to Europe were not in a good position a generation later. Hundreds of Jews in the city my father would emigrate from, Kolomyya, in what was then Austria-Hungary and is now Ukraine, would be rounded up and executed by Nazis in 1941. Fourteen thousand more would be sent to the Belzec death camp.

I don't know if there was a celebration when my mother's family all passed their physicals, or just plain relief. Sheine Gitlitz became Jennie when she arrived in Brooklyn. When Aron Zeiger arrived on the SS *Minnekahda* sixteen years later, in 1923, he became Eddie.

Eddie took a room in the same building where my mother's family lived. That's how they met. There aren't any wedding pictures remaining. The only story passed down from their wedding day is that Eddie and Jennie went to see the play *No, No, Nanette*. I suppose that's more significant to New York Yankee fans than anyone else. The owner of the Boston Red Sox was so eager to bring an earlier version of the show to the stage that he sold Babe Ruth to the Yankees in order to raise the money.

Jennie and Eddie were married in 1927. Jennie gave birth to a son a year later. Then the Depression hit—in more ways than one. Their son, Irwin, was some kind of prodigy. Many years later, I remember hearing that Irwin was at a second-grade level well before his time. His death certificate shows that he died at age four. I can't fathom my parents' devastation. They didn't get Irwin to the hospital quickly enough after he complained of stomach pains, and he died from a burst appendix.

I was born a year later—on November 19, 1933. I never saw a picture of Irwin around the house. My parents didn't speak of him. But the impact of his death showed up in other ways. When I was three years old I became dizzy and had ear pains. I remember being in the back of a cab on the way to the doctor, and my father yelling at the driver, "Hurry, hurry!"

My parents poured their life into my younger brother and me. My mother overprotected us. If she had ever written a book it would have been called *Dress Warm*. My father worked long days at the bar and grill to achieve his dream of stepping up and moving to Bensonhurst. Ahhh, Bensonhurst! To be five minutes from Coney Island! By the sea! Now, *that* was living. Moving from Brownsville to Bensonhurst at the time must have been the difference between bringing home $5,000 and $6,000 a year. But it remained a dream.

My father didn't get Bensonhurst. He got Pearl Harbor instead. I don't know how my mother reacted when my father told her he was going to enlist after the Japanese attack. It didn't matter. My father was rejected because he was too old.

So he sold his bar and grill and went to lend a patriotic hand at a defense plant in New Jersey. His heart attack struck, I was told, while he was in the middle of telling a joke.

Two weeks after the police officers arrived at our apartment to tell us, the next blow struck. My mother's mother died. Jennie Zeiger was a forty-three-year-old housewife with two kids. Eddie hadn't left behind any insurance.

The irony is that not long after my father died, his dream came true. One of my mother's sisters helped us find a tiny attic apartment in Bensonhurst. The rent was something like thirty-four dollars a month. There was one slight problem. We didn't have money coming in to pay for it.

We got by on what was then called Relief. Inspectors used to come to our apartment to look at the meat in our refrigerator. You weren't supposed to have good-quality meat on our income. When you were on Relief, you were inspected to make sure that you stayed poor.

My mother was a great seamstress. She would take in dresses to hem from people on the block for a little extra cash. We weren't supposed to have extra money. If people downstairs saw the inspectors coming, they'd run to tip us off and we'd scurry around and hide the clothes that my mother was altering. When you come up poor, those are the little things you remember.

I began to notice that I couldn't read the blackboard at school right after my father's death. First, the teacher moved me to the front row. Then, my eyes were tested. New York City bought me my first pair of glasses. The way it worked was, you got a slip from what was then the equivalent of the welfare department. You'd take the slip down to the optician's office on 14th Street in Manhattan and they'd give you the glasses for free.

The glasses you got on Relief had wire rims. Getting called

Four Eyes was bad enough. Wire rims made it worse. There was a stigma attached. Everybody who saw you in those wire rims knew that your family was poor. I hated those glasses. Years later, the same style actually came into fashion. But you'll never find a picture of me after the age of ten wearing wire rims.

Looking back, it's no wonder I couldn't see everything that my mother was going through. I was too busy making her and everyone else feel sorry for me. I lost interest in school— just stopped reading. I must have associated books with my father's passing. I'd been a very good student, even skipped third grade. Suddenly, my mother was asking teachers to forgive my missed homework assignments because I was upset over my father's death.

Everybody else who sang the mourner's prayer at Hopkinson Synagogue looked at least forty years old. *Yisgadal v'yiskadash sh'may rabo* . . . I purposely recited it in a way that provoked pity. Years later, a psychologist friend suggested that anger was the reason—anger at my father for leaving me. I didn't go in for analysis. He was just a friend. But I can't think of a better explanation. Why didn't I go to the funeral? Why didn't I cry? I was so close to my father. I can still see myself on his shoulders at the Macy's Thanksgiving Day parade. Why did I use his death to gain advantage over people? It showed even more resentment to make everyone around me feel pity.

If a man asked my mother out on a date, my brother and I would throw things and fight with each other as soon as he walked through the door. We'd make it impossible for anyone to want to come back. Later on, we both regretted that a great deal. Jennie Zeiger might have had a chance at a lot more happiness, and we might have had more happiness, too.

Young, losing a son, losing a husband, losing a mother, without a job—raising two boys. My mother taught me resilience, and she taught me by example. After a short time, she got a job as a factory seamstress. It didn't mean much more money, but we were able to get off Relief.

I never saw my mother buy anything for herself. She lived for her sons. She cooked and served dinner at the same time every day. Lamb chops, well done, dripping with fat. Breaded veal cutlets. Latkes. Kasha varnishkas. Potato kugel that you would die for. My mother didn't know it, but she was basically cooking heart attacks. If you want to get an idea of what Eastern European Jewish food tastes like, go to Sammy's Roumanian Steak House on the Lower East Side of New York. It's wonderful food. But they hand you Bromo-Seltzer as you walk out.

It's not hard to understand why the portions were so big in Jewish restaurants or why the meals were everything in my home. For centuries, the Jews of Europe lived without security. Any minute your property could be confiscated, your life could be taken, the meal you were eating could be your last. Make your meal the best and eat all of it—that was the way life was lived. The second reason to eat everything on your plate was because of the people who didn't have. Not eating what was in front of you while people were starving was the biggest shame of all.

If you didn't eat, you insulted my mother. Even if you ate the whole dinner and left a bite of cherry pie, she'd say, "Oh, you ate to please me." I don't remember my mother ever eating with my brother and me. She cooked, served, and sat to watch us eat. Then she took the dishes away to wash.

Maybe because I want to remember her happy, the clearest image I have of her comes from after I became a big shot on the radio and was able to move her down to Miami. I can still see her serving me lamb chops.

"How are the lamb chops?"

"Delicious, Mom."

"Ask me how I got the lamb chops."

"How Mom? How'd you get the lamb chops?"

"I went to the butcher shop and I looked in the case at the lamb chops—but they were not very attractive lamb chops. Just ordinary-looking lamb chops. So I said to the butcher, 'Are those all the lamb chops you have?'

"He said, 'That's it, lady, take it or leave it.'

"So I said, 'Perhaps you know my son.'

"'And who is your son?'

"'Larry King.'

"'Larry King is your son?'

"Then he took me to the back room. And *that's* how I got those lamb chops."

That was my mother. She always found a way to be proud and get me the best that she could.

There was another woman who came by to help out when I was young. Auntie Bella, we called her. She was not an aunt by blood. She was Scottish. My brother and I called her Auntie because we loved her. She had white hair in a bun. She was old. Her father had served in the Civil War and she had a letter that President Lincoln had written to him. Auntie Bella cooked for us and cared for us while my mother was working. On one Christmas, she had a relative dressed as Santa Claus come down our chimney right in front of my eyes. We had a Christmas tree in our kosher apartment so that Auntie Bella would feel at home. She was family.

But together, my mother and Auntie Bella couldn't be my father. It was my father who dealt the smacks.

One of the most vivid memories I have from childhood comes from after I'd fallen from the shiny black iron fence topped with spikes in front of our apartment. I had broken my arm and was at home with a cast. I was sitting out front when a huge black car pulled up.

"Hey, kid, c'mere."

I must have gotten a million warnings about staying away from strangers. There was no sin worse than going over to a stranger in a car who offered candy. I moved a step closer, figuring I could run for it.

A guy got out and opened the trunk. If I saw candy, I was outta there. But curiosity got the best of me and I peered in. There was no candy. There were comic books. The whole trunk was filled with comic books. And I loved comic books!

"I told my kid if he misbehaved one more time he was going to lose his comics to the first kid I see," the guy said. "You're the first kid."

I took the treasure up to our apartment.

"Daddy, look," I said when he got home.

"How'd you get them?"

"A man pulled up in a car."

"You went to the car?"

"Yeah."

"What did I tell you about strangers?"

"But—"

Whack!

There was another time when I didn't go to Hebrew school. I came in for dinner as if everything was normal and joined the family at the table.

"How was Hebrew school?" my father asked calmly as he ate his soup.

"Fine."

Whack!

I fell right off the chair.

"Eddie!" my mother gasped. "What are you doing?" Someone had seen me on the street at the time of Hebrew school and tipped my father off at the bar and grill.

"Don't lie!"

They say that discipline is a father's way of showing love.

There were times later in my life where a few more of those whacks might have come in handy. My mother's love did not come with smacks. Her biggest weakness was that she felt sorry for my loss and spoiled me. If I had blown a hole in a bank and taken thousands of dollars, she would have asked the police, "Did somebody make a mistake in his checkbook? Maybe my son had a good reason."

She apologized, gave excuses, and got me out of every mess I got myself into. Which enabled me to get into the next mess because I knew that somehow she'd get me out of that one, too. Over the years, so many people came forward to try to fill the hole left behind by my father. I don't know if they could sense what I'd lost. It's a good question. But in the beginning, the emptiness was not filled by a man. It was filled by the radio.

My days started and ended with the radio—a dark brown Emerson shaped like an arch, with speakers on both sides. Sometimes my mother, my brother, and I would sit around and stare at the radio as the sound came out. It sounds crazy. What did we do when the radio was on? We looked at it.

I'd mimic the shows in my deepest baritone. *Who knows what evil lurks in the hearts of men? The Shadow knows . . .* The Shadow wasn't invisible. He had the power to cloud men's minds so that they couldn't see him. He'd learned it in India. There was Captain Midnight, brought to you by Ovaltine. All of us in the Captain Midnight club had our special decoder. *And now boys, here's your message for tomorrow. Thirty-six.* You'd work the decoder. T. *Fifteen.* E. . . . *Terror tomorrow on Caaaaaaaptain Midnight!*

We didn't have television then. But radio was more exciting than watching television because your mind could picture anything. Listening to a gavel pound at a convention was much more dramatic than watching it. I remember talking about this many years later with Rod Serling, who was famous for writing *The Twilight Zone*.

"We used to think the scripts on radio were better than on television," he said. "They weren't. Radio just allowed you to imagine better. Let's say I'm doing a radio script. I write, 'There's a dark foreboding castle at the top of the hill.' Your mind can see that castle any way you want. If I write the same thing in a television script, I've got some guy coming over to me, saying, 'Mr. Serling, how would you like that castle? You want steeple tops?'"

I became a radio freak. I knew exactly what was on and when. One of my favorite shows early on was *Uncle Don*. He did a great kids' show. He would read the comics on Sunday in a wonderful voice. I had my Uncle Don piggy bank. It was green and yellow and had his picture on it. "Don't forget, kids, to save your money." I loved Uncle Don. He had this theme song:

Rippity-ripscar-hi-lo-zee
Homonio-figgidee-hi-lo-dee
Rodee-kazolts with an alakazon
Sing this song with your Uncle Don
Good night, little boys and girls!

One night, I must have been ten years old, Uncle Don signed off with his trademark, "Good night, little boys and girls!" and then we heard, "That should hold the little bastards until tomorrow."

I took my Uncle Don piggy bank and threw it out the window. My mother went crazy. "What are you doing? There's money in there!" She ran down three flights of steps to pick up the coins. I've never been much for psychobabble. But I'd be hard-pressed to argue with any psychologist who linked that moment to my financial problems later in life. "Even at an early age, Larry was throwing his money right out the window." When I look back, I don't see the moment as being about money. To me, it was really about passion.

We never heard from Uncle Don again. But my love for the radio only grew as I got older. I would go to the shows and watch the sound-effects men rub cellophane together to simulate the crackling of fire.

Best of all, there were Red Barber and Arthur Godfrey. Red made baseball come alive. He taught me the game. He described baseball in a way that went straight into your soul. There was nothing like the tension of a great Brooklyn Dodgers game. I can still remember Red Barber on opening day. "Spring training is over," he said. "They now play in hate."

Red was so great with pauses. He could really set you up and make you lean in toward that radio. In the war years, announcers couldn't travel with the team. They used to announce the accounts that came in by telegraph. We'd hear the tick, tick, tick, and think that we knew what they meant. *That's a double!* Sometimes, the ticker would break. I remember Ronald Reagan telling me that when the ticker broke while he was announcing games he'd have the batter foul off eleven straight pitches until the telegraph came back up. Baseball is a sport made for radio. But there's nothing like going to the park. I'll never forget entering Ebbets Field for the first time, being struck by how green the grass was, how brown the dirt, how white the lines. I'd sit in the bleachers of Ebbets Field, roll up the scorecard, and broadcast the game as if I were Red.

Arthur Godfrey was something else. He was the first rule breaker, and he encouraged me to take risks. One day I was home from school with a fever. My mother was working and my brother was at school. Godfrey was on, and he went into a Peter Pan peanut butter commercial.

He said, "I talk about Peter Pan peanut butter every day.

When I tell you how good it is, you can believe me or you can not believe me. But I'm not going to give you the same old message today. What I'm going to do today is I'm going to eat some. I know this breaks the rules, because it's not going to sound right. But I'm going to take this dollop of Peter Pan peanut butter and I'm going to put it in grunddmadrudmdrmgdrrumumnurdurdumdmdm."

I got out of bed, got dressed, went to the store, and bought some Peter Pan peanut butter. I was eating it on the way home.

By the time I was in junior high school, I already knew. You could see it in the school yearbook. They asked me what I wanted to be, and I told them: a radio announcer.

ANOTHER POINT OF VIEW

Marty Zeiger

BROTHER

There's no denying that our situation would have been different if my father had lived. We wouldn't have gone on Relief. There would have been more stability and discipline in our home. And we wouldn't have moved when we did.

So much of Larry's childhood was formed by where we moved—Bensonhurst. It's one of those things. If you make one little change in life, it changes everything that follows.

Chaia King

DAUGHTER

I wasn't there. But when I try to imagine my father at nine, I see the child of Jewish immigrants who's absolutely loved.

I see the classic and overprotective mother. I see him very close to his father. I see the family struggling financially, but with a very strong sense of home. Then in one moment his father is taken, and I think he was crushed in his soul.

He may have been angry at his father for leaving. But ultimately that falls upon the God whom his mother was taking him to worship at temple. Something in him turned that day. I don't know that he's ever cried about his father's death. It's one of my softnesses and pains for him, because if he hasn't cried, then that anger and grief is still stored. It got translated into a go-go-go personality that never stops to reflect. In a way, he turned that grief into good. He turned it into a great career, and he became famous. But that doesn't make that pain go away.

Chapter 4

Home Is Where the Friends Are

P AUL NEWMAN once told me that whenever he arrived in a
city halfway around the world after a long flight, he would
turn on the hotel television to see me. I was his connection to America, he said, his connection home.

A lot of people have made comments like that over the
years. The map that is the backdrop of my CNN set is one of the
most recognized television images in the world. I've been in front
of that backdrop night after night for almost a quarter of a century. Maybe, as Woody Allen once joked, 80 percent of success
is simply showing up. But that sense of home that people talk
about, there's much more to it than just sitting behind a microphone night after night. My guess is, it comes from Brooklyn.

I couldn't imagine a better place to grow up than Brooklyn in the '40s. Back then, Brooklyn had all the benefits of a
small town. The butcher and the owner of the candy store
down the street were like your extended family. There was permanence. After all these years, a photo of my friend Sid and
his all-star basketball team still hangs in a glass case in the
Jewish Community House of Bensonhurst. And yet the Brooklyn we grew up in was bigger than Philadelphia. You could get

on the subway and go to see one of three major league baseball teams. Brooklyn was home to millions of immigrants. So
it was a place where permanence intermingled with change. It's
said that if you're walking down any street in America today,
one out of six people you bump into will have some association with Brooklyn.

I not only realized what a great place it was after I left, I
knew it was a great place at the time. Anybody who spent his
formative years in Bensonhurst will tell you that those years
were the best years of his life. Nobody moved, nobody divorced, and your friends were your friends forever. Fifty years
later, you could be walking down the street, meet somebody
you knew casually from high school, and you'd be best pals in
five minutes. Maybe you can say this about a lot of places. I've
never grown up anywhere else and have no way to compare.
Except that Mario Cuomo once told me, "Everybody heard
about Bensonhurst. I don't know what it is, I grew up in
Queens. I had a lot of friends, and a great childhood, but
there's something about where *you* grew up. We heard about
it in Queens."

Simply walking to the corner of 86th Street and Bay Parkway gave you friends with nicknames.

There was Inky Kaplan, who told a teacher he'd drink the
bottle of ink on his desk before he'd apologize for something
he'd done in class. He had blue teeth for six months . . . and
grew up to become a dentist.

There was Hoo-ha Horowitz. You'd mention somebody to
him and he'd say, "Who?" as if he didn't hear you. And you'd
say, "Hah?" That's how he became Hoo-ha.

Joe Bellen was Joe Bush. I don't know why he was Joe
Bush. But he was Joe Bush, and he'll always be Joe Bush.

I was Zeke the Creek the Mouthpiece because I was always talking and it rhymed.

My best friend, Herb Cohen, was Herbie the Negotiator. Herbie was a troublemaker who specialized in getting us out of trouble after getting us in neck deep. Our chemistry was perfect. I love stimuli. Herbie was a stimulus.

I met him at Junior High School 128 when we both were given signs that said Stop and were assigned to be traffic monitors in front of the school. "How about you keep your side moving," Herbie suggested, "while I keep my side moving." We waved the cars right into each other and created a traffic jam that stretched for blocks.

The principal demanded to see us . . . and our mothers. It was one of many times my mother was forced to make the trek to that office. But at least that time she became friends with Herbie's mother.

There are a million Herbie stories. But the one that tells them all is the Moppo story. It happened while we were in ninth grade. In the New York City system, ninth grade was the final year of junior high school. The following year, we'd be going to Lafayette High.

In the middle of the year, we noticed that a kid we called Moppo wasn't showing up for school. His real name was Gil Mermelstein. But we called him Moppo because he had wild curly hair. A few more days passed, still no Moppo. So we went by Moppo's house to find out what happened. There was me, who wanted to be a broadcaster. There was Herbie the Negotiator, who wanted to be a lawyer. And Brazzi Abbate, who wanted to be a doctor.

All the shades at Moppo's house were drawn. Sitting on the stoop in front of their building was Moppo's cousin, who lived in New Jersey. He was Moppo's only living relative in the Northeast.

There'd been a tragedy, the cousin told us. Moppo had contracted tuberculosis. As soon as they found out, Moppo's parents took him to Tucson, Arizona, with the hope that the climate would help him recover.

The cousin had come from Jersey to tell the school that Moppo had moved, and to wait for the phone company to disconnect the line.

"Listen, there's no reason to hang around until tomorrow to tell the school," Herbie told him. "You can go home to Jersey after you're done with the phone company. We'll go to the office tomorrow and inform them of the situation."

"Will you do me that favor?" the cousin asked.

"Sure."

The cousin left. We were walking down the street. I can still see this, and it still goes through my bones. Herbie said, "I got an idea."

"What? What are you gonna do?"

"We'll tell the school that Moppo died. In the meantime, as Moppo's best friends, we'll go around and raise money to send flowers to his family. We'll collect the money and use it to get hot dogs and knishes at Nathan's. It's foolproof. The school is gonna call the house. But nobody's there. The school don't know about the cousin in Jersey."

"Yeah, but what happens if Moppo comes back for high school?"

"We'll all be at Lafayette by then," Herbie said. "It'll become a joke."

We decided to go along with it. We went to Mrs. Dewar's homeroom the next day looking incredibly forlorn.

"Moppo's dead."

Oh, the crying. The girls. The friends.

Mrs. Dewar reported it to the office. The principal, Dr. Cohen, called the house. The operator told him the phone had been disconnected. The office staff wrote "Deceased" on Moppo's records. Herbie, Brazzi, and I went around collecting money for flowers. Then we headed off to Nathan's and stuffed ourselves on hot dogs and knishes.

A couple of days later, a message was waiting for us at homeroom. Herbie, Brazzi, and Larry were wanted in the principal's office. As we were walking down the corridor, I was almost crying. My father was dead and I was in trouble again. Brazzi was going, "I'll never be a doctor. I'll never be a doctor." Herbie was saying, "No problem. No problem. We'll just tell 'em we *heard* that Moppo died. We'll act thrilled that he's still alive. We'll say we sent the money to charity and we'll do our best to get it back."

We went into the principal's office and Dr. Cohen was beaming. "Sit down, my young friends," he said.

He started to tell us that junior high schools had been looking for a way to attract positive publicity. Most high schools were able to do this through coverage of their sports teams— but not junior highs. At a faculty meeting, a question was raised: What can we, at PS 128, do to show ourselves in a good light?

"Somebody mentioned how the three of you raised money on behalf of your friend Gil Mermelstein," he said. "We thought it would be a good idea to have an assembly. The Gil Mermelstein Memorial Assembly. It'll be a couple of weeks before graduation. We'll present a plaque to the outstanding student in the school. At the presentation, we'd like the three of you to be onstage in honor of your late friend. The *New York Times* has agreed it would make a good feature story."

This would have been the perfect time to confess. But we were either scared, caught up in the ego of the moment, or both.

We left the room, and Herbie actually said, "You know, when you think about it, some day Moppo will die. This award *will* kick in."

Time passed and the day of the ceremony came. The three

of us stepped up to the stage dressed in suits. The whole school filled the auditorium. The winner of the Gil Mermelstein award was there to get the plaque. The principal was giving it his all for the *New York Times* reporter.

That day, that damn day, Moppo came back to school. In the annals of the history of tuberculosis, this was medicine's finest moment. Moppo had been cured.

The corridors were empty as Moppo came into PS 128. He didn't know from nothing. He found a janitor or someone, asked what was going on, and was told that the entire school was at a special assembly.

Moppo went down to the auditorium. There were two ways he could enter: through the side and some Chinese curtains (very inconspicuous). Or through two big brass doors in the rear that opened to the light.

Moppo opened the brass doors just as we finished the Pledge of Allegiance. The first thing he saw was a banner: GIL MERMELSTEIN MEMORIAL.

Herbie immediately spotted him. He was thinking, *Moppo is not the brightest guy in the world. But he knows what "memorial" means.*

Moppo froze. The kids in the back row sized it all up immediately. Moppo was alive. Herbie, Larry, and Brazzi glommed us for money. The kids knew it the second they saw him, because they were New York City kids. New York City kids are a step ahead. Laughter began to fill the room. The principal didn't know what was going on. He didn't recognize Moppo. But the *New York Times* reporter was sitting up front, so there was obvious discomfort. Herbie stood up—to this day he doesn't know why he did this—and said, "Go home, Moppo, you're dead!"

Moppo ran, ran right out the doors. There was pandemonium in the auditorium. In the middle of the chaos, we could hear the winner of the Gil Mermelstein plaque asking, "Do I still get the award? Do I still get the award?"

The principal looked at us and said, "Report to my office immediately!"

We walked to Dr. Cohen's office in panic. I was almost crying. My poor mother. How was she going to get me out of it this time? Brazzi was saying, "I'll never be a doctor. I'll never be a doctor." And Herbie was saying, "Let me handle this."

When we got to the principal's office, Dr. Cohen said, "I've never been so humiliated in all my years in education. You are all suspended from school. Go to your lockers. Take all your stuff out. Go home. Get out of my sight."

Herbie said, "You're making a big mistake."

"What do you mean?"

"It's true, we invented Moppo's death. And you're definitely right to suspend us. But think of the consequences. You'll have to file a report with the school board. Somebody on the school board is going to say to you, 'Let me get this straight, Dr. Cohen. Three nudnick kids come into school one day and tell you that a student is dead. You make one call to the house. The phone is disconnected. You write the student up as dead and plan a ceremony in his honor?'

"Oh, yes"—Herbie was on a roll—"we'll be suspended. But I don't think you'll ever be a principal again in the city of New York." Herbie didn't stop there. Oh, no. "Right now, it's local," he said. "Why don't we just forget it?"

Dr. Cohen shook his head, a beaten man. He went out to talk to the *New York Times* reporter, who viewed the events as more of a *Daily News* story and agreed not to write anything about it. Herbie went on to advise presidents and became a part of the Strategic Arms Reduction Talks team that negotiated with the Soviet Union. Brazzi became a brain surgeon in Buffalo. Moppo is still alive and lives in Florida. And I got my diploma with the rest of them.

Looking back, I could compare our childhood in Brooklyn to improvisational theater. We wouldn't have called it that at the time. We were just making our own entertainment. Herbie and I invented a vaudeville comedy routine called Spark and Plug that cracked up high school audiences. But there really was no better stage for our antics than Sam Maltz's candy store on the corner of Eighty-fifth and Twenty-first Avenue.

Maltz was a grouchy little guy shaped like a snowman. He always had a cigarette in his mouth, though I never remember him taking a puff. In front of his store was a gum-ball machine that dispensed a handful of sunflower seeds for a penny. Four booths lined one wall. There was a jukebox, a place for newspapers and candy. And a counter where you could get the greatest drink ever invented—the chocolate egg cream.

I don't know how the egg cream was named. There is no egg in it, nor any cream. The ingredients are milk, Fox's U-Bet chocolate syrup, and seltzer. There's a right way to make one. First, you pour in the milk, then the syrup. You stir a little. Then you fill the glass up with seltzer until you get a foamy top, then stir again until the foam looks like the head on a beer.

Sometimes I didn't have the required seven cents, or maybe I did, but just wanted to bust Maltz's chops. So I'd order a two-cents plain. That was ordinary seltzer. I'd take a drink, lean over the counter, and say, "Maltz, do you think you could squirt in just a little syrup?"

Maltz would grunt and give me a quick pump of syrup. I'd stir, take another sip, and say: "Maltz, would you happen to have just a little milk?"

The joy wasn't so much in the drinking, it was in the drama of watching how far we could push Maltz before he exploded.

One day we noticed that we didn't need to put a penny into the machine with sunflower seeds out front. If we turned the knob, a handful of seeds spilled right out. So we all sat and ate sunflower seeds the entire day. Oh, the buildup. Anyone who came through the door would get a cupped hand over his ear and a whisper: "Free sunflower seeds . . ." We watched Maltz smile all afternoon as he glimpsed the run on his machine. It was empty when we left.

The next day Maltz cornered us in a craze.

"You robbed me! I saw you eating sunflower seeds all day long! I had dreams of five hundred pennies in the machine! But there were no pennies! And my dreams did not come true! You robbed me!"

"Not so fast," Herbie said. "Can you prove this in a court of law, Maltz? Do you have any witnesses?"

Maltz sold the store not long afterward, and it was said that we'd run him out of Brooklyn.

The guy who bought it was fiery and we loved to drive him crazy even more. Moe, his name was. One day we played Frankie Laine singing "The Cry of the Wild Goose" on the jukebox.

My heart knows what the wild goose knows,
I must go where the wild goose goes
Wild goose, brother goose, which is best?
A wanderin' fool or a heart at rest?

It's one of those songs that just spin around in your head and won't ever come out, which was bad enough, but we played it over and over on the big Wurlitzer, maybe thirty-nine straight times. It must have seemed like a hundred and thirty-nine to Moe, but when he tried to stop us, Herbie refused.

"We're good-paying customers," Herbie said. "We have a right to listen to the jukebox and play anything that's on it!"

That was too much for Moe. He snapped, nearly leaped over the counter, and yanked the mighty Wurlitzer out of the socket, pushing and kicking it out the door as he screamed: "You want to know where the wild goose goes? This is where the wild goose goes! Now play what you want on the jukebox, my little lawyer shyster. Out! Out!"

There's another story that I've got to tell even though it happened a few years later. I love the Carvel story. So I'm going to tell it now.

It happened in November of 1951. I was eighteen years old. Me, Herbie, and Howie Weiss were standing around the corner arguing the merits of ice cream. Its cost and its taste. We were arguing, arguing, arguing, back and forth.

Herbie said, "You can't beat Breyers and the cost is pretty good."

I was saying how I liked Borden's.

And Howie said, "Yeah, but we gotta talk about Carvel."

Carvel is a chain of ice cream stores. They were all over back then. They had soft ice cream and they had hard ice cream that you could get in scoops. The company was created by Tom Carvel. I came to know Tom very well. Years later, he came on my show to talk about this story.

Howie said there was a Carvel in New Haven, Connecticut, where you could get three scoops for fifteen cents. Herbie said that was a lie. I said it was a lie. Nobody gave you three scoops for fifteen cents. It just couldn't be done. So we were betting Howie that this Carvel in New Haven didn't serve three scoops for fifteen cents.

The only way to prove this, of course, was to go there. So we called our parents and told them we were going to New Haven. But, of course, we couldn't go to New Haven without taking Hoo-ha. You had to take Hoo-ha. Hoo-ha added to any scene he stepped into.

He wasn't funny. Well, he was funny, but he didn't know he was funny—just like Yogi Berra. Yogi Berra never said anything to be funny. When someone once asked him, "Do you know what time it is?" and he said: "Do you mean, now?" he meant that seriously. There are shadows in the outfield of Yankee Stadium. When Yogi said, "In Yankee Stadium, it gets late early," that was a very definitive statement. Everything Yogi said was 100 percent right. "Nobody goes to that restaurant because it's too crowded."

Just listening to Hoo-ha's voice made everything he said better. Hoo-ha's voice is comically deep and earnest and impossible to describe but not hard to imitate. Once you hear it, you'll never forget it. I'll do it on the audio book. Herbie used to imitate it for his kids. They grew up thinking Hoo-ha was a character Herbie had invented. Then one day, Hoo-ha showed up at their house and one of the kids ran to the other and said: "Hoo-ha is real!"

When we got to Hoo-ha's house he was just sitting down to eat dinner.

"Hoo-ha, you want to go to Carvel?"

We could have said, "Hoo-ha, you want to go to Afghanistan?" and he would have gone.

His mother said—she called him Hoo-ha, too—"Ve're eating."

Hoo-ha said, "It's Carvel, Mother. It's dairy and we're having dairy. It's OK." His family kept kosher. "Carvel is two blocks away. I'll be right back."

He got in the back of the car. We didn't say anything. We just started driving along. We pulled onto the Belt Parkway and into the Brooklyn Battery Tunnel. Hoo-ha had no objections. We were talking football, talking baseball.

We were on the West Side Highway. Then we were on the Major Deegan Expressway, passing a sign that said: "Massachusetts/Connecticut."

Hoo-ha said, "I hate to interrupt this very stimulating conversation. But about three hours ago, you came to my house and said, 'Hoo-ha, you want to come to Carvel with us?' I said, 'Yeah.' And now I see that we're going to either Massachusetts or Connecticut. Will somebody tell me what the hell is going on?"

Herbie said, "Hoo-ha, Howie says that there's a Carvel in New Haven that serves three scoops for fifteen cents."

Hoo-ha forgot about his mother. He forgot about his father. He said, "I'll bet you, Howie. I'll bet you they don't. Nobody serves three scoops for fifteen cents."

So Hoo-ha bet him. Now, Howie had about twenty dollars in bets.

We pulled into New Haven and it was snowing. It was an early-season snowstorm.

Howie said, "Hold it. That block! There it is! Right there!"

We could see the guy inside closing up. We drove into the parking lot. But Herbie said, "Hold it. This could be a trick. Howie might know this guy." That's just the way Herbie thought. "Howie could go out, tell the guy about the bet, and set the whole thing up. Larry, why don't you go out, order three scoops, and see how much it costs."

"OK," I said. I got out of the car and went into the store. I stepped up to the counter and said, "Three scoops, please."

The guy said, "Fifteen cents."

I went back and told Herbie and Hoo-ha we'd lost the bet. We decided it didn't have to be a total loss—this was some bargain. We decided to eat the guy out of Carvel.

Hoo-ha said, "You know, if I have twenty of them, I'll be even."

So we were ordering and ordering. Finally, the guy looked up and said, "Fellas, can I have a word with you?"

"Sure," we said.

"I'm having my best day since the Fourth of July . . . and it's snowing. What are you doing?"

"Well, we came to your Carvel."

"You live around here?"

"No."

"Where do you live?"

"Brooklyn."

"Brooklyn? There's hundreds of Carvels in Brooklyn."

"Yeah, but we wanted to come to *your* Carvel."

"Why?"

"Cause Howie said that you served three scoops for fifteen cents."

The guy said, "Doesn't everybody?"

"No."

He said, "No wonder I'm losing money!"

Now the story gets a little bizarre. We'd never seen New Haven, so we went downtown. God, I can see this like yesterday. We were driving down a street and suddenly cars stopped in front of us. Cars pulled in behind us. People came out of doors and they were putting signs on cars. The signs said: REELECT MAYOR LEE. They put these signs on cars in front of us. On cars behind us. They put a sign on our car.

It was election eve. There was a rally for Mayor Lee supporters at New Haven High School, and we were caught in the middle of it.

Herbie left the sign on his car and Lee ended up getting write-in votes from Brooklyn.

We went to the rally at the New Haven High School gym. They had all these seats set up. Chairs were set up onstage for the speakers. They had coffee and doughnuts. Hoo-ha was putting doughnuts in his pocket. He was way ahead of the game now. He had doughnuts to bring home.

Someone came over to me and said, "You know what your

friend Herbie is doing? He's going around telling everybody how hard you work. He's telling everyone you're the hardest working kid in New Haven for the mayor."

"He's doing that?" Well, then I was going to talk about him. So I went around telling people about Herbie.

I swear to God, the PR director for the campaign came over. "Fellas, come here. The mayor's going to speak. We'd like to have the two of you onstage with him as a symbol of youth in politics."

So we went up on the stage. Howie had wet his pants he was laughing so hard. Hoo-ha was in the back with him.

There was the PR director. There was the mayor. We didn't know him from Adam. We shook hands. Herbie said to the PR director, "I've got an idea. Why don't we let Larry introduce the mayor? It'll be great."

The place was mobbed. The PR guy got up and said, "We have these two hardworking young men, Herbie and Larry, with us tonight. And Larry's going to introduce the mayor."

I stood up. I think it was the first time I had actually been in front of a microphone. It had to be. I was looking around, thinking, What am I doing here?

"Uhhhh. I've been asked to introduce Mayor Lee. Uhhh-hhhhh. But I think it's better that my friend Herbie has the honor." I turned the mike over to Herbie.

Herbie got up—and he did twenty minutes.

He did the Declaration of Independence, and he didn't stop there. "I give you not just the next mayor. No. Not just the future senator. No. Ladies and gentlemen, I give you . . . maybe . . . the future president of the United States."

The crowd was going crazy.

The mayor came up and spoke. The rally ended.

Now it was about one in the morning. Everyone was

leaving. The lights were out in the gym. The only light coming into the gym was from the moon. I can still see this. Mayor Lee said, "Fellas, can I have a word with you?" The mayor asked the stragglers to go outside so he could speak to the four of us.

The mayor remembered this all his life. Years later, when he was close to ninety, he invited me back to New Haven for an event to commemorate the evening. People knew about it because I told the story on national radio. After the first time, people would call in asking to hear it again. So I'd tell the story about once every six months.

Herbie, Hoo-ha, and Howie and I were standing there. The mayor said, "Fellas, I've heard how hard you work. But at the same time I have to mention something to you."

Hoo-ha said, "Go ahead, Mayor, get it off your chest."

The mayor said, "I have lived in New Haven all my life. I have two campaign offices that I visit every day. Please don't take this personally. But I have never seen either"—he looked at me, looked at Herbie—"of you in my entire life."

And Hoo-ha said, "We don't know who the hell you are either."

The mayor said, "What?"

Hoo-ha said, "We've never been here before. This is our first time ever in New Haven. Except for Howie. Howie was in New Haven before."

"Where you guys from?"

"Brooklyn."

"Brooklyn? You have relatives here?"

"No."

"You go to Yale?"

Ha! Ha!

"No," we said, "we don't go to Yale."

The mayor said, "What brings you here?"

And Herbie said, "Mayor, Howie said that there was a Carvel in New Haven that served three scoops for fifteen cents."

And Mayor Lee said, "That's impossible! They can't serve three scoops for fifteen cents."

So we told the mayor where the Carvel was, we said good-bye, and we left. We drove back to Brooklyn. We were driving down Hoo-ha's street. Hoo-ha had never called home. It was now snowing in Brooklyn.

Standing in front of the apartment were Hoo-ha's mother and father. This was Jewish masochism. *Our son has not come home. We will stand out here in the snow. We will get pneumonia. We will suffer. We will die. And he will feel it for the rest of his life.*

We got out of the car. The snow was coming down. Hoo-ha's mother said to Hoo-ha, "Don't lie to me! Don't lie! I'm going to ask you a question! Just answer. Answer! Vhere vere you tonight?"

Hoo-ha said, "Carvel."

"Don't lie. Don't lie. Don't lie! I made your father put on his galoshes. I made him go to the Carvel. The owner said that my Bernie vasn't there. So, vhere vere you? Vhere? Vhat Carvel vere you at?"

"New Haven, Connecticut."

She said, "I'm gonna die! I'm gonna die!"

People were opening up their windows and looking down.

Mr. Horowitz came forward, grabbed Herbie, pulled him next to him, and said, "Vhat the hell did you go to New Haven for? Vhat da hell? You're a bum! You're a bum! You're a bum! Bum! Bum! Bum! Bum! Vhy did you go?"

Herbie said, "Well, Howie said that there was a Carvel in New Haven that served three scoops for fifteen cents."

And as God is my witness, Mr. Horowitz said, "That's impossible!"

ANOTHER POINT OF VIEW

Herbie "The Negotiator" Cohen
FRIEND

Friends are chosen people. You stay friends with someone over a long period of time because they make you feel better than you are.

I've been friends with Larry for sixty-five years. I've known him longer than my wife. My wife once asked me, "Who's the number one person in your life?" I said, "Let me see. In terms of longevity and closeness, Larry is number one. Hoo-ha is number two. But you're three—and moving up."

You can imagine how she reacted to that . . .

Growing up in Bensonhurst gave us our basic values. One is that people are unique and different. If there were anybody here exactly like you there would be no reason for being here. There was nobody like Larry. Larry would stand on the corner and announce cars going by. We called him Zeke the Creek the Mouthpiece because his mouth was like a creek that was constantly running.

One of my major slogans in life is: A nose that can hear is worth two that can smell. I don't even know what it means, but I say it a lot. How did it help Larry? Larry understood instinctively that not conforming to the norm was an asset. He had that gruff Brooklyn voice. When you turned on the radio and heard that voice, you knew it could only be Larry.

Marty Zeiger

BROTHER

Larry was not a good student. He barely got out of high school and never went to college. "You realize your brother has attention deficit disorder," my son said to me a few years ago. The observation caught me by surprise.

But then I started to think about it. My mother—she should rest in peace—used to be called to the school all the time. But what were the criticisms? Larry was restless. Inattentive. He couldn't stay focused. He was always talking to other kids. If there had been Ritalin back then, maybe he wouldn't have become Larry King. Think about it—he would have been calmed down. They would have made him a good student because he was smart. It might have changed the entire direction of his life.

I remember Larry once saying to me, "Marty, you go into the office for eight hours, and you stay in the office?"

I said, "Sometimes I go to lunch. I go to the bathroom. I walk around."

He said, "I couldn't do that in a million years."

I was telling a child psychologist about my brother a while back. She said, "When intelligent adults with ADD have to concentrate they are usually very good at what they do."

If you see Larry at the studio, for that hour he is totally engrossed. When he has to keep up with four people on the screen at once, his mind is right at home.

Chapter 5

Baseball, Girls & Passion

N OW THAT WE'RE BACK from New Haven, let me back up for a moment. I've never been very good at backing up. I don't stop and look back. I've been a *Let's go! Let's go!* kind of guy ever since I was a kid. I can remember going over to my friends' houses early in the morning before Dodgers games and shouting *Come-mahhhhn! Let's go!* If the game started at 1:05, I was pleading with them to get moving to the park at 9 a.m.

I was never, ever, ever, ever late for a Dodgers game. I was never late for a batting practice. We needed to take two subway lines to get to Ebbets Field. There was usually a long line to get into the bleachers, and we always wanted to be among the first ten or twenty. I can remember so many days of standing in line with everyone, yelling, "Open the gates, you creeps! Our sandwiches are spoilin'!"

Then the gates would open, we'd rush through the turnstiles and make a dash for the first two rows. Those were the best seats for anyone who was paying with coins like us. I wasn't fast. Herbie wasn't fast. Hoo-ha wasn't fast. But Natey Turner was, and he'd get there first and hold seats for us.

From the time I started listening to the Dodgers on the radio, my hero was the feistiest guy on the field—Leo Durocher. Leo was the Dodgers' manager. They used to say that when you played against Leo, you played against ten men. He was angry and fiery, the first one out of the dugout to argue a call or back up his players. Early in his career, when he played for the Yankees, he got into a fistfight with Babe Ruth. That's why the Yankees traded him. You didn't fight with Babe Ruth. But that was Leo—gambler, hustler, pool shark, high-living Las Vegas kind of guy. He was married to a Hollywood starlet.

I wasn't a very good ballplayer, but I always wore number 2 on my little uniforms—just like Leo.

These days, Joe Torre is a great manager and a nice guy. But you look at him in the dugout and you don't know if he's winning or losing. Leo was the complete opposite. Stick it in his ear!

That's the kind of attitude you needed if you were going up against my nemesis, Davy Fried, a snarling rat of a New York Giants fan. Or Herbie, Sid, and Asher, who rooted for the Yankees. Look up the word *gloat* and you'll see Herbie's picture in the dictionary. Yankee fans were arrogant, conceited dolts who were above it all. Their attitude was, *Why are you and Davy even bothering to argue? We're gonna beat whoever wins between you.* Most of the time, they were right. The Dodgers became very good. But the Yankees were always a tick better—and luckier.

There were Dodgers fans who even believed the Yankee Stadium grounds crew put little objects like nails in the infield grass. So that when a Yankee hit a ball, it would strike the nail and bound over the fielder's head. It had to be a plot! Between 1947 and 1953, the Yankees won the World Series six times. Four times in that span they beat the Dodgers, and all we could do was fume, "Wait 'til next year!"

That's when my come-mahhhhn changed. It went from, "Come-mahhhhn, we're gonna be late for batting practice," to "Come-mahhhhn, you bums, you're breaking my heart!"

But Dodgers fans had something special. We had Jackie Robinson. We had the guy who broke the color barrier. My friend Aaron Sobel and I kept a newspaper scrapbook of the entire 1947 season. But looking back, I'm not sure we understood how monumental Jackie's achievement truly was. There wasn't any prejudice in my house. I can remember one of my cousins marrying a black guy and her parents disowning her. But my mother had my cousin and her husband over and always made them feel welcome. So I saw Jackie the way Leo saw him just before Leo got suspended for consorting with gamblers at the start of that '47 season. "I don't care if this guy is yellow or black or if he has stripes like a zebra," Leo said. "I'm the manager of this team and I say he plays."

We knew about the death threats. We knew how the manager of the Phillies tried to rattle Jackie by having the players in his dugout aim bats as if they were machine guns and act like they were shooting at Jackie when Jackie came up to the plate. We knew how Jackie had to hold his temper when other players spiked him and called him nigger. We heard how our captain, Pee Wee Reese from Kentucky, put his arm around Jackie when the crowd in Cincinnati shouted every insult under the sun at him during batting practice. We heard all about it from the voice of Red Barber, who was from the Deep South. As time passed, we heard about Jackie and Don Newcombe and some of the other black Dodgers integrating the Chase Park Plaza hotel in St. Louis. But it wasn't until I spoke with Dr. Martin Luther King Jr. years later that I understood the magnitude of what Jackie had accomplished. It was Jackie, King said, who started the civil rights movement. It was Jackie, King said, who made his job easier.

To a kid arguing with Herbie at Maltz's candy store, Jackie was the second baseman who in his MVP 1949 season hit .342 in 593 at bats with 38 doubles and 37 stolen bases. Statistics was something else baseball gave me that would help later on when I was a broadcaster. You had to know your numbers cold if you were arguing with Herbie. You had to be precise. Get caught with the wrong statistic in an argument with Herbie, and you were dead. How could anything else you said be believed? Where I grew up, statistics were ammunition. The only time in my life I ever got into a fistfight was after Herbie argued that the Yankees' second baseman, Snuffy Sternweiss, was better than Jackie.

Looking back, I can only marvel at how lucky I was to grow up announcing into a rolled-up ten-cent scorecard at Ebbets Field. To see Billy Cox at third base with his beat-up old glove. He'd hold that glove in his right hand while the pitcher pitched. Then he'd slide it on his left just in time to catch the ground ball that the hitter smashed his way. He'd make the catch, and look at the ball before throwing to first base. How lucky I was to see Duke Snider and Willie Mays and my brother's favorite player, Stan "The Man" Musial. To take the subway to Yankee Stadium and watch Joe DiMaggio. No matter how much you hated the Yankees, you couldn't hate DiMaggio. It was the best of times even when it was the worst.

The saddest moment of my life came in the 1951 season. It was even sadder than the day my father died because I wasn't sad when my father died. I was *angry* at him for leaving me. For pure sadness, nothing could compare to what happened to the Dodgers in 1951.

We had a thirteen-and-a-half-game lead in August with only a month and a half to go. Day after day, the Giants chipped away at that lead. Curse of curses, their manager was none other than Leo Durocher—who'd left the Dodgers and gone across town. The worst part was that we weren't blowing our lead. The Dodgers would win two out of three, but Leo and the Giants would win three out of three.

The Giants caught up to and passed us, but the Dodgers managed to tie on the last game of the season when Jackie hit a home run to beat the Phillies in the fourteenth inning. A three-game playoff was scheduled. Even if you're not a baseball fan, you've probably heard about it. The Giants won the first game. The Dodgers won the second. I'll never forget the newspaper column Dick Young wrote before the final game. The entire column listed the word for *one* in what seemed like every language.

We were ahead 4–1 in the ninth inning. We were one damn inning away from the World Series. I was listening to the radio in the office of a job I had at the time. Of course, the Giants started chipping away. Ralph Branca was brought in to pitch. Bobby Thomson came to the plate. Now we were ahead, 4–2, and the Giants had two men on base. Everyone was poised. Nobody had any idea that Leo and the Giants were reading the catcher's signs from center field. Then Thomson hit a fly ball. In a lot of ballparks that's all it would have been—a fly ball. But the Polo Grounds was a funny park. There was an overhang in left. The ball went over the fence. There was Leo jumping up and down at third base.

Most people heard the voice of Russ Hodges: "The Giants win the pennant! The Giants win the pennant!" But I was listening to Red Barber, who must have prepared for this, because he put it into perspective by talking about all those families who had lost boys in Korea. The sun was still going to come up tomorrow for Dodgers fans, he said, but I was in a daze. I left work, got off at the subway station in Bay Parkway, and bumped into the last person in the world I wanted to see. Davy Fried. All he did—son of a bitch—was laugh. Never said a word. It was a horrible laugh, a demoralizing laugh, and my shoulders sank. I'll never forget it.

Years later, long after the Dodgers had finally beaten the Yankees to win the 1955 World Series, I emceed a banquet attended by a lot of the players from the Yankees, Dodgers, and Giants. At the end, I called up Branca and Thomson. I looked at Branca. Then I looked at Thomson. And I said to Thomson, "I still hate you."

ANOTHER POINT OF VIEW

Herbie "The Negotiator" Cohen

In 1951, the year of the Giants' miracle run, Larry would get in arguments every day with Giants fans. Not only with our friends, but with our friends' fathers. Larry was like an encyclopedia of baseball. He'd throw out statistics and get these fifty-year-old men frustrated to the point where they were frothing mad.

After Bobby Thomson hit the home run, Larry disappeared for three days. Every Giants fan in the neighborhood was saying, "Where's Larry?" They couldn't wait to get at him.

Then the Giants went into the World Series and started to lose to the Yankees. Suddenly, Larry appeared and continued to harass these Giants fans about how their team had let down the National League. These were old men. He would drive them crazy.

As if there weren't enough passion in baseball and Maltz's candy store, girls entered the picture when I was about age sixteen. Women have always mystified me. The more I know about them, the less. I once talked with Stephen Hawking, the physicist, the guy who could tell you about black holes in space. At the end of the interview, I said, "You've been called the smartest man on the planet. What don't you know? What puzzles you?" He said, "Women."

For me, it's always been a little like the song in *My Fair Lady*.

Why can't a woman be more like a man?
If I forgot your silly birthday, would you fuss?

I never really talked to my mother about girls. Mothers aren't women anyway, they're mothers. My affairs with the opposite sex didn't get off to a good start at Lafayette High when Herbie bet me five dollars that I couldn't get Iris Siegel to walk out of school with me. Iris was the most beautiful cheerleader, a far-off fantasy, but the bet was winnable because I simply had to walk down the front steps next to her.

"I don't have to hold her hand or anything?"

"That's right," Herbie said. "Five bucks."

I went straight to Iris and asked her. But she told me she was in a hurry to get to cheerleading practice. I confessed the bet to her, told her I'd give her the five bucks. But she went on her way. It didn't get any lower than handing Herbie the cash in front of all our friends at the bottom of those steps.

At least I thought so at the time. My first kiss turned out to be even more embarrassing. It was a cold night, and I had just started smoking. Hoo-ha's date lived on one end of the block, Herbie's on the other. Mine lived in the middle. Judy, her name was. I must have been about seventeen. I was walking Judy home with a cigarette dangling from my mouth because

I thought it made me look like Humphrey Bogart. We headed up the steps. She turned around, closed her eyes, and puckered. Holy Shit, I'm gonna be kissed. So I kissed her . . . with the cigarette in my lips. She screamed. All the lights in the neighborhood came on. Herbie and Hoo-ha came running. The girl's father raced downstairs. Judy was crying. I was apologizing from the bottom of my heart. "I just started smoking. I'm so sorry, I didn't know what I was doing."

Herbie looked closely at Judy's lip and said: "Don't worry. That hole will be gone in two years . . ."

About twenty guys in our neighborhood formed a club called the Warriors. We had jackets with a *W* over the heart and a club room in Hoo-ha's basement with a Victrola to play records for parties. One time, Herbie and I sneaked in two girls. Teresa and Angela. Teresa said, "I don't neck unless I have music."

Our Victrola was broken. So Herbie said to me, "Go upstairs and get Hoo-ha's radio. It's in his bedroom."

I got the radio. I was coming through the kitchen to go down to the basement, and there was Dora, Hoo-ha's mother, making chopped liver.

"Vhere you goin' with my son's radio?"

"Downstairs."

"Vhy?"

"I want to listen to the baseball game."

She looked at me through squinted eyes. "I think you've got girls down there."

"Mrs. Horowitz, I'm going down."

"No, you're not!" She stood in front of the door.

At just that moment, one of the girls yelled, "Are you coming with the music?"

Now Mrs. Horowitz was really blocking the door. So I busted right by her. She fell, and as she fell, the chopped liver in her hands shot up to the ceiling and crashed down on the floor. The kitchen was covered with chopped liver and we all had to leave.

I don't know what a psychologist would make of that moment. To me, I was seventeen years old and feeling the heat. The next day, I was standing on the corner with Herbie and there came Hoo-ha, raging mad.

"Did you beat up my mother?"

"Hoo-ha, it was kind of an accident."

"You beat up my mother. You know what I'm gonna do?"

"What?"

"I'm gonna go to your house and kick your mother in the face."

"Hoo-ha, you go to my house and kick my mother in the face, and I'm gonna go to your house and kick your mother in the stomach."

"You kick my mother in the stomach and I . . ."

This went back and forth until Herbie said, "Look at this. These two guys will kill each other's mother, but they won't touch each other."

Ellen David

SISTER-IN-LAW

Can you imagine what it must have been like for this kid who grows up poor in Brooklyn to years later sit at the same dinner table with Angie Dickinson, the sex symbol of the time? There must have been an element of disbelief.

Maybe I wasn't the best candidate to be drafted for the Korean War. Plus, it was the Navy that drafted me—and I couldn't even swim. Once, when I was young, I'd gone out in the ocean and been flipped over by a wave. I found myself gasping for air on the sand and I never wanted to go back. I had no college prospects after graduating from Lafayette. I never cared about school from the day my father died. The draft notice came, the Warriors threw me a farewell party, and I went for my physical. I was placed at the end of the line during the eye test—they didn't want the guys with glasses slowing up the rest. We were waiting to be sworn in, and I heard, "Zeiger—go home."

"Go home?"

"You failed the eye test. Your eyes are so bad, if you lose your glasses in war, you'd shoot up everything around you. If we swear you in, we'd have to give you a medical discharge and pay you."

I went home. I told my mother. She was thrilled. I went out, turned the corner, and all my friends were there.

"What happened?" Hoo-ha wanted to know.

"I'm 4-F."

"That wallet I gave you." It was a going-away gift. "Give me back my wallet."

"But Hoo-ha, I've already used it."

"No, no, no, no," he said. "That wallet was for the Navy."

Truth is, from that day on, I was lost. Childhood was over. Herbie went into the Army, and all my friends seemed to be leaving the neighborhood. My mother had to endure the comments of friends and relatives who sent their kids off to a bright future in college or to the service to become a hero. Seeing me flounder at home had to be difficult.

When my younger brother, an excellent student, arrived at Lafayette, the dean walked over to him. "Martin Zeiger. Are you Larry Zeiger's brother?"

"Yes," Marty said.

The dean put his hands on my brother's shoulders and asked, in the most sympathetic voice imaginable, "How's your mother?"

Herbie's father would take me for walks around the neighborhood to offer guidance. For years, I wanted to be Herbie. He had a father. He had money. He had a television set. Herbie's father asked me what I was going to do with my life.

I told him I wanted to go into broadcasting. "What are you," he said, "a pipe dreamer? What are you, Arthur Godfrey? What are you, nuts? Get a job."

Herbie's father had a little factory that made bindings for hats. "I'll give you a job in my factory," he said. "You'll learn to be a binder. And someday, *someday*, you could be foreman. Foremen get three weeks' vacation. Like this, you can be somebody."

I went through a bunch of odd jobs. My Uncle Lou hooked me up with the United Parcel Service. I was an assistant on the truck that delivered packages. We had a driver—Crazy Krauss—who liked to drive down the street and clip off the side-view mirrors of parked cars. I sold Borden's milk for a little while. But the best success I had was working the phones for the collection division of a department store.

I invented the word *congealiate*. There's no such word. But it sounds like a word. It was very effective in the collection business. I used to call up people and say, "If you don't have your payment in here by Thursday, we're going to congealiate the whole account." Or "I may be forced to recommend congealiation. The sheriff will congealiate your account forthwith."

I remember one guy pleading, "Don't congealiate me! Please, don't congeliate me!"

I was at work listening to the radio when the Dodgers finally beat the Yankees in the World Series. It was 1955. The most amazing thing about it was how anticlimactic the ending was. The Yankees came up for the final time, and every Dodgers fan was thinking, *We'll make an error. The Yanks will score three runs*. But the Yankees went down one-two-three. It was great, but not the same with Herbie already away in the Army.

There were some good moments after Herbie left, but it was a lonely time. Most of my friends were gone. I was alone. I met a girl named Frada through my cousin Julie. A plain girl, the type who doesn't wear makeup.

You know the joke about the Jewish guy who's going to get married? He goes to his mother and says, "I'm gonna test your intuition. I'm gonna bring three girls home. My future wife, and two of her friends. See if you can pick which one I'm going to marry. I'm not going to say a thing during dinner to give you a hint."

They have dinner. The girls leave.

The guy asks his mother, "Which one?"

She says, "The second one."

"How'd you know?"

"Because I couldn't stand her."

The joke doesn't apply in this case. There was nothing about Frada to dislike. The reality is, the source of our attraction was that she was lonely just like me. My brother was the best man. Frada and I got an apartment in Queens and a white couch. But it never amounted to anything. We were together for maybe six months. I wonder what ever happened to Frada.

ANOTHER POINT OF VIEW

Marty Zeiger

I was the best man at Larry's wedding to Frada. It seems like a hundred years ago. Frada was a nice girl. She had a high-pitched laugh. Funny, what you remember; I recall thinking that the marriage was hasty.

Herbie "The Negotiator" Cohen

I came back from the Army and Larry was married. I said, "Why did you marry her?" He said, "Well, everyone was away and nobody was around. It was cold that winter. So I got married." That was his answer.

Marty Zeiger

I don't remember the circumstances of how it fell apart. But I wasn't surprised when it did.

Sometimes I'd go to New York, stand in front of the buildings housing CBS or WNEW radio, and hope. What I wanted was right in front of me and so far away. Yet anyone who really knew me could see that I already had what I needed to be successful in broadcasting. It had been set inside me by my parents and my childhood in Brooklyn. I was funny and likable, just like my father. I was open and loyal, just like my mother. I had tons of friends. I had the passion to transmit, and for as long as I could remember people had always said that they loved my voice. I'd learned to pay attention to details through baseball and knew how to come up with just the right ones to win an argument. What's more, Brooklyn had taught me how to ask good questions. Like, How could that new restaurant be called the Famous when it just opened?

One day, I ran into James Sirmons, a staff announcer at CBS. "Mr. Sirmons," I said, "I'm twenty-four years old. I've always wanted to be in radio. I've never given it a try. What do you recommend I do?"

"Go down to Miami, kid, and give it a shot," he said.

"They've got a lot of stations. It's easier to get started in Miami because there are no unions down there. In Miami, people are either on the way out or they're on the way up."

I had an Uncle Jack living in Miami Beach.

It was time to go.

Chapter 6

Miami Hello & Jamaica Farewell

I TOOK THE TRAIN to Miami and stepped off with about eighteen dollars in my wallet. I can still remember what I saw. Two water fountains. One said COLORED. The other said WHITE. I walked over to the one that said COLORED and drank out of it.

Then I went to stay with my Uncle Jack in Miami Beach. I was so excited that I started knocking on doors the next day. I stopped at a small station on First Street, WAHR. The guy in charge liked my voice. "We get a lot of people coming and going," he told me. "If you hang around, you'll get the first opening."

I sat and watched in fascination for a few weeks. It was a tiny operation, but the sight of the UPI and AP machines furiously clicking out news made me feel like I was on the brink of something big. Miami Beach was like a dream. The palm trees. The ocean. I remember walking past Joe's Stone Crab. Joe's is more than a restaurant, it's a landmark. It was full when I arrived in 1957, and I guarantee you, people will be waiting in line tomorrow night. I stopped outside the front window with only a few dollars in my pocket, unable to afford a meal, looking at the happy faces, wondering what it would take to get into a place like that.

Then came my big break. There was a morning deejay named Tom Baer. He was making sixty dollars a week and his alimony was sixty-five. He claimed to be living off the coconuts falling from trees. He quit on a Friday, and the general manager told me I could start on Monday.

I must have rehearsed the entire weekend. I don't even think I slept. On Monday morning I showed up at WAHR with the record that would play my theme song, "Swingin' Down the Lane."

The general manager called me into his office to wish me good luck. "By the way," he said, "what name are you going to use?"

"What do you mean?"

"You can't use Larry Zeiger," he said. "It's too ethnic. People won't be able to spell it or remember it. You need a better name."

There was no time to think about whether this was good or bad or what my mother would say. I was going on the air in five minutes. The *Miami Herald* was spread out on his desk. Faceup was a full-page ad for King's Wholesale Liquors. The general manager looked down and said, "King! How about Larry King?"

"OK," I said. This was the opportunity of a lifetime. I wasn't going to blow it.

"Fine. You'll host *The Larry King Show*."

Nine o'clock was approaching. That's when the news came on. A few minutes later, *The Larry King Show* would make its debut. I went through the control-room door, sat down, and set up my record. The news ended. I started my theme song, then faded down the music so I could introduce myself. I opened my mouth. It was as dry as cotton. For the first time in my life, I couldn't speak.

So I brought "Swingin' Down the Lane" up again and faded it once more. Again, not a single word came out of my mouth.

I could only wonder if listeners were hearing the pounding of my heart. I'd waited for this moment my whole life. How could I be blowing it? Once more, I cranked up "Swingin' Down the Lane"—but not a word came out of me.

The next thing I knew, the general manager was kicking open the door to the control room. "This is a *communications* business!" he roared in a way that only a general manager can. Then he turned, walked out, and slammed the door behind him.

Shaken, I leaned in to the microphone and said, "Good morning. This is my first day ever on the radio. I've always wanted to be on the air. I've been practicing all weekend. A few minutes ago, they gave me my new name. I've had a theme song ready to play, but my mouth is dry. I'm nervous. And the general manager just kicked open the door and said, 'This is a communications business!'"

That's how my career started on May 1, 1957. Years later, Arthur Godfrey would tell me, "The only secret in this business is . . . there is no secret." He was right. I learned a great lesson on my first day. There's no trick to being yourself. I don't think I've ever been nervous on the air since then.

I can't remember if Uncle Jack heard me or if I met anybody else who did on that first day. It didn't matter. I was on a high. My dream was reality. I couldn't wait to come back the next day, and the one after that. I so loved being on air that I'd do anything. The people at the station knew I was a glutton. Sports. News. Whatever came up, someone would say, "Larry will do it."

One day, the general manager called and said the all-night guy was sick. "Would you like to fill in tonight?"

"Sure," I said. "No problem."

"OK, you're on from midnight to six. You play music, you chatter a little, and you say the regular guy will be back tomorrow."

I went in at night. WAHR was a small station. At night, I was the only one there. I started playing records, and the phone rang.

"WAHR."

A lady's voice came through. I can still hear her voice. She said, "I want you."

"What did you say?"

"I want you!"

I was a long way from losing that bet to Herbie for not being able to walk Iris Siegel down the front steps of Lafayette High. All I could think was, *There are a couple of extra pluses to being in this business.* So I told her, "I get off at six!"

And she said, "Nah, that won't do, I gotta go to work. You've gotta come now."

"But I'm on the air!"

"I'm only eleven blocks from the station." She gave me her address. "If you can make it, please, I *really* want you."

There was no Mrs. Horowitz blocking the door. So this is what the audience heard.

"Folks, I'm only sitting in tonight. So I've got a real treat for you. You're going to hear the entire Harry Belafonte at Carnegie Hall album uninterrupted."

Now I had thirty-three minutes—which was all the time I needed. Until this day, that's still true.

I put the record on, rushed to my beat-up '51 Plymouth, drove to her house, pulled in. The light was on. She said the door would be open, and the door was open. She was sitting there wearing a white negligee. A little lamp was on and I could barely see her face. The radio was on. Harry Belafonte was singing from Carnegie Hall. She opened her arms. I ran to her and my cheek was against her cheek as Belafonte sang "Jamaica Farewell."

"Down the way where the nights . . . where the nights . . . where the nights . . . where the nights . . . where the nights—" The needle was stuck in the record.

I pushed her back. I rushed to the car. I drove to the station. And—this was Jewish masochism—I kept the radio on the entire eleven blocks. "Where the nights . . . where the nights . . . where the nights . . . where the nights . . ."

I was petrified. I got back to the station and took off the record. The phones were ringing off the hook. I was apologizing to people one after the other. The last call, I'll never forget. An old Jewish guy.

"This is WAHR."

He said, "Vhere da nights! Vhere da nights! Vhere da nights! I'm going c-razy! I'm going c-razy! I'm going c-razy!"

I said, "Sir, I apologize. But why didn't you change the station?"

He said, "I'm an invalid. They set the station on the radio and I can't reach the knob."

The story may be funny now, but foxhole humor is never funny when you're in the foxhole. The next time I walked into the station, I couldn't help but think, "Oh, God, this is the end." But sometimes in life, the worst never happens.

How I got out of that one, I still don't know. The only thing I can think of is: *Management doesn't listen.* I say that in jest. But in this case it might have been true. Remember, this was a small radio station. It didn't have a great signal. The manager may have lived far enough from the station not to hear. Plus, it was three in the morning. Nobody said a word about "Jamaica

Farewell" the next time I came in, and my life seemed to get sun-
nier by the day. I got a second job, announcing at the dog track
in the evenings. I got into an affair with a beautiful woman who
was ten years older than me. And does it get any better than being in Florida when spring training rolls around?

The Dodgers were arriving in Miami to play an exhibition
game in 1958 when the sports director at the station called me
over. He asked me if I wanted to go out to the park and interview one of the Dodgers before the game. *Would I?* After all those
years as a kid wearing number 2 on my uniform, here I was
phoning my hero, Leo Durocher, to try to set up an interview.

Leo was working with the Dodgers at that time. Of course,
he didn't know me. And he wasn't around when I phoned. So I
left a message to call Larry King, then I went on the air. When
I got off, there was a message waiting for me. "Leo Durocher
called." My *hero* called me back! I saved that slip of paper for
years. So I called Leo back, but missed him. Then he called me
back, but missed me. We went back and forth like this all morning, but never connected. Now I've got five messages from Leo
Durocher.

I went out to the stadium with the huge portable tape
recorder that we used in those days. It was so heavy you had to
sling it over your shoulder. Even though I can picture the scene
in my head, it's a moment I'd love to have on videotape. Thousands of people were at the park to watch the teams warm up.
I stepped out on the field, and there he was, number 2, at home
plate hitting ground balls.

I walked over and said, "Mr. Durocher?"

"What do you want, kid?"

"I'm Larry King."

He looked up and screamed loud enough for the people
sitting in the top row of the park to hear, "What the *fuck* do
you want?"

I must have flown back ten feet—tape recorder and all.

"Larry King!" he howled. "Who the hell *are* you? And *why* do you keep calling me?"

Remember, I was still a kid, and this was my first interview, so I had to have been a bit shaken. Come to think of it, if Leo had said, "What can I do for you, kind sir?" that really would have stunned me. I still would have jumped. But nobody likes to be yelled at in front of three thousand people.

I didn't say, "I'm sorry, goodbye." I managed to calm him down and we went to the dugout to talk. It was the first of many great conversations we would have over the years. Leo was always a wonderful interview because he was expressive and opinionated. Years after our first talk, he did the game of the week on NBC, and he was so honest that the network didn't know what to do with him. He'd say things like, "See this pitcher? I can hit him—and I'm sixty years old."

I couldn't have had a better first interview. There are people who are disappointed when they meet their heroes because their heroes don't live up to their expectations. But the Leo I met was the Leo I loved. At the end of the interview, I said: "Leo, one thing I don't understand. You didn't know me. If you didn't want to talk to me, why did you call me back?"

Leo said, "Your name sounded like it was somebody important."

There's no telling if I would've become who I became if I'd remained Zeiger. Would Tony Curtis have become Tony Curtis if he'd stayed Bernard Schwartz? Would Frederick Austerlitz and Virginia McMath have been on movie marquees if they hadn't become Fred Astaire and Ginger Rogers? We'll never know. I can tell you one thing. If I'd been black or Latino, I don't think my career would have been allowed to take off at the time.

There's another thing about my life that I should point out even though I can't explain it. I've always been around famous people and circumstances—even when it had nothing to do with work. I'll give you an example. Shortly after I got to Miami, I drove three disc jockeys from our little station to see Palm Beach. We had somebody's convertible—a rinky-dink old car. I was behind the wheel. We drove up along coastal route A1A, past these beautiful homes, on a magnificent Sunday morning, clear as crystal. There were hardly any cars on the road as we turned onto Worth Avenue, and I was moving very slowly as we looked around at all the stores. We were approaching a light, and because I was looking around I didn't stop quickly enough. The car bumped into a convertible in front of us—not hard—but the driver's head bounced forward and then back. The guy got out of the car and it was John F. Kennedy.

It was unmistakably John F. Kennedy. Only two years earlier, Adlai Stevenson had thrown open the vice presidential nomination at the Democratic National convention and it came down to Kennedy and Estes Kefauver. Kefauver won. Which, it was said later on, was lucky for Kennedy. Because he didn't run on a losing ticket and was therefore in a better position to get the nomination for president in 1960.

I'll never forget. Kennedy walked over to us and said, "How? How could you hit me? It's ten o'clock in the morning. It's clear. There's nobody on the road. I'm the only car. How could you hit me?"

I said, "I'm sorry, Senator, would you like to exchange licenses?"

He said, "I'll tell you what. Raise your right hands, all of you. Say, 'I swear to vote for John Kennedy in two years.'"

We solemnly swore, and with a smile he drove off. But before he did, he said, "Stay a distance behind me."

I'll never know if the owner of a local restaurant intuited my ability to bump into famous people, or if he just liked listening to my show. But Charlie Bookbinder had an idea that changed my life. Charlie's restaurant was a Jewish deli called Pumpernik's. It was open twenty-four hours a day. But the hour after breakfast, between ten and eleven, wasn't bringing in much business. So Charlie got this idea to have me broadcast live from the restaurant. I'd do a morning show from the studio of WKAT between six and nine, all the while promoting the fact that I'd be broadcasting live from Pumpernik's between ten and eleven.

I had no idea how the switch from WAHR would develop my style. What really got my attention was the increase in pay. WKAT was offering a hundred dollars a week!

I showed up at Pumpernik's on the first day and found a sign in the window for *The Larry King Show* and an elevated stage. That was it. There was no producer. Just me. It turned out to be a wonderful breeding ground. Who knew? I'd never really interviewed anyone apart from my one experience with Leo Durocher. Now I was interviewing anyone who came over—waiters, customers on vacation, conventioneers. Anything could happen. There was no way to be prepared, because I never knew who was coming over next. This forced me to think on the fly.

I mean, when was the last time you heard a plumber being interviewed? I can still remember doing forty-five minutes with one. The guy said, "People don't think about it, but plumbing is the key to your house. Without plumbing, your house can't function. Your bed falls down, you can sleep on the floor. But if your plumbing is screwed up, you need me. I make your house work."

"Is there an artistry to plumbing?" I asked him.

"Definitely. What makes one fixture better than another? You have to size things up. Do you know why New York City has the best water in the world? Because when they built the system years ago, they made it with copper. Copper is the best piping you can have. Copper doesn't rust. The water stays pure. You make sure copper is in your bathroom, and you'll have much less trouble . . ."

The specialness of an interview like that is how unspecial it is. It's the essence of what I do. I'm an everyday guy, and my interviews attract the everyday guy. But they also attract the everyday guy in people who can do things that are special.

After I'd done about two weeks at Pumpernik's, the singer Bobby Darin walked in. He had trouble sleeping at night, and he had been up at six that morning, listening to me promote the show. I loved "Mack the Knife" and the rest of Bobby's music, but, again, there was no way to prepare. I interviewed him for an hour, and it worked out great. He told me he was embarrassed to have written "Splish Splash." Afterward, we took a long walk down Collins Avenue. This was really an experience for me. Little Larry Zeiger from Brooklyn was walking down Collins Avenue with the singer of a number one hit, and he was confiding in me. Darin was born with a rheumatic heart. He was telling me that he knew he was going to die at an early age. That's why he worked so hard and tried to pack so much into his life. He knew he was on borrowed time. He wanted to do everything yesterday.

One of the newspapers wrote about Bobby Darin going on with Larry King at Pumpernik's. Before long, Jimmy Hoffa walked in. When you talk to plumbers, you make friends with teamsters. The Teamsters union was in town for a convention, and a few guys I knew brought in Hoffa. Once Hoffa started to talk, the restaurant began to fill. Hoffa was a character. Tough as nails.

I asked Hoffa what kind of truck driver he was and found out he wasn't a truck driver. He was a loader. Which is why, he said, whenever he went in to negotiate a contract, the first thing management had to do was promise to heat the loading platforms. He used to freeze his ass off at four in the morning loading trucks in Detroit. "If you don't heat the loading platforms," he said, "I don't talk to you."

These are the sorts of things you learn when you don't have time to prepare.

Hoffa said he never wanted to ride in the back of a limousine. These union leaders who go around holding straps, he said, are no different from the guys running the corporations. He always rode in the front of a Chevrolet. He had a funny way of referring to himself by his own name. He'd say, "Hoffa says." When he did, I'd say, "King responds." He had a good sense of humor about it. When the show ended, I noticed that Pumpernik's was jammed.

Soon, Danny Thomas and a bunch of famous people started coming around between ten and eleven. Saturday was children's day and people brought their kids in to be interviewed.

Pumpernik's became *the spot*, and I became Mr. Miami. It wasn't planned. I didn't have a PR person. People liked me. Lenny Bruce and Don Rickles liked coming by. Once Lenny came in wearing an outfit from the state prison.

Miami was one of the few places where Lenny didn't have a lot of trouble with the cops. I said, "Lenny, why are you wearing this?"

He said, "I like to wear prison uniforms."

"Why?"

"I like to walk up to cops and ask them directions."

"Why?"

"To see their reactions. Because you know what they're thinking. The first thing they're thinking is, *Is this an escaped con asking for directions?* The second thing they're thinking is, *Nah, can't be an escaped con. Why would an escaped con ask a policeman for directions?* Third thing they're thinking is,

What if he's a brilliant escaped con who thinks that I'm not thinking what he's thinking?"

And Rickles said, "Lenny, get a job."

The Pumpernik's hour was funny and loose, and that really started to come out in my early morning show between six and nine. If I had stayed with it, I'd have ended up a major morning disc jockey like Imus.

One time during my show I was listening to the morning traffic report. The guy giving the report told drivers that I-95 was backed up, so they should use Seventh Avenue. I thought, Well, he's alleviating I-95. But he's congesting Seventh Avenue. So I invented this character to rectify the situation, Captain Wainright.

It was my voice, I just hit a control that distorted it and made it sound funny. So Captain Wainright came on and said, "I just heard that traffic report, Larry. All you listeners, I want you to know that I-95 is open and clear. Get back on I-95." Then Captain Wainright gave a little laugh. *Heh, heh, heh.* Five minutes later, Captain Wainright came back on with that same laugh and said, "I got 'em backed up to Broward County."

Captain Wainright was my alter ego, and everything a cop shouldn't be. When Gulfstream Park racetrack opened, Captain Wainright said, "Don't go to Gulfstream. Bet with any Dade County police officer. They'll take your bet. Leave your money where you live."

I'd get Miami's state attorney Dick Gerstein on the phone and Captain Wainright would say, "Dickie baby, where are you? Today is payoff day, and if you're not in the office in five minutes, I'm going to call out the boys."

Whenever I'd pass a detour sign where roadwork was being done, I'd have fresh material. "If you're on I-95 and you turn toward Miami Beach, you'll see a detour sign," Captain

Wainright would say. "Disregard that detour sign. We're on our way to take it down. Go straight through it."

A guy working for the city called me and said, "Larry, if we didn't love you, we'd kill you." Looking back on it, I probably wasn't doing anything different from when Herbie and I clogged the streets as traffic monitors in junior high. Only this time, I didn't have to go to the principal's office. Now there were bumper stickers around town that read, DON'T STOP ME, I KNOW CAPTAIN WAINRIGHT.

Requests to speak at Rotary Clubs started coming. I would emcee the opening of every new movie theater. A small television station gave me a weekly interview show. The *Miami Herald* gave me a column. I'd walk into Joe's Stone Crab and stand at the end of the bar among the crowd as if I'd been on the waiting list all night. The wait might be two and a half hours. Within five minutes, I'd hear, "Mr. King. Larry King."

But it was a bus driver who would take me to the next level.

Chapter 7

Jackie & Frank

THERE ARE TIMES when I watch reruns of *The Honeymoon-ers* before I go on the air at CNN. They always give me a lift. Jackie Gleason has lifted me up from the day I met him.

One of my favorite episodes is called "Better Living Through TV"—and it's a nice coincidence that I met Jackie around the time I got my first local television show in Miami. The plot goes like this: Ralph and Norton come upon a kitchen utensil that can do everything. Everything from core an apple to open an aluminum can. The Helpful Housewife Happy Handy, it's called. So Ralph and Norton decide to go on television dressed like chefs to sell this gadget. It had to be the first infomercial, which shows you how ahead of his time Jackie was. Ralph and Norton were going to make a fortune selling the Helpful Housewife Happy Handy.

Except that the producers bump their segment up, tell them they're on in two minutes, and Ralph freezes before the camera. Hummana, hummana, hummana . . . It takes him longer to core an apple during the demonstration than for Norton to do it the old-fashioned way. When he tries to open a can, he slices his finger. By the end of the demonstration, Ralph has crashed down the whole kitchen set. It's still hilarious fifty years later. Which gets to the essence of Jackie. I remember Bishop Fulton Sheen speaking at a dinner honoring Jackie. Sheen talked about children and humor, how children love to see something funny over and over again. They could watch it a hundred times and never get tired. Then he turned to Jackie and said, "That's what I say to you, Jackie. We're all children. Do it again. Do it again." There was something about Ralph Kramden the bus driver that touched not only every man of that social stratum, but everyone.

I met Jackie on a train coming down from New York. Jackie wanted to play golf all year round, so CBS agreed to move *The Jackie Gleason Show* to Miami. The press was invited to take the trip and I went for the ride. *And awa-a-a-a-y we go!*

When we arrived, there was an official reception to welcome Jackie to Miami Beach. I was the emcee. Jackie and I got close that night, and he started to listen to my radio show. Though he was fifteen years older, we had similar backgrounds and a chemistry that made for good friends. We were both ethnic kids from Brooklyn. His father ran away. My father died. He didn't have a phone. I didn't have a phone until I was fifteen years old. We both liked attention. Jackie once told me about the time his mother took him to see a show. At the end, during the applause, Jackie turned around and faced the audience. He knew in that moment that he preferred to look at the audience instead of the stage.

"You know," he once told me, "there can be fifty people in this room funnier than me. But they can't get up in front of a camera. Because that takes something else."

I said, "You're telling me you have an enormous ego."

"Of course," he said.

"Are you conceited?"

"Confident."

Conceited to Jackie meant someone who wanted the spot-light but didn't have talent. When that light goes on, he said, that's my world. He saw that same quality in me. He liked the way I took control of a show, and I learned a lot watching Jackie.

One night, we planned to go out to dinner after the film-ing of his show. I was standing offstage while he was doing a scene. As the scene shifted to Norton and Trixie, he stepped off the stage and came over to me. "Call Raimundo," he said. "Tell him we're coming over to eat right after the show."

"Fifteen seconds . . ." a crew member alerted him.

"Tell him I want the soft-shell crabs the way I like them with the min—"

"Ten seconds!"

"With the minestrone soup, all right, and I want that fresh bread."

"Five seconds, Jackie."

"And tell them to make sure that fresh bread is well, well baked. NORTON!" And he stepped onto the stage at exactly the right moment.

I'm thinking, *Whoa, does this guy know his stuff.* I've got a clock in my head just like Jackie had a clock in his head. You have to have that clock if you're going to work in radio. You tell me thirty seconds, and I know what thirty seconds is with-out having to look at my watch. But Jackie taught me how to take command of that clock. He taught me how to have a pres-ence. The confidence I got from watching him paid off big time when my first television show came along.

A lot of radio people fail at television because they look at it as *Television! Oh my God, I'm on television!* They forget that it ain't brain surgery. You're just sitting at a table asking questions, only there's a camera on you.

If you start laughing, people will see you crack up instead of just hearing you. Once, a guy in the radio studio took off his clothes and was sitting there naked eating a banana. I looked over at him and lost it on the air. But there would have been no difference if he'd been sitting naked and eating a banana off camera during a television show. I'd have laughed just the same. The essential difference between radio and television is that there is no difference.

My first television show was weird, though. The show came on Channel 10 at midnight every Sunday and it had no time limit. When the subject we were talking about was finished, the show ended. It gave me a chance to ask questions that you don't hear on my CNN show now. When I'm interviewing people now, it's often for fifteen minutes or half of the hour. The open-ended time frame of that first show gave me the chance to explore. For example, I might have asked Michael Phelps, the guy who just won eight gold medals in the 2008 Olympics, "When did you start to swim? Did you like swimming right away? Did you ever think of swimming as a way to make money? What about swimming in salt water?" You'd never ask those questions on a television show now. Now it's *bam!* "What was winning today like?"

It's very different to have General Petraeus on and ask, "What's happening with the surge?" than it is to ask, "Why did you make the army your career? What do you like about it? What do you like about strategy? How good are the Iraqis as fighters? How do you motivate an army?"

Naturally, I'd love to ask those questions if I had the time. That was the pleasure of that Sunday night show in Miami. I could go as far as my curiosity would take me. Sometimes the show would go to 2 a.m. Other times it would end at 3. We took calls, but we didn't have the technology to broadcast them. So messages and questions were written down and handed to me for discussion.

The first show was a debate about whether China should be admitted to the UN. I was placed at a table between two guys with opposing viewpoints. Big mistake. Major blunder. Because I was sitting in a swivel chair. Every time I'd turn to the other speaker, I couldn't stop. The whole show, I was trying to stop myself. It was weird to be swiveling, and weirder to know that I was being seen swiveling. I was further conscious of it because I had come to understand the power of television during the Kennedy-Nixon presidential debate.

I heard that debate on the radio. My conclusion was that these were two intelligent guys who basically agreed. When I got to the radio station to do my show, everyone was saying, "Oh, Kennedy mopped the floor with him."

"What?"

"Kennedy destroyed him."

They felt that way because they'd seen the debate on TV. Nixon looked drawn and gray, and wasn't well made up. Kennedy was in a sharp suit and stood more erect. It had nothing to do with the quality of what they said and everything to do with how they looked. That's when I realized television's impact as a visual medium.

So I knew there was going to be no mistaking my swivel. The *Miami Herald* wrote something like: "In an age when the television talk show host is beginning to be prominent, we now have a new feature. A swiveling, smoking host." Someone at my radio station actually said, "It's so different from any show we've ever seen. Why don't you leave the swivel chair in?"

Gleason watched the show and then came in to be interviewed as a guest. He arrived before I did, broke in to the general manager's office to find a couch, got a chair, found a different lamp. I can still see him standing on the set. "That don't go, pal. This goes here. That goes there. We'll move this over here." He went into the control room and prelit the set. What were we going to do, stop him? He was an aesthetic genius. I wonder if there is anyone today who could come as a guest to a television show and change the set?

And he was a great guest. He was a ponderer, a philosopher who grappled with his thoughts. He was curious about life and death. He used to call himself a roaming Catholic. He was torn between the idea that you could go to a heaven where all would be well—and the logic that defies that. He was interested in religious leaders and how they found faith. He had a lot of time to think about these things because he was an insomniac. He never read novels, only nonfiction. A mind like his appreciated good questions—and that might have been the core of our friendship.

The actor-director-novelist Peter Ustinov once told me he loved good interviews. When I asked him why, he said they made him think about things he hadn't thought about—that's what a good interviewer does. My style meshed perfectly with Jackie. That night, the show lasted for *five* hours.

When another local channel made a better offer and I moved, Jackie helped me out by doing a promotional spot for the new show. "You're all lucky," he said. "Larry King's coming to Channel 4."

But one of the greatest things he did for me came from a simple question he posed. Jackie liked to make games out of questions. The game one night was, What in your profession is impossible?

There was a doctor with us that night. The doctor said, "In my profession, they will never make blood in a laboratory. It's impossible. You can go ten million years into the future and you'll see that blood will never be made in a lab."

Jackie looked at me and asked, "What's impossible in your profession?"

"Well," I said, "I do a local radio show every night between nine and twelve. Frank Sinatra doing my radio show for three hours on one night—that's impossible."

This was 1964. There was nobody bigger in the world than Frank Sinatra and he *never* did interviews. Sinatra was the only person I knew of at the time who would not return a call from the *New York Times*.

Jackie immediately said, "Frank is performing at the Fontainebleau next week. What night is he dark?"

I said, "On Monday. He doesn't work Monday."

Jackie said, "You got him."

I said, "What are you telling me?"

He said, "You got Frank Sinatra on Monday night."

I said, "Look, if I've got Frank Sinatra on my radio show next Monday night, I've got to tell people. I've got to promote it."

"Promote it!" Jackie said.

So I went on my radio show that night and said, "Ladies and gentlemen, next Monday night we'll have Frank Sinatra for three hours."

A station exec called me up the next day and said, "Are you kidding?"

I understood exactly where the exec was coming from. To give you an idea how remote the possibility of getting Frank on my show was at the time, imagine that Vladimir Putin had never given an interview in the United States. Now imagine Barbara Walters, Katie Couric, Charlie Gibson, Brian Williams, Diane Sawyer, and Larry King asking and being turned down. And then one evening, Putin agrees to do a local radio show for three hours. Well, this exec obviously wasn't aware of Gleason's definition of clout, which is the best definition there is:

"If you think you have it, you have it. If you think you don't have it, you don't have it. And if you think you don't have it, and you have it, you still don't have it."

I said to the exec, "Jackie Gleason told me we'd have him."

"OK . . ." he said, but I could tell he didn't believe it.

Friday came along. The exec called. He said the station was taking out a big ad in the *Miami Herald* on Monday. "Full page ad," he said. "Gonna cost a lot of money. Here's the problem. We've been calling the Fontainebleau Hotel and leaving messages to confirm that Frank will be on the show. But Frank hasn't returned any of our calls. We're getting a little nervous."

So I said, "OK, I'll call Jackie."

I dialed up Jackie. "Jackie, they're nervous at the station."

Jackie said, "*Are you questioning me, pal?* I told you he'll be there, and he'll be there!"

"OK, Jackie," I said, "I'm sorry."

So the station ran the ad. Monday night came. Nobody went home. The secretaries—they all worked nine to five. They all waited. Everybody at the station stayed.

It was five minutes to nine. No car. Nothing.

It was four minutes to nine. Three minutes. Nothing.

I was supposed to go on at five after the hour. At nine o'clock sharp, a limo pulled up. Out of the car stepped Frank's PR guy, Jim Mahoney, and there he was—Frank Sinatra. He came up the stairs. He said, "Which one's Larry King?"

Timidly, I raised my hand. "Me."

"OK, let's do it!"

As we were going into the booth, the PR guy pulled me aside. He said, "I don't know how you got him. But I'll tell you one thing. He pays me big money *not* to do this!"

I stepped toward the booth and the PR guy pulled me back. "Just one thing," he said. "Don't ask about the kidnapping of his son."

So I was thinking, better not ask about the kidnapping or Frank will walk off.

"OK," I told the PR guy. "It's none of my business."

So Frank and I went in the booth. We sat down. The light went on. We were on the air.

Now a lot of talk show hosts would have said, "My guest tonight is an old friend—Frank Sinatra. Great to see you again, pal."

That's bullshit. I learned a long time ago never to lie to a radio audience—or any audience.

But you've got to understand, there was something in the air. The whole audience was wondering. Larry. Frank. Larry? Frank? It didn't make sense. Frank was at the top of the world. Larry was a local radio guy making $120 a week. How did he know Frank?

I wasn't going to pretend that I knew him. So I was honest. As soon as I introduced him, my first question was, "Why are you here?"

It was a good question. He had to tell me something, right? I think Frank appreciated the honesty.

He said, "I'll tell ya. About a month ago, just before a closing night, I got laryngitis. Couldn't sing. Couldn't speak. I didn't know what to do. We had a packed house.

"So I called up Jackie Gleason. I said, 'Jackie, will you come and do the show?'

"He said, 'OK.' So he came and did the show. It was wonderful. After the show, I walked him out to his limo, leaned in, and whispered, 'Jackie, I owe you one.'

"When I checked in to the Fontainebleau Hotel there was a message to call up Jackie. So I did. I said, 'Jackie, it's Frank.' He said, 'Frank, this is the one.'"

Well, Frank and I really got along. Frank was a great interview. Ella Fitzgerald had no idea where her voice came from.

With Louie Armstrong, it was: "I just play." But Frank—he could break it down. I remember him telling me, "I lay there listening to Heifetz play the violin. I didn't know the song. I didn't know classical music. I'd never heard the melody. And I'm crying. And I said to myself, 'What is he doing?' Or, I'd watch Tommy Dorsey play the trombone. And his jacket wouldn't move. Wouldn't move! And these amazing notes are coming out. All with that great breath control. I tried to ape that. How could I ape that sound? How could I interpret that music? Could I make *you* cry?" Frank would think about things like that.

Frank became really comfortable during the interview. So, you see, there's a lesson in being honest and remaining who you are. In the middle of the interview, I said to him, "Frank, the thing between you and the press. Has it been overplayed? Or have you been bum-rapped?"

He said, "Well, it's probably been overplayed. But I've been bum-rapped, too. Take my son's kidnapping . . ."

I looked over at the PR guy and thought he would faint.

Frank told the whole story of the kidnapping and how the press treated him!

Why? Because he felt comfortable. Years later—after we'd done many other radio and television interviews—he wrote me a letter that included a sentence that would have made Jackie Gleason smile. It said, "What you do is you make the camera disappear."

I became very friendly with Frank as a result of that first interview. After it was over, after three hours, he said, "Hey, kid, you wanna come see the show?"

"YEAH!" I said.

"Come tomorrow night. You're sitting ringside. Bring a guest."

Now, I could choose any woman in town to go with me, and I knew I was going to get laid. *You wanna come see Frank*

Sinatra sing? We're sitting ringside! Could it get any better than that?

I asked this pretty girl I liked, and we went to the show. We were sitting right in front of the stage having a wonderful dinner and listening to Frank Sinatra. It was great. But here's the thing. In the middle of every show, Sinatra always had a cup of tea and talked to the audience. I had no idea what was coming. All of a sudden, while he was drinking his cup of tea, he said, "By the way, I don't do interviews. But I want to tell you about a young man in the audience tonight. I owed a favor to Jackie Gleason and Jackie introduced me to this guy and I did an interview with him and he was terrific. It was a great interview. I want him to take a bow. You're going to be hearing a lot about him. Larry King, stand up."

Now, the girl and I were in the middle of dessert. I was eating cherries jubilee. I had no idea Frank was going to introduce me. In my haste to stand, I bumped the table, the cherries jubilee went flying and landed all over my white shirt and pants. There was nowhere to hide. Cherries jubilee is *very* red. Sinatra started to laugh. The band was laughing. The audience was laughing. The girl was laughing.

It was really embarrassing. What could I do? I wiped myself off and we enjoyed the second half of the show.

The performance ended and it was time to drive the girl home. I knew it was going to be a good night.

After paying the bill, I had eighteen dollars left in my pocket. I knew I needed three dollars for the car. So I left fifteen dollars as a tip for the waiter. When I gave the valet three dollars for the car, I had absolutely nothing left. But that was OK. The girl had already invited me home.

On the way, she said, "Oh, I don't have any coffee. Why don't we stop and bring home a couple of containers?"

What was I going to do with this dilemma? I was a big

shot who just took her to see Frank Sinatra, and I didn't have a cent in my pocket.

So I pulled in to Royal Castle. I told her to wait in the car, that I'd be right back. A few minutes later I came back to the car without anything.

She said, "Where's the coffee?"

I said, "They can't change a hundred dollar bill."

Chapter 8

Chasing the '60s

SOMETIMES I USED TO WONDER: *Where the hell did all the money go?* I didn't do drugs. I wasn't a drinker. I wasn't into nightclubs. I just lived beyond my means. I should have owned a Chevy. I drove a Lincoln. A new Lincoln. Every year. There were women. Days at the racetrack. All I can tell you is, the bigger I got, the more money I owed.

My real problem was that money just didn't mean anything to me. If I owed a hundred thousand dollars and somebody called me up in a pinch and asked for some cash, I'd give him what I had. I was never good at saying no even when it was the smartest thing to do. Not only was I borrowing from Peter to pay Paul, I was lending to Pat at the same time. It was a flighty way to live. But I was able to get away with it. Bank presidents signed off on loans without a credit check because they were fans.

Talent got me out of one jam after the next. If I heard it once, I heard it a hundred times. The station manager would call me in and say, "Larry, the furniture store phoned. You are so good at what you do. Why aren't you paying what you owe to the furniture store?"

"Oh, I'll be better," I'd say. "I'll try."

If I meant it, I didn't do anything about it. I don't think I ever looked at myself and said, *There are going to be some changes here.*

Some part of me must have liked living that way—on the edge. I should have known better. I'm not dumb. Why do smart people do dumb things? Even worse, why does a smart person repeat a dumb mistake? That's the definition of insanity—repeating the same behavior and expecting a different result.

It's like one of the great gambling jokes. This guy is leaving Las Vegas. He's lost a lot of money, and he's totally depressed, whacked out. A voice comes to him, saying, "Go back to Las Vegas."

He shakes his head, pulls in to a gas station, gets some gas. Again, the voice appears out of nowhere, "Go back to Las Vegas!"

The guy turns to the attendant and asks, "You hear anything?"

"No," the attendant says.

So the guy's certain that God is talking to him. He makes a U-turn. Drives back to Las Vegas. As he's driving down the Strip, the voice comes to him again. "Go to Caesars Palace."

He pulls in to the parking lot and walks into Caesars Palace. The voice comes again. "Go to the roulette table. Play the red!"

The guy goes to the cashier, writes a check for everything he owns—thousands of dollars—and puts it all down on the red.

The roulette wheel spins.

Comes up black.

And the voice says, "Shit!"

I don't think I was addicted to gambling. I stopped playing blackjack after I caught myself cursing at a dealer who gave me bad cards. It wasn't his fault. The dealer *wanted* me to win. That way, he could get a nice tip. I felt much better yelling at horses that couldn't hear me. I can still remember the pain of having the winning ticket at the racetrack only to learn my horse had fouled another and been disqualified.

No matter how bad my finances got, once my show started, all my problems and pressures vanished. When I was on the air, I didn't have to make a payment. I was in control. I was live and in the moment. And you couldn't help but lose yourself to the moment during the '60s—especially when the moments started to come faster and faster. My life has always been go, go, go. But I could never seem to catch up during the '60s.

Sometimes you don't know you're living in a crazy time until after it's over. During the '60s, we knew we were in a whirl. Every day I'd wake up and think, *What now?* And every day something else would happen. The '60s was the most amazing decade in American history. It all started with John Kennedy becoming president. I can remember tanks rumbling down the street outside my window when our intelligence dis- covered nuclear weapons in Cuba and we had the showdown with Khrushchev and the Soviet Union. Then came Kennedy's assassination. The Vietnam War. "I Have a Dream." The Bea- tles. Malcolm X. Muhammad Ali. The Cold War. The Civil Rights Act. Women's lib. Israel's Six Days' War. Hippies. Drugs. Burning bras. Vietnam War protests. Martin Luther King Jr.'s assassination. Bobby Kennedy's assassination. Police brutality at the '68 Democratic convention. Black-gloved fists raised on the Olympic victory stand. Race riots. Cities burn- ing. The *Eagle* landing on the moon.

There were no twenty-four-hour news networks to cover all this. We had CBS, NBC, and ABC. News from Vietnam came a day late. All these events needed to be placed into context and understood. The best places to hear them talked out in Miami were my radio and television shows. I was at the center of the swirl. Once you've had Sinatra on your show, you can get anybody. A friend of Richard Nixon's, Bebe Rebozo, was a big fan of my show. So Nixon came on when he visited. All the major players of the '60s would pass through Miami on vacation, and every one of them came on my show.

Not only did I have clout, but my life seemed to be personally intertwined with everyone else's. When I saw the footage of John Kennedy's assassination, saw the force of the bullet strike and his head lurch forward, I recalled the moment in Palm Beach when my car hit the back of his convertible.

I was driving to lunch when the news came over the radio that the president had been shot. I had an instant of denial. *That can't be, I just saw him a few days ago.* In fact, Kennedy had given a speech the week before at a conference in Miami. When he recognized me in the third row, he winked. But my instant of denial was just that. I made a U-turn to get back to the radio station over a cobblestone bridge-walk and nearly wrecked my car.

America was never the same after that. Kennedy was the first president born in the twentieth century. He brought us youth and possibilities. He told us we would land a spacecraft on the moon by the end of the decade. His assassination was such a terrible awakening. I'll never forget how Nixon found out. Nixon had lost the presidential election to Kennedy in 1960. By coincidence, Nixon flew out of Dallas on November 22, 1963, just as the city was preparing for the arrival of the president. He was traveling commercial. Back then, even vice-presidents didn't receive Secret Service protection. That came after Kennedy's assassination. As Nixon's plane took off, the guy sitting next to him said, "A couple of thousand votes and it could have been you arriving today."

"I don't even think about it," Nixon told the guy.

When he landed in New York, the car that was supposed to meet him was at the wrong terminal. So he got in a cab. The cab left the airport but made a wrong turn and ended up on a street in Queens. A woman came running out of her home screaming. Nixon rolled down the window and asked, "What's the matter?" The woman saw him and fainted. Nixon got out of the cab to help her. People came running over, and that's how he found out that Kennedy had been killed.

The aftershocks kept coming, and they often hit in ways that couldn't be immediately understood. I got back to the radio station and began phoning people who knew Kennedy. I reached the former ambassador to Ireland, Edward Grant Stockdale. His wife was a prominent poet, and they lived in Miami. The ambassador was disconsolate to the point where he couldn't get a word out. He was moaning and groaning over the phone. I didn't even know if he heard me. Later on, he jumped out of the window of a downtown office building and killed himself. The only thing on his desk was an issue of *Life* magazine with Kennedy pictured on the cover.

Talk of the assassination must have filled my radio and television shows for two weeks straight. I did one show with Dick Gerstein—the state attorney who in happier times had been a target for Captain Wainright's humor on my morning radio show. Gerstein talked about how Kennedy had been protected in Dade County when he'd come to give the speech I'd seen a week before the assassination.

The more time passed, the more implausible the shooting began to seem. Here was this young, vibrant, sexy, dynamic, rich guy—and some little punk shoots him? It had to be bigger than Lee Harvey Oswald. I later became involved in the whole mystery because I knew the district attorney of New Orleans, who was convinced that JFK was assassinated in a gigantic conspiracy. My involvement with that district attorney would turn my life upside down in the early '70s. But that's for another chapter.

Kennedy's assassination seemed to set in motion everything that followed. As I look back, I don't know how I kept up with it all. Just staying on top of the civil rights movement was a full-time occupation in the '60s. There was an incident with Martin Luther King Jr. that remains etched in my mind. King was attempting to integrate a privately owned motel in Tallahassee. He'd made a reservation. I knew the lawyer who was going to represent him in Florida. It was understood that if Dr. King walked into the motel and insisted on a room, he would be put in jail. The lawyer asked if I wanted to come along.

I was right next to King when he walked into the motel. It had maybe twenty rooms. He walked up to the desk and said, "I have a reservation here. Dr. King."

The clerk said, "We don't accept Negroes."

Dr. King walked out and sat on the stoop. The squad cars came up. The owner of the hotel came out. The owner said to Dr. King, "What do you want? *What-do-you-want?*"

Dr. King looked up and said, "My dignity."

I froze.

Nothing bothers me more than bigotry. What should skin color have to do with anything? A job? An election? A game? A house? What do you care? I never could understand it. I wrote about my feelings in the *Miami Herald*, and a guy responded with a letter to the editor. In this letter, he wrote, "What if your daughter married a black?" I printed his letter in my next column and responded, "I'd have to warn her about guys like you." Even with Barack Obama winning the presidency more than forty years later, we're still dealing with it. We've come a long way, and yet we haven't.

But back then, tensions that had been boiling for four hundred years were suddenly on the surface. Stokely Carmichael told me he'd been at a school that was getting integrated. A cop made a black student get down on the ground, then he put a boot to the kid's neck, pulled out a gun, and said, "You go into that school and I'm going to shoot you." From that day forward, he told me, he never was calm again.

I had to contain myself when the Alabama governor George Wallace came on my television show. Wallace had stood in front of doors at the University of Alabama to block black students from entering. As he walked in to the television station, Wallace looked around, smiled, and said with a smirk, "I don't see any black people."

"They own the station," I said. "They're out to lunch."

Whenever I've had to interview people I've strongly disagreed with, I've always pushed myself to go beyond my feelings and seek the best answers. But with Wallace, I became argumentative. I told him a story that the leader of a civil rights group called the Congress of Racial Equality (CORE) had told me. The CORE leader had been stationed in Galveston, Texas, with an all-black detail in the Army during World War II. When a German submarine had problems and surfaced, the black soldiers took the German crew prisoner. They stopped at a restaurant to get food on the way to Beaumont. The German prisoners were allowed to eat inside. The black soldiers were forced to eat outside. "Tell me why I shouldn't be angry," the head of CORE said.

"What would you have said to that man, Governor?" I asked Wallace.

"I don't have time to talk to everybody," Wallace responded. It would be many years before he had the capacity to confront that question, and when he did, he changed his ways.

I can remember interviewing John Howard Griffin—a white guy who had his skin artificially darkened so that he could see what it was like to be black in the South. He wrote about the experience in *Black Like Me*. I had him on with the writer James Baldwin.

Griffin commiserated with Baldwin, saying that after three months he couldn't wait for the color to disappear. He knew it would take a year, and he could barely endure living in his artificial skin for the remaining nine months.

"You knew you were going to change," Baldwin said. "My color is not going to change. I'm going to live with it every day of my life."

What do you say to that?

I had that powerful moment, then I bumped into J. Edgar Hoover, the FBI chief who I later learned was spying on Dr. King, at Joe's Stone Crab. We got into a conversation and I mentioned that I was traveling to San Francisco for the first time. Hoover asked me when. When I landed, an FBI agent was waiting. He showed me around the city for four days. When I say he showed me around, I mean he showed me around. The agent was waiting with the car when I got out of the theater. He knew all the best restaurants. That, I found out, is how J. Edgar Hoover handled public relations.

I had that experience, and then I was blown away on my show when I asked the police chief of Los Angeles, William Parker, about the FBI. Parker was a no-nonsense guy. The police building in downtown L.A. is now named after him. Usually when I asked police chiefs about the FBI, their comments were laudatory.

"J. Edgar Hoover is not a cop," Parker said. "He's the best PR man in the country. I'd put any one of my L.A. policemen against any FBI agent on any investigation. They're frauds and phonies." Not long afterward, two FBI agents were at the station doors asking for the tape.

One day, I was talking with generals selling the Vietnam War. Another day, I opened the mike to Abbie Hoffman, who once attempted to stop the war by organizing a rally in which fifty thousand people tried to use psychic energy to levitate the Pentagon. Israeli leaders like Moshe Dayan and Golda Meir stopped in while fund-raising. And then there were fierce protests against me by Jewish listeners when I invited an

Egyptian delegation on my show. As if an Egyptian point of view was unthinkable.

If you were living in Miami, I was everywhere you looked or listened. In 1962 I moved to WIOD, the largest radio station in the area, and my interviews could be heard on weeknights from nine to midnight. I'd also climbed to the top of the ladder in local television, leaving Channel 10, the coming-of-age ABC affiliate, and joining Channel 4, the CBS affiliate that dominated the market. I now had interview segments at six and eleven every Saturday and Sunday evening. My Sunday shows were on each side of *60 Minutes*, which actually bombed at its inception because it aired on Tuesday nights opposite *Bonanza*. One of the reasons it was moved to Sunday night was that it did well in that time slot in Miami. I was churning out my newspaper column for the *Miami Herald* and speaking at events across the city. When William F. Buckley, a founder of the conservative movement, came to visit Miami, he joked, "I can't escape you."

Again and again, my talent and clout kept me out of trouble. The station manager might call me in with complaints from the husband of a woman I had an affair with. "Larry, you're so good. Why do you have to do things like this?" But what could he do? I was Mr. Miami. When the Dolphins arrived as an NFL expansion team and the first color commentator on the broadcast crew wasn't very good, who did management turn to in order to draw more listeners? *Hear Larry King, Sunday on Dolphin football!*

My social life was as out of control as my finances. David Letterman has made fun of me for being married seven times to six different women, and he didn't know that it was really eight marriages to seven. I can't explain it. But I can tell you something I've always believed. What you're like at twenty is not what you're like at thirty. And what you're like at thirty is not what you're like at forty. And so on. When you look at the world that way, three marriages in a lifetime might be healthy. But no matter how you look at it, eight is not.

I never told anybody about the first time I got married in Florida. Not even my brother. There was no wedding party. I was this young kid, and I got into an affair with a beautiful woman ten years older than me. Annette was thirty-four. I had never known such a thing in Brooklyn. Going out with a woman ten years older than me? Come-mahhhhn! But she was a mentor in a way. It was crazy, and it was probably made more adventurous by the fact that she was married when I met her.

Annette had three kids. Her marriage was obviously not working out. After she got divorced, she told me that she'd done so because of me and insisted that I marry her. She could be very controlling, and I was never good at saying no. We were married at Broward City Hall. But I was young, and I wasn't going to be boxed in. I never lived with her. I can't remember seeing her much after the wedding—maybe a couple of times. Divorce papers were filed as a matter of course.

One thing I've learned is that you can never plan to fall in love. You simply cannot say, *Today, it's going to happen. I'm going to fall in love.* And if you do meet someone and it does happen, you can't get out of it. Events may push you out of it. But *you* can't get out of it. Nobody's ever explained it. Shakespeare tried. The best I can do to describe the feeling is this: Falling in love is when you meet someone and she says, "I'll call you at six." Five after six comes, she hasn't called, and you're out of your mind.

That's what it was like with Alene. I met her while I was doing a show at Pumpernik's about Playboy Bunnies. She came with her cousin. Alene was too young to be a Bunny at the time—the age requirement was twenty-one and she was twenty. But she would become one, and I was attracted to her right away.

The only experience I had to compare it with at the time was what I felt for the Dodgers. When you develop an attachment to a team, your emotional well-being is dependent on the actions of others. The Dodgers could make me very happy. Or they could hurt me terribly—without their even knowing it. An innocent girl can do the same. *Oh, I'll call you later.*

The courting stage was not simple. Alene had a five-year-old son when I met her. That wasn't a problem; Andy was a great kid. And he made me feel like a little bit of a big shot. I'll never forget the day the adoption became official. The judge asked Andy if he liked his new name. When Andy told him yes, I felt a surge of pride I'd never known. All of a sudden I was telling people that I had a child. I've always considered myself a good dad. I just wasn't a very good husband. I was always off in my own direction. Even when I was married, a part of me always felt single. Then again, this was not your *Ozzie and Harriet* kind of marriage. I'd step into the bathroom and find Bunny costumes hanging.

The Playboy Club was a new type of experience back then. The sexual revolution was getting under way. As a Bunny, Alene was making three times my income in tips. She had a very low voice and didn't talk a lot, and she came off very mysterious. I may not have been very good at fidelity. But I was intensely jealous at the same time. Once, Alene came home and told me there was a guy who came every day for lunch, sat at her table, and tipped her fifty dollars no matter what he ate. Playboy Bunnies weren't allowed to wear wedding rings, and he assumed she was single. The guy was shy, and obviously enamored of her. She wasn't sure how she wanted to handle it. I showed up the following day with a couple of friends and took over the next table. "Hey, there's the wife!" I shouted as loud as I could, and broke this guy's heart.

It's impossible to know what happens to that feeling over time. Where does it go? Alene and I divorced. After we were separated, I introduced her to a guy who had a jazz show on the radio station, a sort of Pied Piper of the times, free love and all that went with it, and he took Alene off to Iowa. It was a blow to my ego, which might explain why I rebounded by marrying a woman who worked at the radio station. The marriage did not work out for long and to this day the woman wishes to remain anonymous. I'm going to respect her wishes. But I can't overlook something that's difficult for me to talk about. We had a daughter. When this woman fell in love with another guy, she asked that he be allowed to adopt the child. Outside of my time in front of the microphone, my life was out of control, and I went along with the woman's wishes. It seemed like it was the right thing to do. So I did it. When Alene returned from Iowa, the sparks came back from wherever they'd been, and we married again.

Sometimes I wonder if the entanglements, the poor handling of money, and all the stress that came with it made me better on the air. Was I scrappier? I'll never know. The only thing I can tell you is that the microphone was my sanctuary. I couldn't screw it up and it was never going to stab me in the back. People could be calling me for money. My marriages might be dissolving before my eyes. Bobby Kennedy and Martin Luther King Jr. could be taken away from us all in the blink of an eye. But when I stepped behind a microphone, I was in control.

My marriage to Alene did not work the second time either. But life is yin and yang. Sometimes great benefits come out of difficult times. Alene got pregnant. I was driving on Biscayne Boulevard en route to North Miami General Hospital in 1967, when two of the best sentences I ever heard on WIOD came over a newscast. "Bulletin just in. Larry King has a seven-pound, three-ounce baby girl." Happiness could have blown me straight through the roof.

I pulled in to the hospital lot, ran into the room, and a doctor was holding up a little girl. We called her Chaia. Alene had loved the book *The Chosen* by Chaim Potok. And my mother's mother was named Chaia. It's like the Hebrew toast, "To life." The loss of my own father when I was young has always remained with me. Even after Alene and I divorced for the second time, I was a good absentee father. I still have images in my mind of taking Chaia to the opening of Disney World and of her brother Andy smiling on the sidelines during Miami Dolphins games.

Maybe it's just the way I see the world. But as a tumultuous decade came to an end, two recollections stand out in my mind. They speak to laughter and promise. Maybe it has to do with being born Jewish. No matter how difficult the times, comedy always survives to triumph.

I had Mel Brooks on the night that we landed on the moon. Brooks is probably the funniest man I've ever met. There was nothing better than his comedy album *2,000 Year Old Man*.

I said to him, "OK, let's play 2,000 Year Old Man. You're two thousand years old. Tonight, we landed on the moon. What do you think of that?"

"The moon is my favorite thing in the whole universe," he said. "Nothing better than the moon. I worship the moon. The moon is my friend."

"Why?" I asked.

"Because for four hundred years I thought I had a cataract. Then one day this guy named Irving said, 'Isn't the moon beautiful tonight?' And I said: 'The wha—?'"

The other memory is from the beginning of 1970, when Don Shula was named head coach of the Dolphins. I was the emcee at a welcome lunch. All the players were in the crowd.

We were on the dais and Don said to me, "Which one is Griese?"

He didn't know which one was the quarterback, Bob

Griese. I pointed Bob out, and Don asked me to have Bob come up.

So I had Bob come up.

"I want to sit with you and get working on the offense," Shula said. This was in the off-season, months before practice started.

Griese said, "Great, how about next week?"

Shula said, "How about tomorrow?"

I knew then, this guy Shula was going to be something special. In time, he would mold the Dolphins into the only team ever to have a perfect season. It's still talked about thirty-seven years later in the sports world, and to anyone who lived in Miami at the time it will remain as unforgettable as the moon landing.

But I wasn't really a part of it. It was about the only time in my life I would ever ask myself, *What am I doing not there?*

ANOTHER POINT OF VIEW

Marty Zeiger

I used to joke, "Larry, you know how George Washington was the father of this country? You're sort of the husband of this country."

He's sensitive about it. The thing is, Larry is actually very traditional. He didn't believe in living with women. He married them.

So the multiple marriages can be explained in part by what happens when tradition meets impetuousness and restlessness. It was leap before you look. There was nothing anybody else could do but watch it play out. Then it becomes, *What was that about?*

Herbie "The Negotiator" Cohen

To be honest, I wasn't very surprised about all those wives. I'll tell you why. First of all, Miami was a crazy place at that time. It was the Las Vegas of America before Las Vegas. Sinatra was there. Jackie Gleason was there. In that culture, it was much more accepted to see women and have relations.

Now combine that with the fact that Larry is in love with being in love. If Larry loved someone, instead of sleeping with her, which would be the way most people would handle those situations, Larry married her. Strange as it may seem, getting married that much is his conservatism. It's sort of like the Elizabeth Taylor way of doing things—only I think he surpassed Elizabeth Taylor.

Andy King

SON

One thing you have to understand about my dad is that his life brought him an overwhelming number of choices. Just growing up with him was like being in a fantasyland.

Whatever your fantasy was, it would come true. You want to meet Joe Namath? "We're having dinner with him." I'd go to see Muhammad Ali at the Fifth Street Gym and he'd throw a jab at my head and kid around with me because he was a friend of my dad. My dad would ask, "What do you want to be when you grow up?" Whatever the answer, he could arrange for me to talk with an expert in that field. He'd interview someone in aviation and they'd offer him free pilot lessons. He'd say, "No thanks, but my son might like that." Next thing you know, I had a pilot's license. There were so many options presented. Life was, "Here's everything."

I believe I've been to just about all of my dad's marriages. I can't think of any that I wasn't at—that I'm aware of. My dad has always been an in-the-moment kind of guy. So I guess I thought early on that there was no right "one" for my dad.

He would meet somebody new and ask me, "How do you like her?"

My answer to him was always, "Does she make you happy?"

He'd say "Yes," because in that moment, he was happy.

And I'd say, "Be happy."

Marty Zeiger

Everyone will bring their own experience into how they're looking at Larry. It's sort of like the movie *Rashomon*. The same scene is interpreted very differently by many sets of eyes.

I remember how beautiful Alene was. I remember being the best man at the wedding that came after the first one to Alene. My recollection of that wedding is of their laughter. There is happiness at every wedding. But there was something frivolous about the laughter at that wedding. It gave me the feeling the marriage wasn't going to last.

Knowing Larry, it had to be very painful for him to give up the child that came out of that wedding for adoption.

Chaia King
Daughter

In the early days, my dad was known as a penetrating interviewer. You don't see that as much now because society has changed. Now the show has got to move fast. There are bullets at the bottom of the screen and panels of people. But his gift is in one-on-one interviewing and getting to know what's behind a person. That really is his talent. He can go deep into others in a nonthreatening way. But he won't turn that on himself.

I'm not saying I know what's at the bottom of my father's many relationships. I'm certainly no expert on marriage. But I know one thing. If you take a risk and you love somebody, if you're really committing yourself, you're opening yourself to be hurt. Which is why I think my father's experiences all relate back to when he lost his father at such a young age. You can look at what he's been through as a form of running to protect his heart.

Chapter 9

Trouble

I'VE SEEN the mug shot. They publish it sometimes in the tabloids under the headline FAMOUS ARREST PICTURES. It's been run next to Sinatra's. A lot of famous people have been arrested.

I'm certainly not proud of that picture. The police didn't treat me like a criminal when it was taken. They all knew me and were very nice. I was fingerprinted, photographed, and released on my own recognizance within ten minutes. Some of the guys helped sneak me out the back door to avoid the press.

When I look back on that moment, it's hard to believe that it happened. Boy, was I playing in a league way over my head. JFK's assassination. A multimillionaire. A district attorney. A state attorney. Stacks of hundred dollar bills in brown envelopes. And little Larry Zeiger from Brooklyn. What was I doing there? I ended up the fall guy. But the fall was a long time coming. I'd been playing musical chairs with my finances for years. At some point, the music was bound to stop. I just didn't count on being arrested when it did. Here's what happened.

One of the fans of my radio and television shows was a guy named Lou Wolfson. Lou was a prominent financier who grew

up in Jacksonville and later lived in Miami. His family had a history as liberal Democrats, and he played football at the University of Georgia. Lou became known as "The Great Raider" in
the '60s for the sort of corporate takeovers that gained notoriety in the '80s. He ultimately created an industrial and commercial empire that was said to be worth more than a quarter of a
billion dollars, and would come to own the Triple Crown–winning
racehorse Affirmed. He even tried to buy Churchill Downs.

You couldn't live in Florida in the '60s and not know who
Lou Wolfson was. One day I was walking to place a bet at
Hialeah, and someone called out my name from a private box.
It was Lou Wolfson. Lou Wolfson was calling *my* name.

Lou told me how much he liked my shows, and we made
plans to have dinner the following week. He was under suspi-
cion by federal authorities for stock market manipulations at
the time—this was 1966. But what did I know?

A complicated friendship grew out of that first dinner. Lou
was a generation older than me, and he had the air of a father
figure. When he heard that I was a step ahead of the IRS, he
genuinely wanted to help. He proposed funding an interview
show for me that would be syndicated to bring in more money
than I was making.

There were pluses in the budding friendship for Lou,
too. Lou believed that there was nothing more powerful in
America than the media. "I can have all the money in the
world," he once told me. "But I don't have entrée. *You* have
entrée." I would later come to understand the power he saw
in my connections.

Here's an example of the kind of guy Lou was. Lou heard
a show I did with Ralph Nader. This was back when Nader was
making a name for himself suing automotive companies for
building unsafe cars. General Motors hired private detectives
to discredit Nader. But Nader won the lawsuits and in the

process changed transportation laws. You now wear a seat belt because of Ralph Nader.

Lou wrote Nader a check for twenty-five thousand dollars, and sent it with a note that said something like, "My friend Larry King tells me you're a hell of a guy. I'd like to support Nader's Raiders."

A week later, Lou called to tell me that Nader had returned the check. Ralph had attached a note explaining that he wouldn't accept any donation more than fifteen dollars. If he took too much money, Nader explained, he'd be forced to return phone calls. Lou lived in a world where tipping the maître d' got him the table he wanted, and he was astonished to find someone who wouldn't accept a gift or a favor.

Our friendship developed naturally over dinners and on trips. Occasionally, Lou called me for entrée. Occasionally, I'd introduce Lou to friends and acquaintances in need of money for good causes. "How much do you need?" Lou would ask, reaching for his checkbook. As we grew closer, Lou lent me money so I could stay ahead of my debts.

The trouble started after Lou became intrigued by an interview I'd done with the New Orleans district attorney—Jim Garrison.

Garrison believed that Lee Harvey Oswald had not acted alone in the assassination of John F. Kennedy. He believed there was a giant conspiracy that had roots in New Orleans, and as district attorney he had amassed a lot of facts not known by the public. It would take me three hours to tell you all the intricacies of his theories. Believe me, it'd be easier for you to rent the movie *JFK*. Oliver Stone's film is an accurate depiction of Garrison's beliefs.

There was no bigger event in the '60s than the Kennedy assassination. Not only was it shocking at the moment, it didn't end. It was an unsolved mystery. Everybody wanted to know what really happened on November 22, 1963. I interviewed the cop who arrested Oswald. I asked him if Oswald had said anything to him. "I'm a patsy," Oswald told him. Meaning, of course, that he'd been set up. When the Warren Commission issued a report that said Lee Harvey Oswald had acted alone, much of the public didn't believe it. I remember interviewing Gerald Ford about it—he was a member of the Warren Commission. Anybody who might have something new to say about the assassination made a great guest because the public hungered for the truth. Nothing ever added up correctly. John Connally, who was riding with his wife Nellie in the convertible in front of the president and Jacqueline Kennedy that day, came on my show. He couldn't even agree with his wife on how many shots were fired because he said he didn't hear the shot that hit him. I can still remember Connally showing me the wound in his wrist. And the last words Nellie said to the president over the cheers of the crowd before the shouts rang out: "Mr. President, you can't say that Dallas doesn't love you."

It was only natural that a guy like Wolfson, who had strong links to the Democratic Party, would be intrigued by what Garrison had to say. Lou called me after that show and asked if I could set up a dinner with Garrison. He also asked me to bring along my pal, the state attorney in Miami, Dick Gerstein. Gerstein's job was very similar to Garrison's. Lou thought that a legal mind like Gerstein's would be able to spot any holes in Garrison's theories.

We went to a steak house in Miami Beach—Lou, the two attorneys, and me. Garrison stated his case. Lou questioned him from appetizers to dessert. Dick and I sat and listened.

At the end of the dinner, Lou looked at Dick and said, "Do you believe him?"

"Well, I haven't seen the evidence," Gerstein said. "But I have a lot of respect for Jim. Off what he says, I'd certainly want to know more."

We went to Garrison's hotel room to listen to tapes of people he'd interviewed. I wish I could re-create the eerie mood in that room. The more we listened, the more we just had to know.

Garrison's problem was that the State of Louisiana wouldn't finance his continuing investigation. Remember, the shooting took place in Texas. Garrison was working for the taxpayers of New Orleans. "There are a lot of people who think I'm too caught up in it," he told us. "They don't want me to go any further. I've gone as far as I can go. I need more money to continue."

"How much do you need?" Lou asked.

"About twenty-five thousand."

If Lou had just pulled out his checkbook right then and there and written Garrison a check for twenty-five thousand dollars, my mug shot never would have ended up in the tabloids. It would have been perfectly legal. But Lou came up with another way of getting Garrison the money. His idea was to break the total up into five installments, which he would pass on in cash through me and Gerstein. The idea of transferring cash from me to Gerstein to Garrison may seem crazy now—but not so back then. According to Garrison, people who knew of the conspiracy to kill JFK were showing up dead. There were many good reasons to avoid a paper trail.

I was so caught up in the passion behind Garrison's investigation that I didn't think twice about helping it along. Neither did Gerstein. We felt like we were on the inside of something huge. Plus, it made sense logistically. There were times when Gerstein and Garrison were scheduled to be in the same place. So the arrangement didn't seem at all farfetched.

Every word Garrison said seemed to make his conspiracy theory more ominous. I'll never forget driving Garrison to the airport. He got out of the car, then leaned back in and said: "Within a year, they're going to kill Robert Kennedy." Then he walked away.

Lou gave me a brown envelope filled with five thousand

dollars worth of hundred dollar bills. I passed it on to Gerstein. He passed it on to Garrison. The second or third payment—I can't remember which—came at a time when I
missed connecting with Gerstein. It was also a time when I
owed a tax payment. So I called Lou and asked if I could use
the money to pay my taxes. I had money coming in, and I told
Lou that as soon as it arrived I'd get the five thousand dollars to Gerstein. Lou said that would be OK.

Not long afterward, Lou was convicted of selling unreg-
istered stock. It was a very complicated case.

Lou began to realize he'd need more than his lawyers to
figure a way out of jail. I was with him when his secretary put
in a call to the Supreme Court justice Abe Fortas.

Fortas had represented Lyndon Johnson in 1948 during
a challenge to Johnson's slim margin of victory in the Texas
Democratic primary. Johnson got his Senate seat because of
Fortas, and Fortas became one of his most trusted advisers.
Years later, when he became president, Johnson wanted Fortas to become chief justice of the Supreme Court. There was
only one problem. Fortas was Jewish. Back then, you couldn't
have two Jews on the Supreme Court. It was an unwritten rule
that has since changed. So you know what Johnson did? He
asked Arthur Goldberg to leave the court. He gave Goldberg
an appointment as representative to the UN—just to get Fortas on the Supreme Court. Goldberg didn't have to leave. It's
a lifetime job. But Johnson told him that he really needed
him at the UN—which was bullshit. A hundred other guys
could have been named UN ambassador. Goldberg gave up
his position just so Johnson could put Fortas on the Supreme
Court.

Lou Wolfson was sending Fortas checks for twenty thousand dollars through his foundation. Fortas would speak to
a Jewish organization, and Wolfson's money would defray the

expenses. There was nothing illegal about it. My point in all this is that it wasn't long before Fortas returned Wolfson's call.

The conversation didn't last long, and the expression on Lou's face told me he hadn't gotten the response he wanted. Lou said two words after he hung up, and they were very cold. "That's friendship."

Lou was going to be sentenced, and I guess he was down to his last option. Me.

Richard Nixon had just won the 1968 presidential election. I'd interviewed Nixon many times over the years and knew his friend Bebe Rebozo. Bebe put together a celebratory breakfast at Nixon's vacation home in Key Biscayne and invited about two dozen people. I was on the guest list.

Nixon had a few private moments with each of us at that breakfast. When he got to me, he said, "Larry, I know we don't always agree on the issues, but I've always been treated fairly on your show. Now that I have the chance, is there anything I can do for you?"

Could there have been a better opening?

"Well, Mr. President, there is."

I told him that Lou Wolfson was a friend of mine. Nixon indicated that he knew of Lou. I explained that Lou felt that he'd been convicted of a crime that he didn't commit, and that Lou had documents to prove it. Nixon called over a bald, pudgy guy and introduced him as John Mitchell, his campaign manager. He told me to send along any documents to John and that John would get back to me.

As you can imagine, Lou was thrilled when I told him about what had happened. He gave me documents and called me constantly over the next month to see if I'd heard back from Mitchell. But when Mitchell did call me, the news was not good. Mitchell said he'd have nothing to do with Wolfson.

This put me in a position of making a call I did not want to make. Lou was the type of guy who wouldn't take no for an answer. And I've always been the type of guy who has a hard time saying no. Looking back on it now, I can see how the situation played right into one of my biggest weaknesses.

I did something I'd never do on the air.

I lied.

I told Lou that Mitchell was interested in his legal dilemma.

Now Lou was ecstatic. And he played right into another one of my weaknesses. He gave me thousands of dollars to forward to Mitchell's law firm to look over the case. Not only that, but he told me something that's never come out until right now. Lou said, "Here's what I'll do. Tell them that I'll set up an organization called Democrats for Nixon. I'll fund it at a million a year for four years."

This was getting out of control—but not as out of control as my own financial situation. I used the money Lou gave me to pay off some debts. My game of financial musical chairs continued. And I waited for another opening to figure a way out of this mess. You know me: *Somehow, I'll get out of it.*

The court was about to sentence Lou as Nixon's inauguration approached. Nixon was in New York, staying at the Pierre Hotel. I flew to New York, called the hotel, and asked to speak with the president-elect. I was put on hold. I held and held and held. Knowing what I was about to do, a part of me was actually relieved that nobody was picking up.

"Hello, Larry." Nixon's voice was unmistakable. "What can I do for you?"

I told Nixon it was urgent that I see him. Nixon said that he was flying to Washington later that same evening, but that he was going out for a short walk to pick up his wife. He invited me to join him.

I went to the Pierre. The lobby was filled with reporters, cameramen, and Secret Service agents. When Nixon came down, one of his attendants saw me and brought me over to him. Little Larry Zeiger headed out with the president of the United States inside a ring of Secret Service agents.

The night was cold, and as we began to walk, Nixon joked, "Whatever this is, it must be important for you to be here in this weather when you could be in Miami."

There are uh-oh moments in everybody's life, and this was one of mine. I was about to present the president of the United States with Lou's four-million-dollar offer to create Democrats for Nixon. In a roundabout way, I was about to ask him to pardon my friend.

"Well, Larry, what is it I can do for you?"

The words just wouldn't come out of my mouth. If I'd made the offer, you wouldn't be seeing me on TV today. Because I'm sure that it would have come out in some form. And if it had come out, I would have been caught in a conspiracy to bribe the president. I don't even want to think of the consequences. The only thing I could think of that night was to tell Nixon it would be a big thrill if he'd do my show after the inauguration.

"Why didn't you just ask me on the phone?" he said.

"I just had to do it in person."

The rest of our walk was a little awkward—but nowhere near as awkward as it was for me to walk through Lou Wolfson's front door when I returned to Florida. He was sure Nixon would take the money.

There was no escape from the situation. My mother couldn't get me out of this one. Nor could Herbie the Negotiator. No banker could come to the rescue. There was just no way out. I looked Lou in the eyes and told him the truth about everything that had happened. He didn't scream. He didn't show any outward anger. But I could feel the rage burning inside him.

"Get out of my house," were the last words Lou Wolfson ever said to me.

Lou was sentenced to a minimum-security prison. Before he was sent away, one of his associates set up a repayment schedule for all the money I owed him. I tried to stick to the schedule, but it was hopeless.

I just wished the whole thing would go away. It was such a strange time. I was bigger than ever on the air now that I was the color man for the Miami Dolphins radio broadcasts. I managed to keep my game of financial musical chairs going by constantly borrowing money. But Wolfson always seemed to be in the air. In 1969, an article appeared in *Life* magazine detailing Wolfson's payments to Justice Fortas. Those payments weren't illegal. Fortas was a good and honorable man. But it doesn't look good when a Supreme Court justice accepts money from a felon. Fortas was forced to resign. The whole thing just wouldn't go away.

After Wolfson got out of jail, my life became a theater of the absurd. I scraped up the five thousand dollars that I had taken and sent it back to him. But Lou didn't want it back. Lou wanted something else.

He filed a complaint against me through the office of state attorney *Dick Gerstein*. Think about that. He filed the complaint with the same guy who had taken money from me and passed it on to Garrison. And, as it turned out, there had been several missed connections between Gerstein and Garrison. Gerstein himself had never gotten one of Lou's five-thousand-dollar installments to Garrison. He'd held on to the money for a year before sending it back to Wolfson.

Gerstein certainly didn't want to file charges against me. He was my friend. And, of course, he didn't want his own involvement to come out. Eventually, he was forced to recuse himself from the case. But it didn't look good for him. There were calls for him to resign.

On December 20, 1971, I was charged with grand larceny

and had that mug shot snapped at the police station. As I drove to do my evening radio show that night the lead item on my own station's newscast was my arrest. The general manager met me as I walked to the studio. He said it might be best for me not to go on the air that night. I was suspended, pending the outcome of the charges. The television station where I worked followed suit. As did the newspaper that ran my column. I argued that in America a man was innocent until proven guilty. But nobody would listen.

The trial was set for a Monday morning a month later. The night before, the presiding judge had a heart attack. JUDGE COLLAPSES READING KING BRIEF wasn't exactly the newspaper headline I was counting on.

My lawyer thought we could beat the charges straight up. But there was a more direct strategy. The statute of limitations had run out. A couple of months later, the same judge dismissed the case. I was ecstatic—but not vindicated. The general manager at WIOD said there'd been too much notoriety surrounding the case, and that I couldn't have my job back. The television station and the newspaper had the same attitude.

The only times I've felt in control of my life have been when I was on the air. Now my life was in disarray, and I couldn't control a single second. My friends were sympathetic and a few newspaper writers came to my defense. But I was filled with shame. It was painful even to visit my mother. My mother, who had once gotten the best lamb chops in the butcher shop because she was going to cook them for *Larry King*, couldn't even speak about what had happened. "What have they done to my poor son . . ." was all she could say.

I was thirty-seven years old. I had no job. I had a couple hundred thousand dollars in debts. And a four-year-old daughter. I'd take Chaia to our secret park on our visiting days. That's when the pain cut the deepest—looking at my daughter and knowing I had no way to support her.

Things got bleaker and bleaker. I became a recluse. By late May, I was down to forty-two dollars. My rent was paid only until the end of the month. I locked myself in my apartment wondering how bad things could possibly get. Pretty soon I wouldn't even be able to afford cigarettes. I remembered a night when I was a young man in New York, alone, cold, and without cigarettes or the money to buy them—I had smashed open a vending machine to get a pack.

A friend called up and told me to start living like a human being again. He invited me to the track. I had nothing better to do, and I figured it would be good therapy to get out and have lunch with a friend and watch the horses come down the stretch.

I'll never forget that day. I put on a Pierre Cardin jeans outfit that had no pockets and drove to Calder Race Course. I can still see the horses warming up before the third race. There was a horse called Lady Forli—a filly running against males.

Normally, female horses don't beat males. We're talking cheap horses. I scanned the board and saw that she was 70–1. But my eyes really opened when I looked at the racing form. Racetrack people talk to each other. So I turned to the guy next to me and said, "You know, this horse, three races back, won in more or less the same company. Why is she 70–1?"

"Well," the guy said, "there's a couple of new horses here."

"Yeah, but she should be, like, 20–1. Not 70–1."

Screw it. I bet ten dollars on the horse to win. But I kept looking at the horse. The more I looked at this horse, the more I liked it. So I bet exactas. I bet Lady Forli on top of every other horse and below every other horse. Now I had what's called a wheel.

I kept looking at the horse. *Wait a minute,* I told myself, *I've got four dollars left. I have a pack of cigarettes. I've gotta give the valet two bucks. That still leaves me with money to bet a trifecta.*

My birthday is November 19. Lady Forli was number 11. So I bet 11 to win, 1 to place, and 9 to show.

Now I had bets in for 11 on top, 11 on bottom, and 11 to win. And I had a trifecta—11-1-9.

When the race began, I had two dollars left to my name— and that was for the valet.

They broke out of the gate. The 1 broke on top, the 9 ran second, and the 11 came out third. The 11 passed the 9, passed the 1, and they ran in a straight line all around the track. There was no question about it. The 11 won by five lengths. The 1 was three lengths ahead of the 9. I had every winning ticket. I had it to win. I had the exacta. I had the trifecta. I collected nearly eight thousand dollars. *Eight thousand dollars!*

It had to be one of the happiest moments of my life— certainly the most exciting. But I had no pockets.

So I stuffed all the money in my jacket. It was bundled up. I didn't know what to do with it. I ran out of the track. The valet attendant came over and said, "You leaving so early?"

"Yeah."

"Bad day, Mr. King?"

I tipped him fifty dollars. The guy nearly fainted.

I had to go somewhere, to stop and make sure it was real. I drove to a vacant lot, which is now called Dolphin Stadium. I parked among the weeds and opened up my jacket. All the money spilled out. I counted out about seventy-nine hundred dollars.

I paid my child support for the next year. I paid my rent for a year. I bought twenty cartons of cigarettes and stacked them up in my apartment, and I filled the refrigerator.

It's so much easier to recall every detail of that wonderful day than it is to think about all the pain surrounding it. There was still no job when I got home, and a mountain of debt. What

I really needed was a fresh start. A friend was working at a race-track in Louisiana that needed a publicist, and I got the job.

There were nice people in Louisiana. The work enabled me to send child-support payments. The World Football League started, and I became the color man for the Shreveport Steamers. The locals couldn't believe it. Here was the Miami Dolphins announcer doing *their* games. I'd tell Sinatra stories over dinner and people would look at me in disbelief. So there were mixed feelings. I felt like a big man, but I also came to fully understand everything that I'd lost. I never spoke with Sinatra or anybody else I'd interviewed back in Miami. I was ashamed.

I was in Louisiana for more than a year, and during this time, the Watergate scandal broke. Who was in the middle of it? That bald, pudgy guy named John Mitchell, who had become the attorney general. I was off the air when the burglary was uncovered and Nixon resigned. Part of me was dying inside. I wanted to participate. I wanted to be on the air. After you've been in the action, the hardest part is being out of it.

The racetrack changed hands, and my job went with it. But I lined up another one announcing football games for the University of California. I figured I'd start a new life out west. There were a few months before the season began, so I drove back to Florida to see my mother, Chaia, and Andy.

By this time, my mother had kidney problems. I was helping her get to the bathroom one day when the phone rang. I answered it and a secretary said, "Hold on for Joe Abernathy."

Joe was the new general manager of WIOD.

"Hi," Joe said, "What are you doing?"

I told him about my plans to start afresh in California.

"I've heard your work," he said, "and I read what happened. I really don't understand why WIOD let you go. Would you consider coming back?"

I stood there flabbergasted.

"We can't pay you much, but I'll take care of you."

My mother wept. I didn't have to move across the country. I could be near her.

Soon I was watching the clock count down from the swivel chair in WIOD's glassed-in studio. The engineer gave me a signal. As usual, I had no idea what I was going to say. But as I leaned forward into the microphone, the first words that left my lips told me I was at home and in control again.

"As I was saying . . ."

Looking back, I can be grateful for everything that happened. Sometimes you have to go down before you can go up.

ANOTHER POINT OF VIEW

Andy King

When I got in trouble as a kid, I would be sent to my room. When I came out, we would be on to the next thing. My dad would never hold a grudge. He would be very forgiving.

I guess that's how I saw him during his time of trouble. I was disappointed that he made such bad decisions. But I didn't hold anything against him. It's not that he was an evil person. He just made some bad choices.

Herbie "The Negotiator" Cohen

These were the years of his life when I lost contact with Larry. But I could see the financial problems coming from when Larry was a kid.

Larry was always broke. Hoo-ha had money because his brother had a TV repair store in Corona. Larry would say, "Hoo-ha, loan me five dollars."

Hoo-ha would loan Larry the money. Then they'd get into an argument. They were always getting into arguments. Larry was quite verbal and really articulate. Hoo-ha was—let me put it this way—somewhat slower than Larry. When Hoo-ha would start losing an argument to Larry, he'd change the subject and say, "Where's my five bucks? I want my five dollars now."

Of course, Larry didn't have it. When Larry did get some sort of job and come up with the money, he would say, "Hoo-ha, here's your five dollars."

But Hoo-ha wouldn't take it. He'd say, "I don't need the money, Larry, you keep it."

The next time they'd have an argument, Hoo-ha would say, "Where's my five bucks?"

But he'd never take the money when Larry had it. He wanted the leverage for when they got into their next argument.

Larry always had problems with money, but not so much because of what he was spending. He had problems because if someone asked him for money that he didn't have, he'd give the guy the money anyway. Then he'd have no money and he'd have to borrow money to pay off the people that he owed. He had these tendencies in Bensonhurst, but it really got crazy when he was in Miami.

I think deep down, Larry believes if he had confided in me during that time he would not have had those problems. When we renewed acquaintances in the '70s our relationship came back stronger than ever.

In a moment of despair, he once said to me, "Herbie, do you think I'm ever gonna be able to handle money?"

I said, "You will. You're gonna make a lot more money. When you make a lot more money, you'll hire someone to manage your money. When you do that, you won't have money problems." And that's what happened.

Chapter 10

Timing

A NOTHER OLD JOKE. This one gets to the essence of comedy and maybe even life itself. You say to someone, "Ask me, What makes a great comedian?"

When the person is in the middle of repeating the question, you shout, "TIMING!"

Timing is inborn. You don't have it, you're out of luck. When you do have it, everything seems to come naturally. For some reason, timing always breaks my way.

In late 1977, I got a phone call that changed my life. It came from a guy named Ed Little, who was running the Mutual Broadcasting System. Ed was larger than life; he was 250 pounds of fun and a great salesman.

If you had the chance to see him in action, you instantly knew why he was so successful. I was at his office once when he had three quarters of advertising sold for a Notre Dame football game—but not the fourth quarter. So he called up the head of a beer company, got him on speakerphone, and asked in the most befuddled voice, "Why didn't you call me back?"

"What do you mean?" the executive asked. "I never got

a message." He couldn't have gotten Ed's message, because Ed had never called him.

"Oh, Jesus. Jesus. Jesus," Ed moaned. "I had the last quarter of Notre Dame football open for you. But you didn't get back to me. And now it's taken."

"Wait a minute, Ed," the exec said. "You called to offer it to *me*. I've got a right to that fourth quarter! You called *me* and left the message. That's not fair, Ed!"

"Well, I don't know what I can do."

"Can't you move things around?"

"I don't know," Ed said. "It'll be tough. But I can try . . ."

As the saying goes, Ed could sell air-conditioners in Alaska. And if Ed couldn't sell them, then nobody could. Which is why, in late 1977, when Ed Little thought about the future of advertising on AM radio, he sensed that it was going to die.

FM was overtaking AM. The clarity of the reception was better on FM; it simply no longer made sense to listen to music on AM. It was clear to Ed that it would be increasingly hard for his AM stations to sell advertising, and that a day was coming when it would be virtually impossible. Ed believed that AM radio needed to reinvent the wheel. And he saw me as the new wheel. He asked if I'd be interested in hosting the first national radio talk show.

I knew the Mutual Broadcasting System from when I was a kid. *The Lone Ranger. The Shadow.* Back in the '30s and '40s, the Mutual radio network was a compendium of independent stations that put out exciting shows to compete with NBC, CBS, and ABC. I remembered seeing the Mutual microphone in front of Franklin Delano Roosevelt in the black-and-white photos snapped during the Depression when he delivered that famous line in his first inaugural address, "The only thing we have to fear is fear itself."

It's hard to know if Ed Little could have envisioned Rush Limbaugh and the right-wing fanatics who have taken over AM talk radio today. But Ed was adamant that the national talk show was AM radio's best chance to survive. Not everyone agreed. What interests people in Miami, critics warned, is not what interests people in Denver. But Ed was a step ahead. "I think an all-night national talk show will work," he told me, "as long as the host is interesting across the country. The show can't be just politics or just entertainment. It has to have everything." Maybe Ed knew how many insomniacs there are out there. He asked if I'd give it a try from midnight to five in the morning.

The timing was just right. I doubt that I would have left for Washington if my mother hadn't passed away. I had visited her all the time in her final years. And a little more than a year before the Mutual offer, I'd married Sharon, a former math teacher. She had encouraged me to look into the all-night show, and she was supportive of the move from Miami. I'd met just the right guy to guide me—Bob Woolf. Bob was an agent who represented a lot of baseball players and eventually would handle contracts for the basketball star Larry Bird. I had Bob on my show as a guest, we got to know each other, and he took me on as a client. But describing Bob as my agent is just not adequate. Bob was married to his clients. I talked to him every day, and he stabilized my life.

My attitude toward money was basically still the same. As my friend Herbie says, "People don't change, circumstances change." Miami was not historically a high-paying town. If I'd remained there, I'd be broke and up to my ears in debt to this day. Bob realized that my circumstances needed to change. He negotiated a higher salary with Mutual and arranged for an investment firm in Boston to watch over my money.

The new show launched in Miami. Jackie Gleason and Don Shula were my first guests. Only twenty-eight small stations around the country took the feed that night. There were no overnight ratings in January of 1978. Not that I remember, anyway. All I knew was the show felt right from the start. It was serious, but it didn't take itself seriously. That was the beauty of it. It could go from a profound insight to hysterical laughter in a finger snap.

There was nothing like it on the air. There may have been local personalities who did their own shtick in the morning. But none had a hodgepodge of humor, serious interviews, and listeners from around the country calling in. The format remained the same for years. I interviewed a guest (or guests) for an hour. Then the guest (or guests) answered phone calls for two hours. Then there were two hours of open phones during which anything could come up.

After a couple of months, the show moved just outside Washington, D.C. Not only was the timing perfect, so was the place. I don't know how, but I always seem to be where the action is. The best way I can explain it is like this: Years ago, there was a great middle linebacker for the Chicago Bears named Dick Butkus. He had a tremendous sense for the ball. "Wherever the ball is," people said, "that's where Butkus is." I have that same sense in my own field.

Washington was the hub of power in the late '70s and early '80s, and back then, the word *media* was not in disrepute. The media got respect. Woodward and Bernstein's investigation into the Watergate burglary had forced President Nixon to resign only a few years earlier. The two reporters were seen as heroes, and were played by Robert Redford and Dustin Hoffman in *All the President's Men*. There was no better time or place to be a journalist than Washington in the 1970s. Politicians might spin through town as if through a revolving door. But journalists didn't leave office. They had a cachet that doesn't exist today. They got good tables at restaurants.

Everybody who was anybody in Washington ate at Duke Zeibert's. Ben Bradlee, the editor of the *Washington Post*; George Allen, the coach of the Washington Redskins; Edward

Bennett Williams, the great trial lawyer and owner of the Baltimore Orioles; all the politicians. Duke and I really hit it off when we met. He stayed up to listen to my show, and soon I had the center table, the one that everyone saw as they came inside. I ate lunch at Duke's every day. He refused to let me pick up a check.

It wasn't long before my show was feeding in to the top fifty markets, and Ted Koppel was listening on his way home from his *Nightline* television show. Callers from around the country made our show a great place to feel the pulse of America. Ed Little was right on the money. The country was becoming a smaller place. The mayor of New York was interesting to the guy in Phoenix. Super Bowl matchups intrigued people from coast to coast. People laughed at the humor of the show in Mississippi just as much as they laughed in Wisconsin.

Then came November 4, 1979. Anyone who couldn't imagine the entire country tuning in to one radio show hadn't been counting on November 4, 1979, either. That was a day that grabbed every American and wouldn't let them go for 444 more.

At six thirty in the morning on that day, half a world away, a female student in Iran with a pair of metal cutters hidden beneath her chador approached the gates protecting the U.S. Embassy in Tehran. After she cut the chains, roughly three thousand militants stormed inside. Sixty-six embassy staff members were taken hostage. On the evening news, America watched them being led blindfolded through the streets. Every single call in to my show that night was about the hostages. So was every single call the next. And the night after that. I never heard such anger in all my time in radio. First, that a bunch of terrorists could humiliate the United States. Second, that we seemed powerless to do anything about it.

The militants were demanding the extradition of Iran's old leader, the Shah, who'd received medical treatment in the United States and then gone to Morocco. They wanted an apology from the United States for supporting the Shah and his actions, and they wanted the Shah's assets. Looking back now, it's clear that we all failed to understand the magnitude of the Shah's overthrow. When Ayatollah Khomeini had returned from Paris to become Iran's religious leader less than a year earlier, it appeared to be the overthrow of a regime like so many others throughout history. We had no idea that America would be in conflict with radical Islam from then on.

There was great support for Jimmy Carter when the hostages were taken. Talk about bad timing. The president had just achieved the impossible, bringing Israel and Egypt together for a historic treaty signing at Camp David—an accord that still stands to this day. But when the hostages were seized, Carter made a mistake that was similar to John McCain's just before the most recent election. When the economic crisis hit, McCain said, "I'm suspending my campaign." When the hostages were taken, Carter basically shut down his presidency. He made no speeches about anything else, and kept the lights on the White House Christmas tree dark except for the star at the top. The fate of the hostages consumed him and everybody else in America more and more each day.

My friend Herbie came on my show and pointed out what an error it was to put such a high value on the hostages. "This is not the way to negotiate," he said, and Herbie knew what he was talking about, because he made a living as a negotiator and had written a bestselling book called *You Can Negotiate Anything*. "The Iranians have a culture as merchants," Herbie said. "So it's like going into a rug store. If you tell the merchant, 'I love that rug in the window. I want that rug in the window. I just have to have that rug in the window!' What do you think is going to happen to the price?"

Some of the female and ill hostages were released as a humanitarian gesture. But when Carter couldn't bring the remaining fifty-two hostages home, Americans started to turn on him. In the early morning of my Mutual show one day in April of 1979, a bulletin announced that a rescue attempt had ended in failure with an aircraft crashing in the desert and eight servicemen dying. There were no twenty-four-hour news networks to frame and update what was going on. Our show became the news. We woke up Senator Henry Jackson, who drove out to the studio to take calls, furious that he hadn't been informed of the rescue attempt by the president. Though the calls that night were upbeat—at least we tried something!—the national mood darkened when the failure sank in.

Any pollster who monitored the calls to my show could see that Carter had no chance to be reelected. But, as always, humor found a way into the show. As the 1980 election approached, Carter pulled out of a debate scheduled for Syracuse with Ronald Reagan because Reagan insisted on including the independent candidate, John Anderson. There was talk that an empty chair would be left onstage to symbolize Carter's absence. Wiser heads prevailed, and the president was not humiliated by an empty chair. That night, I got a call from Syracuse.

"Larry, this is the Chair. I'm really down in the dumps. I got all shellacked, varnished . . . this was going to be my big break, and at the last minute they cancel me."

The guy was clever, so I kept it going. "Well, things look bad for '80. Do you have any plans for the next election?"

"I'm thinking of giving it a try in '84," he said. "I have to start looking for an ottoman to run with me."

Those were the things you could get away with deep into the night.

There was talk of an October surprise, a last-minute maneuver to release the hostages and save Carter's presidency. But it didn't happen. Reagan won in a landslide. Minutes after he was sworn in, the hostages were released. When they arrived in the U.S. they were kept a long distance from the press. After stopping to meet their families at West Point, they were flown to Washington for a heroes' welcome. Talk about being in the right place at the right time. The hostages were put up at the Marriott in Crystal City, Virginia, the building next to the studio where we produced my show. Staffers found some of the marines who'd been taken hostage dancing in a disco and convinced one to come over. If he wanted to go on the air, he was told, great. If he wanted to watch, that would be fine, too. He decided to do the show. He spent two hours talking about how the hostages communicated to each other on toilet paper and describing other amazing details of their captivity.

Boy, how Ed Little was right. Not a single listener in Miami or Denver would have turned the dial on that conversation. And nobody listening in Berlin or Seoul through the American Forces Network would have shut it off, either. My influence was spreading far and wide as I got closer to the center of events.

Sixty-nine days after Reagan's inauguration, the president was wounded in an assassination attempt roughly five blocks from Duke Zeibert's restaurant. I don't know why, but when I heard the news I sensed that Reagan would be OK. And he felt the same way. As he told me years later during an interview, he didn't even realize he'd been shot. He thought his rib had been broken when the Secret Service agent jumped on him, pushing him into a car for protection. Reagan had no idea that a deflected bullet was the origin of his pain until he reached down and discovered blood.

The shooting occurred near a gray stone wall outside the Hilton Hotel. The Hilton had the biggest ballroom in town. We all knew it well. It was on a street that everybody walked. If I'd stayed in Miami, I'm sure the assassination attempt would have been a big topic of discussion. But now I was at the center of it all when I walked by the roped-off crime scene on my way to Duke Zeibert's. The gunman, John Hinckley Jr., would be defended in court by my friend and mentor, Edward Bennett

Williams. Soon I became good friends with Ronald and Nancy Reagan.

The show took on a life of its own. Senator Al Gore would drive over late at night to come on as a guest. A caller from Portland became a regular by doing nothing but laughing uproariously. We called him the Portland Laugher. I'd ask him a question and he'd laugh so contagiously that anyone listening couldn't help but join him. When the Portland Laugher hadn't called in for a while, other listeners would phone in wondering why. The show became like family for night watchmen, hospital workers, pilots, police, and college students up late studying. One night I got a call from Arkansas. It was the governor, Bill Clinton.

"We'll get to your point in a second, Governor," I said. "But first, what are you doing up at two-thirty in the morning?"

"Never mind . . ." he said.

Stephen Colbert claims he lost his virginity while listening to the show.

When you tuned in, you didn't know if you were in for laughter or tears. One night I had on the actor, singer, and comedian Danny Kaye. At three in the morning, a woman called in. She said, "Danny, in my whole life I never thought I'd ever talk to you. How would I ever get a chance to talk to Danny Kaye? I just want you to know that my son loved you. He used to imitate you. He sang all your songs. He went into the Navy, and he was killed in Korea. They sent home all the belongings in his footlocker. The only picture he had in that footlocker was of you. I took that picture and put it next to a picture of him in a double frame. I dust it every morning. Now I'm talking to you. I just thought you'd like to know that."

Danny Kaye started to cry. His brother was there, and his brother started to cry. I started to cry. Then Danny Kaye did something brilliant. He asked the woman, "What was your son's favorite song?"

She said, "Dinah." He sang it to her right then and there. It was one of those precious moments that you can never get back but always remain with you.

When John Lennon was killed, all I did for five hours was take calls about him. There was a lot of crying. I didn't realize the impact that the Beatles had until that night. Milton Berle called in. I began to sense that my show was a place that allowed the nation to come together and grieve.

But it was the humor that I loved the most. I would do psychic readings at four in the morning. Of course, I didn't know what the hell I was talking about.

"Tomorrow," I once told a caller, "you will be in Houston."

"But I'm in Detroit," the guy said.

"That doesn't matter. Tomorrow, you will be at the airport in Houston. You will meet a woman named Martha. She will become the love of your life."

"But I'm already married!"

"Trust me."

The people filming the movie *Ghostbusters* called and asked me to play myself in the movie. They shot me, cigarette in hand, behind the mike. The poet Rod McKuen came on without any idea of the size of my audience. "I have a new book coming out, and anyone who buys it, cuts out the corner flap, and sends it to me will get a free copy of my latest record," McKuen said. Two hundred and fifteen thousand people sent him the flap. Cost him a fortune.

The newspaper *USA Today* started in 1982, and its founder, Al Neuharth, asked if I'd write a weekly column. *USA Today* was the newspaper for people who got their news through television. The vending machines on corners even looked like television sets. People made fun of *USA Today* at the start. They called it McPaper. But it was another sign of how America was shrinking, My show added affiliates by the hundred. *USA Today* is now the nation's largest selling daily newspaper by a mile.

I was doing my all-night radio show, writing for *USA Today*, and doing a local television interview show every Saturday night. But let me show you how good my timing really was. The local television executives liked my weekend show so much, they made plans to package it as a syndicated show five nights a week. They were going to run it in the early evening, before prime time. I had dinner with the general manager of the station and he was very excited.

"I'm committed to another show for four weeks," he said. "So I have to carry it for the next month. It's a daytime show that they're trying out at night. It's got no chance! After four weeks, it'll be canceled and you'll come on."

The show was *Wheel of Fortune*. Daytime show! No chance! It's turned out to be the longest-running syndicated game show in American television history. Twenty-five years later, and it's still running.

But think of it. If *Wheel of Fortune* had failed and my daily show had come about, I never would have joined CNN. Sometimes, what's bad is good. Sometimes the best trades in baseball are the ones that aren't made.

Even though I didn't like the mugginess of the summers or the harshness of the winters, I loved Washington. My marriage to Sharon didn't work out. The move from Miami was a little rough at first. I came home one morning to find that our two daughters—my stepchildren—had tied my socks into knots. But the kids adjusted well over time. The real problem was that my relationship with Sharon was either a ten or a one. It was never a six. Even after Sharon and I divorced, we still dated.

My daughter Chaia wanted to live with me. By that point, Sharon and I had separated, and Alene agreed that Chaia needed a father in her day-to-day life. So Chaia came up from

Miami. That was a little adjustment. I'd never had to raise a kid on my own before. Suddenly I was taking care of a twelve-year-old daughter all by myself.

I'll never forget the first night. I picked her up at the airport and brought her back to my one-bedroom apartment. It would be another week before we could shift into a two-bedroom. For the first week she had to sleep on a cot in the living room while I was in the bedroom.

I went to sleep wondering how I was going to do it. *Oh, man,* I told myself, *I've just taken on this responsibility. I have no idea how to make parental decisions. I work all night long. Who's going to watch her? How am I going to do this?*

I woke up in the morning and Chaia was sitting on the edge of the bed. "Did you get up in the middle of the night?" she asked.

"Yes," I said.

"Did you drink a glass of water?"

"Yeah, there was a glass of water already poured. I drank it."

"You drank my contact lenses."

This was my opening adventure in parenthood. One morning, I opened my eyes to find what looked like a rodent peering up my nose.

"Isn't he beautiful?" Chaia asked.

Chaia wound up with three ferrets running around the bathroom. She worked on Capitol Hill for a summer and joined me at Duke Zeibert's. It was an idyllic time. We went to baseball games with Edward Bennett Williams. I sat with Williams when the Orioles won the World Series in 1983, and befriended the Orioles announcer Jon Miller. One night, Jon told the audience that he was going to do a Larry King impersonation for an inning. None of the radio listeners could see that I was sitting next to him. For the next inning, I lived my childhood dream of announcing a baseball game. On my show later that night, a listener called and asked, "Were you at the game?"

"No," I lied, to see what would happen.
"Did you hear the broadcast?"
"No."
"Well, Jon Miller imitated you."
"How was he?"
The guy said, "Fair."

Then another phone call came at just the right time. I was having such a good time in Washington that I didn't even realize how good the timing was.

ANOTHER POINT OF VIEW

Herbie "The Negotiator" Cohen

Larry's great on TV. But he was incomparable on radio. He would do a five-and-a-half-hour show that every mover and shaker in Washington would listen to. People would work late in the White House and they'd turn on the radio and listen to Larry on the forty-five-minute trip home. Larry's resurrection was unbelievable. He had come back like the Phoenix.

Marty Zeiger

There is a story I heard about Larry going to the racetrack with hardly any money during difficult financial times. He left his car a long way from the track to avoid paying for parking, and he walked.

A couple of months later, he went to the same track with Angie Dickinson in a limo.

Chapter 11

Ted

ONE NIGHT, out of the blue, I got a call from Ted Turner. I liked Ted. I knew him from the Atlanta Braves and the Turner Broadcasting System. He'd been a guest on my radio show. Now he was running CNN.

CNN was just getting off the ground. I don't think you could even get it in Washington at that point. I didn't have it in my home. The only time I ever saw CNN was when I was on the road. I remember seeing it in Atlanta once. It didn't look like much.

I had been a guest once on a CNN show called *The Freeman Report*. Sandi Freeman was on at nine o'clock every night. She did the show out of New York. We discussed all-night radio. She was pretty good.

So Ted called and said something like, "You know *The Freeman Report*? Sandi Freeman's contract is up. Her husband manages her, and he's pissing me off. He's trying to hang me up for more money. I'd love to ship his ass out the door. You want to come work for me? You want to do nine o'clock?"

This was a Tuesday night, and her contract was up on Friday.

I said, "Jeez, Ted, I don't know."

Not only was I caught off guard, I was also hesitant because I really liked my life at that point. I was single, having a good time, going to Orioles games at night. I remember going out with Katie Couric when I was in Washington. She was single and just getting started. She invited me back to her apartment and I was thinking, *This could be good! This could be good!* I wasn't counting on the roommate she said she had who wanted to meet me. After the dates and the ball games, I'd do my radio show at midnight. I didn't want to give up my evenings.

"Ted," I said, "my agent is Bob Woolf."

"I know Bob real well," Ted said. "I've negotiated baseball contracts with him. Tell him to call me. Have him call me *now*."

So I called Bob at home. He called Ted, then called me back.

"Here's what Ted wants to do," Bob said. "He'll give you a three-year contract. He'll give you $200,000—that will double your pay. You're already making $200,000 from radio. The second year, he'll give you $225,000. And the third, he'll give you $250,000. But he needs to know today, because he wants to put the screws to this guy."

I said, "Does he want *me* so much, or does he just want to put the screws to this guy?"

"Well, here's one good point I negotiated. At the end of the first year, if you don't like it, you've got an option to leave. It's your option. Not his option. So if it doesn't work for you, or if you're missing your Orioles games, you can go back after a year."

"Well, that ain't bad," I said. "Tell him OK."

Bob called Ted and set up the deal. Ted called the husband to set up a meeting. Apparently, the husband thought he was going to get the contract he wanted. From the way I heard the story, he was a brusque guy. He came into the meeting and said something like, "Well, Ted, I'm glad you came around to *our* way of thinking."

"*Ouuuuuuur*, kemosabe?" Ted said. "See the door? Say goodbye."

That's how I got started at CNN.

There's nobody like Ted Turner. Nobody. Ted is a madcap guy. He's an instinctive businessman, yet completely childlike. When he's up, he's one of the nuttiest, most adventuresome and fun people you'll ever meet. When he's down, he can get terribly depressed. He can't stay focused on any one topic for too long, yet he can be completely at one with the moment. We saw a golden eagle in Montana once and I thought he'd go crazy. It was as if nothing else in the world existed and time was suspended. But he was never late.

He is notoriously cheap and outrageously generous. He'd drive a Toyota to work. And when he did use a limo, he'd have his driver stop a block away from the hotel just so he could get out and not have to tip the doorman when he arrived. But he'd pay anything to keep a baseball player he liked when he was owner of the Atlanta Braves. He was loyal, sometimes to a fault. He started as a novice sailor and advanced to win the world's most prestigious yacht race, the America's Cup. A guy caught in a storm with him in the middle of the Atlantic for three days once told me the only reason he knew he'd survive was that Ted was at the helm. Yet Ted would almost quiver at the sound of bad news. His voice would actually tremble like a cartoon character. "Please, don't tell me it's bad . . ."

He could be the most considerate friend. Knowing that I'd never ridden a horse, he once rode next to me holding the reins so I wouldn't be afraid. He didn't make fun of me. Didn't put me down. But if he didn't like you, he might trip you on a muddy street. When Rupert Murdoch set his sights on buying the Los Angeles Dodgers, Ted called other owners around the league and tried to convince them to bar the door.

He could exercise the wisdom of Solomon. Two CNN employees in a heated dispute could walk into his office in the morning, have the problem resolved one way or another, and leave without either one of them feeling slighted or taking it personally. Yet on the same afternoon Ted could offend a huge audience without a thought. Once, when he was speaking before a women's group, I heard him say, "I like women. I like women romantically. I like to work with women. I'm not like these countries that clitorize their women. I don't clitorize women. I hire them. I promote them. I don't clitorize." You should have heard the collective gasp from that crowd. The media dubbed him the Mouth of the South. But the commencement speech that he gave at Brown—the school that threw him out when he was a student—couldn't have lasted more than a minute and a half. He stood up and said something like, "I have to leave." Then he pointed to his face. "See this? That's a growth. I'm going to a dermatologist now because it's gotta be removed. You know how I got that? Staying in the sun. I'm gonna leave you with one thought. Stay out of the sun." Then he left the stage. I guarantee you that no graduate on that day will ever forget those words.

Ted couldn't think ahead twenty seconds. Yet he could see ahead twenty years. He was completely honest. He could be so childlike that sometimes he actually looked goofy. As individual traits, all these might have been damaging in one area or another. But when they were combined, they were revolutionary. There was nothing genius about Ted Turner, except that he was a genius. He was so far ahead of his time. He saw the potential of satellites in a way that nobody else did.

A psychologist once told me that the biggest event of the twentieth century for Americans, the most startling event, was not the landing on the moon. It was *Sputnik*—the first spacecraft to orbit the earth. It may not seem that big now, especially when you consider that the Soviet satellite was about the size of a beach ball. But, believe me, in 1957, in the middle of the Cold War, there was nothing bigger.

The Soviets were looking down on us. They were doing exactly what we were supposed to do first. That scared us. That changed us. That's what spurred us into going to the moon. The mood was: somebody else is up there, looking down on us, and that somebody else is not our friend. That's how we saw the satellite—as a spy and a threat.

But Ted Turner came to see the satellite as a way to bring people together. When Ted ran CNN, there were very few rules. One of them was that we couldn't say the word *foreign.* To Ted Turner, there was no foreign country. He probably didn't realize how far-reaching this approach was. Nobody else even talked about globalization back then. It was just simple to Ted. He said to me once, "When I look at Atlanta, I don't think of it as part of the United States. I think of where it is on the globe."

The story of how he came to think this way is amazing. He didn't start out as an open-minded liberal who wanted to give a billion dollars to the United Nations. Ted's father was a right-wing conservative who owned a billboard company in the South. There's no doubt that Ted's father had a huge impact on his life. I once said to Ted, "Your father left you one million dollars. You grew that into billions. What would he say if he could look at you today?"

Ted said, "I'll tell you exactly what he would say. 'Inflation . . .'"

Ted could never please his father, and when his father committed suicide he forever lost the chance. Instead, he built a communications empire. Let me give you an idea of how Ted's mind looked at the world. One day, not long after his father died, Ted was driving by one of his company's billboards in Atlanta when he noticed an advertisement for Channel 17. Ted didn't watch much television as a kid in boarding school, and he wasn't watching much at the time, either. This was the late '60s. But that billboard must have struck Ted just like that golden eagle. Ted bought Channel 17, then used his company's unleased billboards to advertise it. Soon, he discovered a way to really expand its audience.

He got the Federal Communications Commission to allow Channel 17 to broadcast by satellite. Now he had the bird. Channel 17 became known as a superstation, and Ted figured out ways to put on old movies and reruns of sitcoms for cable subscribers. Cable was just getting started. Ted scratched out business deals on napkins. He bought the Atlanta Braves baseball team and the Atlanta Hawks basketball team. Think about it. He put the Braves on the bird, and that was three hours of programming a day. The idea for CNN came, Ted told me, when he tuned in to a radio station in Atlanta called WGST. The announcer said something like, "All the news all the time." Ted thought, *A twenty-four-hour news station. Why couldn't that work on television?* He started CNN in 1980.

Ted thought he'd have anonymous hosts. One of the few things he figured wrong, he told me, was that he never thought the hosts would become famous. He never thought he'd have to pay a lot of money to keep them.

I was probably the first major personality brought in from the outside to go on the air for Ted. At the time, people called CNN the Chicken Noodle News. You couldn't even watch my first show across the street from the studio where it was filmed because there was no cable connection in Washington. I had no idea if CNN would be successful. But I liked Ted and figured it would be fun to go along for the ride. Maybe it was our collective good timing that brought us together. Maybe it was that Ted and I were born on the same day. November 19. Whatever it was, it was right. I've never worked for anybody better than Ted Turner.

The first show was set up at a rinky-dink place in George-town. I had to do makeup in one area, then walk across an al-ley to get to the studio to go on the air. I never pay attention to what goes on in the control room. But Tammy Haddad, who helped produce that first show, remembers that everyone but me was sweating and nervous. The set had been constructed to look like a radio show. You see that a lot now. Imus uses the concept. But back then, it was new. I wore a suit that night. Soon afterward I moved to V-neck sleeveless sweaters. Tammy was afraid that I'd grown accustomed to hunching over the mi-crophone during all my years in radio, and she thought the V-neck would make me look vertical. Later on, the suspenders would do the trick. My first guest was Mario Cuomo.

Mario had given one of the great political speeches of all time at the 1984 Democratic National Convention. I was standing next to the Oklahoma delegation as he gave it. I'll never forget. This guy from Oklahoma said, "I never heard of that guy. But I now know why I'm a Democrat." Edward Ben-nett Williams told me that Mario had given an even better speech at a college commencement where students were seated in front and the parents in the back. Mario said to the students, "You're not going to remember anything I say here today. I know, you can't wait until you get out of here. So, just give me a couple of minutes. I'm going to talk to your parents." In sec-onds, he had all the students turning their seats around to look at their parents. It's great to have an eloquent guest. More than that, Mario was a friend.

My memory of that show is not of a particular question or answer. It's the feeling. The whole thing just felt right. Mario sensed it, too. Afterward, he said, "This suits you." I had no idea that I'd just embarked on the longest run in television his-tory—one host, at the same hour, for twenty-four years and counting. But I knew the platform was perfect. The global backdrop you see on my set today? It's the same one we used on the first night. It just wasn't colored back then.

I was going on fifty-two years old. CNN was only five. My voice was recognized around the country. CNN was just about to be hooked up in living rooms across America and the world. The timing would lift us both. I was able to give CNN a boost from my all-night radio show. I'd go on Mutual Broadcasting, mention my CNN show, and bring over my listeners. The next day I'd go on the television show and promote the radio show. It was really no different from what I'd done in Miami with my early-morning radio show and my live hour at Pumpernik's. Only this time, the overall audience added up to millions, and I was positioned in the heart of prime-time television. All I had to do was everything I'd been doing since I was a kid.

My friend Herbie used to say, "You want to know the key to your success? The key to your success is you're dumb." He didn't mean it disparagingly. "Everybody else on TV is a know-it-all—but not you. You're dumb. So you say to your guest, 'I don't know. Explain this to me. Help me.' You create a vacuum and then you fill it."

It goes back to what Arthur Godfrey once told me. The secret is there's no secret. What you do is what you do. I'm a kid off the streets. I've never been to war. I've never been a plumber. I've never written a brief. I've never tried a case in court. I've never cured a disease. All I do is ask questions. Short, simple questions.

Once, I had a specialist on for a show about diabetes. I asked him what the word *diabetes* meant. He said, "I learned it my third day of medical school and no one has asked me since."

Why do you want to hunt animals?

Why do you take pictures?

What happened in the war today?

Simple questions can get surprising answers. But you really have to listen when you interview like that. Because your next question always depends on the last answer. When I was interviewed by Barbara Walters for my anniversary show, she had every question mapped out. It works for her. But I couldn't work that way in a million years. I've never in my life planned a question. When I say, "Good evening, my guest is . . ." I have no idea what I'm going to ask. You may see me with those blue cards— but the notes on them are really just an adjunct, not a road map. When I go on, I'm back at Pumpernik's. I'm in the moment.

The key is the element of surprise. It's the opposite of being a criminal defense lawyer. A criminal defense lawyer doesn't like to be surprised. In fact, many lawyers have told me that if you're surprised in court you haven't done your job. Nothing said by anybody on either side of the courtroom should surprise you. If you're surprised, it means you've been caught. The only time a trial lawyer wants to be surprised is at four o'clock in the morning in a law library. Me? I'm seventy-five years old and I still want to be surprised every night. When I'm surprised, that's when I know I'm doing my job right.

I guess I have a natural ability to draw people out. I don't know if that has evolved over time. But I do know it has allowed me to check my ego at the door. I try not to use the word *I* at all. In an interview, "I" is totally irrelevant. I'm there for the guest. I may have an opinion. But my opinion isn't important during the show. I'm open. There was once a poll in Miami asking people to guess whether I was a Republican or a Democrat. The response was split fifty-fifty.

Most broadcasters these days would find it impossible to do a show without using the word *I*. You have the O'Reillys, the Limbaughs, and other pompous windbags who are there to satisfy themselves. They have an agenda and it's all about them. Their guest is nothing more than a prop. They've got the gift of gab, and that makes them, in a sense, entertaining. But I've never come away from their shows knowing any more than I knew before. When they ask a question, it's like that old joke about a Howard Cosell interview. "Enough about me. What about you? What do you think of me?"

There are many broadcasters who'll recite three minutes of facts before they ask a question. As if to say: *Let me show you how much I know*. I think the guest should be the expert. Anytime you hear a three-minute question, it's a good bet the interviewer is just showing off. You see it a lot during presidential press conferences. I've found that good, short questions can make an interviewer look a lot smarter than a recitation of facts does.

I remember doing an interview with Dr. Edward Teller—the inventor of the hydrogen bomb. A friend of mine helped set it up. Teller was a firebrand sort of guy. He came into the studio and said to me, "What do you know about physics?"

I said, "Nothing."

He said, "How can we do this?"

I said, "Well, we're taping today. If you're unhappy, we'll end it. You don't like it, walk away."

He said, "That's fair enough."

My first question was, "When we were in school, why were we afraid of physics? Why in school is physics so hard?"

His face lit up, and in his Austrian accent he said, "They teach it wrong. They shouldn't even call it physics! They should call it *life*! Because physics affected everything you did today, Mr. King, from the minute you opened your eyes! Physics is *life*!"

So I said, "How?"

Then he described how.

So I asked, "What's the next great thing in physics?"

He told me it was to learn the power in the inanimate,

about the power in mountains. Where did that mountain come from? How did those granules come together?

I said, "You're the inventor of the hydrogen bomb—"

"It was never dropped! I keep hearing that. The A-bomb was dropped. We never hear about that. We hear that I invented the hydrogen bomb. It's never killed a person!"

Soon, I was asking, "When you invented the H-bomb, did you need to see it blow up? Or did you know that it would work by the math?" And he said, "Yes! I knew by the math. Once the math works, the bomb works! I didn't need to see the test. But getting the math to work . . ."

We finished up, and afterward he said to me, "Why were you kidding me? As if you didn't know anything about physics!"

You know what my dream interview is? "Good evening . . ." Then the door opens and I discover who the guest is. I was talking about this with Bob Costas while he was doing his *Later* show. We decided we'd each get each other surprise guests. No preparation at all. A guy walked in that I'd never seen before. I asked him his name. He said, "Meatloaf." I'd never heard of him. So I asked, "When you arrive at a hotel, do you check in as Mr. Loaf?" I got to know all about his music by good questioning.

I used to say you could put me in a locker room after a game, don't tell me the sport, don't tell me if the team won or lost—and I'd be able to tell you exactly what happened by asking questions. Questions like, What did you learn tonight?

Can you use tonight's game in your next game?

What was the toughest moment?

What surprised you?

You've got to know basics. But if you have the time to draw people out, I find it's better to know very little. You can always get into the whos, whats, and whys. It's not only better than knowing too many of the whos—it's more fun. When you don't use any notes, you're flying on your own. That can be dangerous. You can't get the moment back if you fall. Maybe that's why I love being on live. It's so different from taping. It's sort of like how Al Pacino describes the difference between theater and film. When Al does a movie, he can shoot a scene eight times. It doesn't matter if he screws one up. The director will use the best one. When Al plays Broadway, he walks the tightrope at eight o'clock every night.

One of the nicest compliments I ever got came at a Peabody Awards ceremony. Alistair Cook, the speaker, said, "Ninety-nine percent of the people in broadcasting are afraid to take risks. They go the careful route. They try to do what is right, but basically, it's always, 'Don't take that extra step. Do what you're told.' Ninety-nine percent. The other one percent is in this room."

Looking back, I realize it was probably more of a risk for me to join CNN than it was for Ted to hire me. Sometimes it was hard to line up guests at the start because people didn't know about CNN. Tammy would actually send interns to the escalator of the Eastern Airlines shuttle at National Airport to look for famous people coming off their flights. If the interns spotted someone, they'd ask if he or she would like to come on the show.

If I didn't have a history with a potential guest, they were much more likely to want to appear before the huge network audience of ABC's *Nightline* with Ted Koppel. But even early on, there were moments that told us there was about to be a shift in power. After a TWA flight was hijacked by Muslim extremists, the pilot of the grounded plane was photographed talking to reporters through the cockpit window with a gun to his head. It was one of those images that made the world hold its breath. After the pilots and crew gained their freedom, we booked the pilot on our show. ABC's *Nightline* suddenly found itself in the uncomfortable position of phoning Tammy to ask if we'd relinquish him so that they could have him.

All the networks were starting to notice us. Ted Turner tells a great story about talks with CBS over the possibility of a merger. This guy came to Ted's office and said something like, "I'm here representing Mr. Paley at CBS. We're prepared to buy you."

William Paley was the Ted Turner of his own time. He'd built CBS from a tiny chain of stations in the '30s and '40s into what became known as the Tiffany Network with an all-star newsroom. But Paley was more of an executive, whereas Ted was a mogul. And times had changed.

Ted asked the guy, "Why didn't Mr. Paley come?"

"Because I'm Mr. Paley's representative."

"Well," Ted said, "why don't you go down the hall and speak to *my* representative? Look, I run this company. Tell you what. You go back and tell Mr. Paley that I appreciate his offer. I'd like to know what he wants. He wants to buy me? I'll buy him."

It's hard to imagine now, but CNN was the only public network to carry the launch of the *Challenger* in January of 1986. The major networks didn't preempt their programming. The Space Shuttle had a crew of seven that included Christa McAuliffe, the first teacher in space. Schoolchildren all around America were watching CNN as *Challenger* lifted off at Kennedy Space Center and cleared the tower to cheers and applause.

When I remember it, I can't help but think of the way that Charlie Chaplin described that thin line between comedy and tragedy. You're at a party. There's a man at the top of the stairs. He has a mustache and a funny hat. He trips. He hits the top step. He makes a funny face, and you laugh. He tumbles, hits the third step, his knee turns and you're really laughing. He hits the fifth step, blood comes out of the corner of his mouth and you're changed. That second, it's a tragedy. The *Challenger* had that same feeling.

Seventy-three seconds after the joyous cheers and applause, the O-rings in two solid rocket boosters broke. The *Challenger* exploded before everybody's eyes. It's been reported that within an hour, 85 percent of America knew about the accident. The replay was shown countless times that day. That night, President Reagan addressed the nation. I can still remember that speech. Peggy Noonan wrote it. Reagan talked about how the astronauts "slipped the surly bonds of Earth to touch the face of God."

We must have done a whole week of shows following the disaster. What went wrong? What exactly were O-rings? Were the astronauts conscious as they came down? How were the relatives coping? What about the reactions of schoolchildren who'd seen the explosion? How would NASA go forward?

Over and over, I've been told that my show is the comfortable place people turn to in times of grief. I'd noticed this on the radio when the Mutual phone lines jammed after John Lennon was murdered. I don't know where this quality comes from. But it was magnified by television. There's something about television that makes you an intimate part of the family. Johnny Carson once told me that nobody ever called him Mr. Carson. They called him Johnny because people were in bed when they saw him. I have that same quality. I'm Larry. I'm your friend.

I became everybody's friend just as the demand for nonstop news arrived. CNN began to take off, and my show took off with it. Little did I know that a tumble was coming.

Chapter 12

Your Ferret Died

IN THE EARLY YEARS, I smoked through my CNN show. Viewers didn't know it because I had the cigarette underneath my desk—just like Johnny Carson. If the smoke started to come up, I just pushed my hand down to hide it. That saved time. When the commercial break came I didn't have to wait to light a match.

There were times when I didn't smoke out of respect for the guest. On those occasions, I would run to the bathroom during breaks and grab a couple of drags. One of those guests was C. Everett Koop—the surgeon general under Ronald Reagan.

The warning label you now see on the side of a cigarette pack—it's there because of Koop. The tobacco industry hated Koop. The truth is, Reagan was disappointed in him, too. The president didn't like it when people upset the status quo, and Reagan was a staunch supporter of big business. Why would you speak out against the tobacco industry?

But Koop made himself so independent that he couldn't be fired. His beard made him look like a cross between your grandfather and Santa Claus. He was honest and very likable.

It was obvious that he had no agenda other than to warn you to protect your health. All he set out to do was tell you the facts—and he was a master at it. The reality is, we don't know exactly why smoking causes lung cancer or heart attacks. We only know that it does cause lung cancer and heart attacks. When someone would challenge Koop to produce proof, he'd say something like, "I can't prove to you for a fact that you'll die if you fall out of an airplane. But statistically, the numbers are impressive."

Koop came on my CNN show in February of 1987. After we finished the interview, he turned to me with this very concerned look and said, "You feeling OK?"

"Yeah."

"You still smoking?"

I was still smoking in the shower. I'd been going through three packs a day for thirty-six years.

There was a lot of denial on my part. But I couldn't deny the change in the way cigarettes were being perceived. When I started out in radio, everyone at the station smoked. Look at any old film—all the actors light up. There's a great movie called *The Young Doctors*, starring Dick Clark and Fredric March. In it, there's an argument between Clark, the young doctor, and March, the old doctor, about how to treat a patient. The two of them are blowing smoke in each other's face as they debate back and forth. I don't remember the exact dialogue, but if you look at it now, it's got to be laughable. *We're here for health!*

The strange thing about smoking to me was, it didn't feel like poison. When you're smoking, you never feel like it's going to kill you even though you know it's going to kill you. It's insane. Why do smart people do insane things? I don't know, but I can tell you that smoking produces some very complex behavior.

The actor Yul Brynner filmed a commercial to be shown after he died. In it, he said, "I really wanted to make a commercial that says simply, 'Now that I'm gone, I tell you, don't smoke. Whatever you do, just don't smoke.'" When that commercial appeared, I'd jump to change the channel.

Yet I can also remember a USAir flight I was on from Washington to Pittsburgh. You could still smoke on commercial airlines in the mid-'80s, though restrictions were starting to be implemented. The last three rows were made available to smokers. However, if one person in those last three rows objected, the pilot would declare it a nonsmoking flight.

All the smokers were sitting in the back ready to light up. It was a pretty full flight. We were just about to take off, and one guy came rushing down the aisle. He sat down in the second to last row, and we lifted off. All the people in the last three rows—except one—lit up, and it wasn't long before the pilot's voice came over the intercom, saying, "Attention, people in the last three rows. A gentleman requests there be no smoking. Therefore, this will be a nonsmoking flight."

It wasn't hard to locate that gentleman. You know what we did? We not only kept on smoking, we blew smoke in the guy's face. And then, when we saw the stewardess coming, we'd quickly put our cigarettes out and away before she reached us.

Finally, the pilot spoke over the intercom again. "Will the children in the last three rows stop? If not, we'll have you all arrested when we land."

So I was flipping Yul Brynner's commercial out of my sight. I was blowing smoke in some poor passenger's face. And I was also going along with the actor Larry Hagman when Larry asked to be my partner on Stop Smoking Day. The idea was for your partner to support you through the cravings by calling you constantly. I made it for only five or six hours.

These are only a few of the different behaviors that smoking could bring out in you. It was more than an addiction. I loved to smoke. Besides, Larry King was not going to die. I'll bet that up until the day that Koop came in as my guest I hadn't missed more than a week of work in thirty years. I'd go on the air with laryngitis before calling in sick.

I guess you could correlate smoking and my workday— neither ever stopped. I was doing the CNN show, the all-night Mutual radio show, writing a newspaper column, and doing a lot of speaking engagements. The more I was on, the more of my life I could control.

"I don't like the way you look," Koop said before he left the CNN studio. "Do me a favor. See a doctor first thing tomorrow."

We parted, and I went to do my all-night radio show. My guest that night was David Halberstam, the Pulitzer Prize– winning writer. David's brother was a cardiologist whom I'd interviewed many times—Michael Halberstam. Michael was one of the first doctors to discuss the benefits of taking an aspirin every day.

I don't know if Michael's profession had rubbed off on David. But when we finished the interview, at 3 a.m., there was a break before I started to do Open Phone America, and David turned to me and said, "Are you OK?"

"Yeah."

"You don't look right."

Later, people told me that my face had a gray pallor—one of the warning signs of an oncoming heart attack. But I didn't feel anything out of the ordinary . . . until about an hour later.

At about four in the morning, I got this ache in my right shoulder that began moving down my right arm. I got off at five and drove home. The pain wouldn't go away, and it wouldn't let me sleep. So I called my doctor, woke him up.

Right-shoulder pain is an odd symptom for a heart attack.

There was no chest pain. My doctor thought the problem might be my gallbladder, because the gallbladder can give off refractory pain.

"Wait an hour," he said. "If the pain is still there, come to the hospital and I'll see you as I make my rounds."

An hour passed and the pain didn't go away. Chaia was sleeping. I didn't wake her—which to this day angers her. But I had no idea how serious the situation was. I didn't want to upset her. So I called up my CNN producer, Tammy Haddad, and she drove over and took me to George Washington Hospital at about 7:30 a.m. I smoked on the way.

We pulled up in front of the emergency room. People now call it the Ronald Reagan Emergency Room because it's where the president was taken after the assassination attempt. As I got out of the car, I noticed that the pain had disappeared. Doesn't this always happen? For some reason, the pain goes away as soon as you pull up to the hospital.

"Tammy," I said, as I got out of the car, "wait here for me. The pain has gone. It feels like I'm OK."

I stepped through the doors into the crowded ER. It looked like it would be hours before somebody would see me. So I turned to leave. What could they examine anyway? There was no longer any pain. I walked back toward the car, but there was no car. Security had made Tammy move.

This was years before everyone had cell phones. I couldn't call and tell her to come back and pick me up. So I went back inside. There was a guy there with a clipboard—a spotter. I didn't know there was such a thing. But there are spotters in many large emergency rooms.

What they're trained to do is pick out people in need of immediate care. It makes sense—what if a guy comes in with a heart attack and he's fifth in line behind four people with broken pinkies? In a case like that, this person is supposed to spot him.

Out of nowhere, this big guy comes straight over to me and says, "You a heart patient?"

"No."

"Come with me."

I followed him into a cubicle, the same cubicle Reagan was taken into. An emergency room doctor came in. I described how the pain moved from my right shoulder down my arm. There was an EKG attached to my chest and an IV in my wrist before anyone asked to see my Blue Cross card. Tammy came in, saw what was going on, and went home to get Chaia. My Mutual radio producer, Pat Piper, came over to replace Tammy so that somebody would be with me.

A Dr. Warren Levy came through the door.

"It's gone," I said. "I'm no longer in pain."

"I'll tell you what," Levy said. "If you'll stay, I'll stay with you. Because we want to do some tests when the pain comes back."

I noticed that he didn't say *if*. He said *when*.

OK, I told him, I'll wait. He left me sitting there dying for a cigarette. But you can't smoke in the emergency room.

After a little while, the pain returned, and, oh, did it come back—the most terrible pain I've ever felt. Doctors and nurses did their tests, hung the results on a board across the room, and gathered to look them over. I was sitting there when they all turned and came running toward me.

Funny how humor protects you. "I don't think this is a pulled muscle," I said to Pat.

Dr. Levy came over, looked me in the eye, and said, "Mr. King, there's only one way to tell you this. You're having a heart attack."

"Am I gonna die?"

"Good question. That's why they pay you the big bucks. The answer is, we don't know. It's too early. However, you've got three tremendous advantages. You're having your heart attack in a hospital—you're not out on a ski slope. Two, it's a right-side heart attack. In right-side heart attacks, there's a seventy-five percent recovery rate even if the patient doesn't get treatment."

That's just the nature of the right-side heart attack. The artery in question affects only 17 percent of blood flow. It can kill you, but it usually doesn't.

The third reason was that George Washington University Hospital was one of the few hospitals that were using an experimental drug called tPA (tissue plasminogen activator), which breaks up the clots that block blood flow in the arteries. The only problem was that there was a 1 percent chance the drug would cause a stroke.

I didn't care. At that point, I felt like I was dying. The moment I finished putting the *g* in my signature the nurse started the tPA. When I later looked at my signature on that page, it was unreadable. But five minutes after the tPA went in, the pain was gone. Now this drug is in ambulances everywhere.

The cardiologist who took over, Dr. Richard Katz, told me I'd have to stay in the hospital for a week. By this time, Chaia had arrived. She'd paged Herbie, who happened to be flying in to Washington. She'd also called Angie Dickinson.

"Angie," Chaia said, "I have terrible news."

"Don't tell me," Angie said. "Your ferret died."

Herbie landed at the airport, heard his name paged, and immediately knew something had happened to me. To this day, he doesn't know how or why. He just knew. He spoke with Chaia and came straight to the hospital.

There was one problem. I'd been placed in the cardiac care unit. Only immediate family members are allowed to visit you in the CCU. But we're talking about Herbie. It wasn't long before Herbie was striding down the corridor toward my room, looking over at people who weren't there, and speaking to these invisible men and women so that everyone down the hall could hear, "Yes, yes, I'll take care of it! I'll talk to him!"

As he walked in, he saw me, and I must have looked like death warmed over. All he could think of doing was extending his arms outward for a hug. Oh, my friend . . .

I extended my arms to meet his embrace and yanked out every line that was connected to a monitor.

Beep beep beeps resounded through the corridor. The monitors at the nurse's station must have shown that the guy in bed number 12 was dead.

Nurses and doctors came running in and threw Herbie out. They rehooked everything up. There were going to be a lot of changes in my life. I'm sure the doctors told me not to smoke anymore. But they didn't have to. I was so scared that nobody had to say a word. Eating had always been an event for me ever since my mother prepared my first dinner. But I offered no resistance when I was told, "No more fatty lamb chops." I knew what I'd been doing wrong. I did stupid things, but I wasn't stupid.

The rest of my life was going to be Cheerios and bananas for breakfast with skim milk. Salad for lunch. Chicken or fish for dinner with steamed vegetables. A treat was going to be low-fat, low-sugar frozen yogurt.

A week later, I was given the OK to leave the hospital. Chaia drove me home. Along the way, I took the pack of cigarettes out of my pocket and threw it into the Potomac River. I've never smoked since.

A little more than six months later, I went in for a stress test—the first stress test since the heart attack. I wasn't on the machine for two minutes when the doctor watching me said, "Step off."

"What's the matter?"

"You're going to need heart surgery."

"What?"

I was stunned. How could it be? I'd stopped smoking, changed my diet, started to exercise a little, and cut my all-night radio show back an hour. I'd even bought new clothes after moving my spring outfits to the front of the closet and getting a whiff of the cigarette odor all over them. During all the years that I smoked I could never smell the scent on my clothes. I took all my old clothes to the cleaners to be fumigated, but they couldn't get the odor out.

"I'm not going to let you take this test any further," the doctor said. "You have a lot of blockage. You could die during this test."

"I came in for a stress test," I told him, "but this is not the stress I was looking for. I want another opinion."

The data was sent to Herbie's nephew, a great cardiologist in New York. He looked over the results and called me. "Yeah," he said, "you need surgery. If it were me, I'd have it done by Dr. Wayne Isom. Great surgeon. Great guy."

"OK," I said.

But for some reason, I put it off. Not just some reason—I was scared of dying. Denial can make you think crazy things. I actually convinced myself that the cure for my blockage would be invented any day, that I'd pick up the newspaper and see a giant headline that read:

Heart Disease Cured
Larry King Doesn't Need Surgery

There is no way to describe how scared I was. If you'd told me I could avoid the surgery and live comfortably for the rest of my life by swearing off sex, I'd be celibate to this day. But there were no such options. I was stopping to catch my breath as I walked through airports and taking nitroglycerin tablets for the chest pain.

If I was going to die, I wanted to die in New York. Two months after the stress test, the surgery was scheduled with Dr. Isom at New York Presbyterian Hospital.

Many people who'd had the surgery called to tell me it would be a snap. But as the weekend approached, as friends offered humor and support, the only thing I could think was that it would be the last time I'd talk to them.

On my final night on the radio before I went to New York for the surgery, the columnist Art Buchwald was the guest. He told me that for some reason he always ended up going on shows when the host had little time left. Then he brought up his wife's emergency bypass surgery. "Let's be honest," he said, "no one cares about your surgery. Your friends will listen to you for about three minutes. Acquaintances? Two minutes. Strangers? One . . . unless you have a quintuple bypass."

The next day, a Friday, Jon Miller drove down from Baltimore, where he was announcing the Orioles, picked me up in Washington, and drove me to New York. I don't think I heard a word he said during the entire trip. The only thing going through my mind was: *They're going to open up my chest. They're going to open up my chest.* The surgery was set for Tuesday. I had one last weekend.

I stayed with my brother and his wife, Ellen, in New York. Once, when he was a newborn, I plotted to throw Marty out of a window because he was stealing my parents' attention. As we grew up, our differences became more apparent. I spent money as soon as I got it. Marty was very frugal and hid his money all over our apartment. One day, I found two quarters and took them. When he discovered the loss, he went ballistic.

"I'll give you quarters," my mother told him.

"No, that's not the point. It's the principle. He stole the money!"

"It's not stealing. You're brothers!"

"It's stealing! He should go to jail!"

We drifted apart when I moved to Miami. But there's a closeness that comes when you look at your brother as if it's the last weekend you'll have together. We became even closer six months later when Marty found out he needed the same surgery. Must have been the genes.

I was scheduled to check in at the hospital on Sunday night. Now, with insurance companies in control, you check in on the same day. Sunday arrived, a dark, rainy November day that looked like death.

That afternoon, Bob Woolf joined my brother, my sister-in-law, and me as we went to the hospital. Chaia and Andy were on the way. We arrived, and there was Mario Cuomo standing with the head of the hospital. They were there to wish me well. Mario brought a baseball bat as a gift. I still have it.

"Mr. King," the head of the hospital said, "I want to assure you that you'll be getting the finest of care. Everything is set. You don't have to bother with the paperwork. Mr. Wolf will take care of that. We're going to show you to your room."

We went up this elevator to the eighteenth floor—and what a room! It had a magnificent view overlooking the East River, beautiful cabinetry, and a huge television screen. The only sign that I was in a hospital were the monitors next to the bed.

While we took in all this splendor, the head of the hospital said with a flourish, "The Shah of Iran stayed in this room."

"As I recollect," I said, "*he* died. How about a ward with forty-two patients? All of whom go home."

Everybody had a laugh. Mario left. The head of the hospital left. Which left my brother and his wife, Chaia, Andy, and Bob.

Before my brother went in for his surgery, six months later, I advised him not to have the family come with him when he checked in. It's incredibly depressing. You look at everyone and think, *I'll never see them again.*

I don't believe in God or heaven. I've always liked the joke about the guy who falls into a manhole, breaks both legs, and says, "Thank God I didn't die." Why thank God? He gave you the broken legs.

But you couldn't call me an atheist, because that's a religion. When I told Billy Graham that I didn't believe in God, he said, "I hear you say that. But you're one of the most spiritual people I know. God has a special calling for you, and I feel that with all my being. So you can think what you want, because we're given free will to think. But you're in a special place."

As the surgery approached, I can tell you that I wanted to stay in my special place. I wanted to see all the people I loved again. But it's a very pessimistic surgery. People tell you it's no big deal after they've been through it. But I've never met anyone who checked in and said, "Piece of cake . . ."

The surgeon arrived wearing a ten-gallon hat and cowboy boots. Dr. Wayne Isom.

"Mr. King," he said, "you're gonna do rihhhhhght fahhhhn. Rihhhhhhhhhhght fahhhhhn."

What was this? Weren't all heart surgeons supposed to be Jewish? And I've got the Cardiac Cowboy. I would come to discover that there are only two types of heart surgeons. Jews and Texans. There are no Protestant heart surgeons from South Dakota—they just don't exist.

Dr. Isom came over to me and began a little exam. You know, tapping the chest with two fingers.

I looked down, blinked, then looked again. He had half a right thumb!

How do you respond to that? Here's a guy who operates

on David Letterman and Walter Cronkite, and he's got a stub for a right thumb!

I said, "Dr. Isom, I've had this peculiar habit all my life and I can't explain it. But when I meet people, I count their fingers . . . and with you I get to nine."

He smiled, and he told me how when he was a kid he grabbed a handful of branches while his mother was clipping a hedge. She didn't see him and accidentally cut off the top of his thumb. He said it made him a better surgeon because it helped him become ambidextrous.

"Listen," I told him. "I ask questions for a living. So I gotta know. What are you going to do tomorrow?"

"You sure you want to know?"

"Yeah."

"OK. We're going to take a saw and open your chest."

"BorgWarner?" I asked. "The saw in the commercial with the squirrels on the trees?"

"The answer to that question happens to be yes. Borg-Warner makes the saw."

"Are the squirrels going to come too?"

"Then, we're going to pull your ribs back, hook you up to the heart-lung machine, take your heart and move it so the heart-lung machine can stand in for your heart, and then we're going to take the veins from your legs and—"

"Enough! Enough! Enough!"

That night I had a dream that Dr. Isom cut off his other thumb while shaving. I woke up thinking I had an eight-fingered surgeon.

As they put me under, I didn't see any great circle beyond. No white lights. No memories came to me. I was down for eight hours.

It turned out to be a quintuple bypass.

Waking up was one of the great moments in my life. I opened my eyes and felt a little chill. I was under some blan-

This souvenir photo was taken at Coney Island in 1944 shortly after
my father died. I was ten years old. The wire-rimmed glasses I'm
wearing were the kind issued to families on Relief. Alongside
is my younger brother, Marty, and my Aunt Sylvia.
Photo courtesy of Larry King

Herbie "The Negotiator" Cohen has been my best friend for more
than sixty years now, ever since we directed cars into each other
and clogged up the street as traffic monitors in junior high.
Photo courtesy of Larry King

Bobby Darin was my first big interview when I started doing my
radio show at Pumpernik's for WKAT in 1959.

Photo courtesy of Larry King

PERSONALITY

THE LARRY KING SHOW
6:00 to 10:00 A.M.
MONDAY THRU SATURDAY

wkat / miami / CBS radio

A radio sales sheet
from the sixties.

Photo courtesy of Larry King

LARRY KING - CURRENTLY RUNNING THE TOP OF A SWELLING TIDE OF
ACCLAIM BY THE LOCAL PRESS AND TRADE IS BEING CALLED, "GIFTED,
HOT, BRILLIANT...RADIO'S ANSWER TO MORT SAHL". LARRY'S FAST
WITTY REMARKS, MANY TIMES BITING, RANGE ANYWHERE FROM SABU TO
THE MORNING PAPER.
HIS EXCELLENT MUSICAL TASTES VEER VERY STRONGLY TO THE KEELY SMITH -
FRANK SINATRA - EYDIE GORME SCHOOL.
LARRY IS A RADIO VETERAN OF OVER 10 YEARS AND A PROVEN RADIO
SALESMAN.
AS WITH ALL WKAT ENTERTAINER-SALESMEN, AUDITION TAPES ARE AVAILABLE
UPON REQUEST.

PERSONALITY

I was offered nearly twice as much money as I was making at CNN
to leave in 1989, but I couldn't say goodbye to Ted Turner
and CEO Tom Johnson.
Courtesy CNN

Don Rickles has been busting my chops for half a century . . .
and I've been enjoying every minute of it.
Photo courtesy of Larry King

This photo of Cannon as a baby and Chance (looking at the camera) is one of my favorites.
Photo courtesy of Larry King

Cannon feels right at home in front of the microphone.
Courtesy CNN

I didn't know about Larry Jr. until he was thirty-three years old. That's my son Chance, in his arms, while I hold my youngest son Cannon.
Photo courtesy of Larry King

Bill Clinton pays a visit to the King family at CNN headquarters in New York. That's my wife, Shawn, on the other side of Bill.

Courtesy CNN

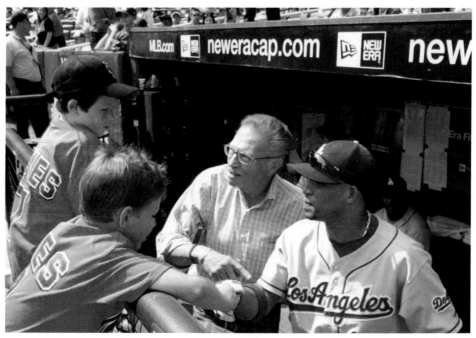

I've given my youngest boys baseball and they've given me youth. Here, Chance and Cannon meet Dodgers' shortstop Rafael Furcal.

Photo by Elisabeth Prantner-Pedrolini, aka Lib Lib

My daughter, Chaia, got her name, in part, because her mother
loved the book *The Chosen* by Chaim Potok.
Photo by Elisabeth Prantner-Pedrolini, aka Lib Lib

Nelson Mandela was easily the most extraordinary figure of the
twentieth century. My executive producer, Wendy Walker,
is in the middle.
Courtesy CNN

Dear Larry- Who is your best audience??
Best- Nancy

Funny, shy and tough, not many people know the real Nancy Reagan.
She's become a great friend over time, and was one of the first to call
when my two youngest boys were born.

Photo courtesy of Larry King

It's always great to talk baseball with George Bush forty-three. This
interview with George and Laura was done in the White House
toward the end of the Bush presidency.

Courtesy CNN

I become a better father every day. That's my oldest son, Andy, on the left. Chance is standing on the swing. Larry Jr. and his wife, Shannon, are on both sides of me with their children, Asher, Max and Stella. Cannon sits in the swing on the far right.

Photo by Elisabeth Prantner-Pedrolini, aka Lib Lib

Longtime friends, Michael Viner, Sid (Yallowitz) Young, and Asher Dan join me at Nate 'n Al deli in Beverly Hills for breakfast.

Photo by Elisabeth Prantner-Pedrolini, aka Lib Lib

kets, and the nurse said, "Mr. King, you did perfect." I couldn't have been happier.

Frank Sinatra had turned my room into a botanical garden. There were so many flowers that I didn't have room for them. We gave them to all the other patients in the hospital.

Angie Dickinson had flown in, and Bob wanted to let me know. "Guess who's here?" he asked.

"Joe DiMaggio?"

Well, Bob *was* a sports agent.

Ted Turner paid a visit. That was great, because the first thing you think about when you have heart surgery is whether you're going to lose your job.

My spirits soared. It wasn't long before I was walking up steps. A week later I was released. It was one of those perfect New York winter days, just gorgeous. I walked back to Marty and Ellen's house. On the way was an OTB. I walked in.

A guy turned to me and said, "Hey, I read about your heart surgery in the papers. How you doin'?"

"Fine."

"Good," he said. "Who do you like?"

You can only know how good a moment like that is after you've just had quintuple bypass surgery.

I spoke with C. Everett Koop many times after the surgery. I did events with him and introduced him at dinners.

"In your life," he told me, "you'll count your heart attack as one of the luckiest things that ever happened to you. You were lucky in where you had the heart attack, lucky in the type of heart attack it was, and you were lucky to be fifty-three when it hit. That's a nice age if you're going to have one. It means that if nothing goes wrong you're going to live a lot longer. And you had surgery with great doctors in a major hospital. If you hadn't had that heart attack, you were on your way to a major one. Sometimes what appears bad is, in fact, good."

It would be years later before I found out how good.

ANOTHER POINT OF VIEW

Chaia King

We were waiting about eight hours. Then the doctors came and told us it was OK, that he was in recovery. They let us go in to see him one at a time. They said, "He's still unconscious. He can't hear you, and he won't respond." So I just walked in to hold his hand. He was wrapped up—he didn't quite look mummified, but almost. He was hooked up to all kinds of machines. I took his hand, leaned over, and said into his ear, "Dad, you made it. I love you. I'm here." Then the hand I was holding squeezed, real strong.

One of the things my dad has taught me is how to pick yourself up.

Ellen David

When Larry stayed in our home around the time of the bypass, it was the first time since they were boys that Marty and Larry slept under the same roof. It was a great time to bond because Larry came out of his surgery absolutely joyful. "Oh my God! I'm alive!"

The first couple of years that I was married to Marty, I could count on the fingers of one hand how many times I spoke to Larry. Now we were having Chinese food every night. I can still remember. Larry would peruse the menu for twenty-five minutes, order the chicken with cashews, and then not eat the cashews. He became family.

During Larry's recovery week we went to see a screening of the movie *Broadcast News*. It was funny.

When you have a bypass you walk around with a pillow to press against your chest because if you start laughing it hurts like hell. *Broadcast News* was very funny. I remember the two of them in the car. Marty would say something funny. And Larry would be laughing and clutching the pillow to his chest in pain and screaming, "Stop it! Stop it!"

To be honest, when Larry left after a week, I can remember Marty thinking that the tightness between them would never last, that once Larry went back to his hectic life, it would go away. But it did last.

Marty Zeiger

I had the same operation six months later. I remember the night before. They'd shaved my chest and I was taking a shower with some medicated soap. I was standing in that shower and saying to myself, "They're going to cut my chest open."

You really realize how vulnerable you are in a moment like that.

Ellen David

Larry came up to be with us for Marty's surgery. Ever since, they talk almost every day. It may be really quick. But they're always checking in with each other. Out of something really terrible came something really wonderful. It was a great gift for both of them.

Chapter 13

Framing the Debate

O F ALL THE THINGS I've ever wanted to do in broadcasting, there's just one I've never done: moderate a presidential debate.

I moderated the Bush-McCain debate in the Republican South Carolina primary in 2000. I thought they were going to kill each other. I've had leaders from Israel, Palestine, and Jordan on split screen. And I've hosted the first debate between a vice president and an ordinary citizen, when Al Gore and Ross Perot went at it over NAFTA back in 1993. But a debate between the Republican and Democratic presidential candidates has never come my way.

I don't think Walter Cronkite ever got a chance to moderate any presidential debates, either. He would have been more famous during his time than the two guys running. Years ago, someone said, "Larry King is a personality. We don't want a presidential debate to become *Larry King Live*." That's certainly a valid point. I don't use Federal Election Commission rules on my show. Sometimes, one guest will say something and I'll just point to another guest for a response. I really just let it flow. So I can understand. But that doesn't stop the urge.

It's hard for me to watch a presidential debate without wanting to be there.

Asking people to go back and forth on the issues is what I do nearly every night during election season. You could make a case that my CNN show has tackled the world's major debates for almost twenty-five years. I sometimes wonder what it was like at the debates between Abraham Lincoln and Stephen A. Douglas. They lasted for hours and had no moderator. Can you imagine what would happen today if there were no moderator in a debate about abortion or gay rights?

I don't know exactly when it started, but I've witnessed a huge change in attitude toward homosexuality. When I was a kid, gay men were fairies and faggots. It was sport to say, "Let's go to Greenwich Village and look at them." Then I grew up and became more open-minded. But my mind really expanded when I interviewed a hero in the Korean War who was thrown out of the Army for being gay. He was removed even though he never engaged in sexual activity on the base. He met with his lovers off base and on his own time. So he never broke any Army law. He sued, and the case was headed to the Supreme Court when the two sides settled.

During the interview, he explained to me that he didn't know why he was gay. There was nothing about his parents that might seem out of the ordinary to heterosexuals. His older brother was married and had several children. But, for some reason, when he was a kid he liked dolls. On the other hand, he also liked guns and uniforms.

As we spoke, a pretty girl came in to serve us coffee. She was wearing a miniskirt. When she walked out, he said to me, "Does that turn you on?"

"Yeah," I said.

"Didn't turn me on," he said. Then he asked. "Do you know why it turned you on?"

"Well . . ."

"OK, she was wearing a short skirt. She had pretty legs. But let's think about this. *Why* did that turn you on? The answer is, you don't know. You grew up and you saw girls and you got excited. I grew up, saw boys, and got excited. And neither one of us knows why. You don't know why you're heterosexual. You didn't make a decision to be heterosexual. You didn't sit down and say, 'Boys/girls? Boys or girls? I choose girls.'"

When he said it, an image came to my mind. I remembered when I was about eleven years old. My cousin Loretta was over at our house for dinner. Something fell on the floor. I leaned down to get it and I saw right up Loretta's legs. I was excited. I had no idea why. What was it that made me feel that way?

So some guys must see a boy, get excited the same way, and not know why. It has to be a gene. You can't alter it. You couldn't make me gay. It would be impossible. But I didn't choose heterosexuality. And who in their right mind would choose being gay? Let's see. Do I want to make it in life? Sure, I'd like to shoot for the presidency. Should I be gay or straight? Straight or gay?

I never forgot that interview. I would bring it up when I spoke with religious leaders like Jerry Falwell, and the point always caught them off guard.

They would say they prayed for gay people. They would insist that being gay is an errant choice.

I'd say, "So these people choose to be gay? It's a choice?"

"Yes," they'd say. "These people have chosen to be gay."

I would pause and ask, "Can you remember the moment when *you* chose to be heterosexual?"

I'd never get an answer.

A guy like Falwell would say, "Well, it's normal."

And I'd say, "What do you mean, it's normal? To the gay person, being gay is normal."

I've questioned nearly every religious leader on gay issues. Elton John came on the show and discussed his life in depth. I remember talking with the actor Raymond Burr. He wouldn't speak about being gay on the air. But over lunch he told me how difficult it was back in the '40s and '50s.

When he was breaking into the movies he was hospitalized with an illness and needed an operation. He didn't know how he was going to pay the bill. As he was leaving the hospital, he found out the bill had been paid. Frank Sinatra had learned of his predicament and taken care of it. The two had worked on a movie together. Burr wondered if Sinatra would have paid the bill if Frank had known he was gay.

Personally, all I can say now is, Who cares if somebody is gay or straight? People should be free to love whomever they wish.

But I try not to let that come across on the air if I'm interviewing somebody in favor of gay marriage. I'll give you an example. During the 2008 election, when Californians faced a proposition on whether or not to ban gay marriage, about eighteen thousand gay couples had already registered as married under state law. The campaign was charged and the public overwhelmingly voted for a ban. Afterward, angry gay activists protested all around California. If one of those activists had been on my show at that time, I might have said, "You lost fair and square. How does protesting help your cause? What are your legal options?"

I try to encourage people on both sides of an issue to see a bigger picture. Abortion is another example. I remember having the vice president Dan Quayle on as a guest. Quayle is against abortion. I asked him, "What if your daughter came to you with the problem all fathers fear? How would you deal with it?"

"I would counsel her and talk to her," Quayle replied, "and support her on whatever decision she made."

Next day, headlines! QUAYLE WOULD GO WITH DAUGHTER
FOR ABORTION.

I wasn't out to snooker him. I just wanted to make him
think. Hypothetical questions are great for that. A lot of
politicians don't like to answer hypotheticals because they're
forced to think in a different way.

I believe a woman has the right to make a choice. I don't
believe that society should tell a woman that she doesn't have
the right to choose. But on the air, I might say to somebody in
favor of abortion, "There are so many other avenues. Why not
give the child to a couple who aren't able to have one? Why
not give the baby to parents who would do anything for a
chance to raise a child? Why would you waste a life?" When
I start talking like that, I can convince myself.

I'm totally against the death penalty. I believe that when
you kill a murderer you're committing the same act. But my
main objection to capital punishment is that there's no redress
of grievance. In all other cases, when the state makes a mistake, it can say, "We're sorry. Here's some compensation." The
state can't do that after it has executed someone.

Imagine what it's like to be innocent and locked up in jail
as your execution day approaches. The Pitts and Lee case in
Florida is a classic example. Two black men were accused of
murdering two white gas station attendants in the Florida Pan-
handle. This was back in the early '60s. There was no gun
found. No evidence at all. Pitts was a twenty-seven-year-old
guy in the service. Lee was a nineteen-year-old cook. Police
beat the two of them until they confessed to committing the
crime. For nine years, they were on death row. Then a white
man admitted he'd done the killing, and passed a lie-detector
test to prove it. Even then, Pitts and Lee were convicted in a
retrial because the judge wouldn't allow the jury to hear the
white man's confession. Only after a Pulitzer Prize–winning

book was written about the case were Pitts and Lee pardoned by the governor.

The problem with capital punishment is that you can't write a law that says if you're identified as the murderer by fourteen people, then you should be given the death penalty. The only person I would capitally punish is someone who asked for it.

But I always look for ways to see the other side. If I had a guest on my show who was against the death penalty, I might ask, "What about Hitler? What if Hitler was captured and jailed in 1940? Wouldn't you have given Hitler the death penalty knowing that if he escaped or was somehow freed he could get back in charge and kill millions?"

By the late '80s, CNN had become *the* place to watch issues like these debated. Now you hit your clicker and see pundits and politicians arguing on channel after channel. But Rupert Murdoch didn't get Fox News up and running until 1996. MSNBC started the same year. Until then, CNN was the only game in town. The exchanges on *Crossfire* led straight into my show. Everything really started to click for *Larry King Live* in the late '80s. We were being beamed around the world and people started calling in from as far off as Greenland and Australia to ask questions. That may not sound like a big deal now. But back then, there was no toll-free 800 number. People in Greenland had to pay for the opportunity . . . and there were long waits on the phone lines to get on the air.

Every time a huge news event hit, more and more people turned to CNN. When I returned from the hospital after the heart attack, it was the Jim and Tammy Faye Bakker televangelist scandal. If ever there was a tabloid story made for television, this was it. Jim and Tammy Faye looked like an adorable couple who had met in grammar school and were joined at the hip. He was a salesman and she was a show. They started the Praise the Lord Club and went on television pitching memberships in a Christian hotel and theme park. They collected millions and lavished it on themselves, going as far as building an air-conditioned doghouse. In the meantime, Jim was having sex with his pretty secretary, Jessica Hahn, and paying her a couple of hundred grand to keep quiet.

We had Jim and Tammy Faye on many times, and Jessica Hahn, too. She was really sexy. I'll never forget. I was single at the time. We were riding in a cab back to her hotel and she was very flirtatious. She lifted her foot toward my crotch and was starting to play around. I held myself back. Sometimes in life I haven't been able to sense those uh-oh moments. But that time I could.

Jim and Tammy Faye Bakker were incredible TV because new revelations and accusations were constantly emerging. Hahn accused Bakker of drugging and raping her. The preacher Jimmy Swaggart came on my show and called Bakker a cancer on the body of Christ. A short time later, Swaggart was discovered in a Louisiana hotel with a prostitute. More than a hundred thousand former supporters of the PTL filed a class-action suit to try to get back their money. Jerry Falwell came running to the rescue and tried to take over the organization. After one successful fund-raising drive, he plunged down the waterslide at the theme park with his clothes on. Tammy Faye didn't like Falwell, but she didn't have a mean bone in her body, so she never let on. Nobody ever blamed Tammy Faye. But Jim was convicted of fraud and dragged off to jail crying, kicking, and screaming.

Tammy Faye stood by him at first. She couldn't get through a show without mascara streaming down her tearful face. But while Jim was in jail, Tammy Faye divorced him. She went on to march in Gay Pride parades and became a favorite of the gay community. I got to be friendly with her. Tammy

Faye got colon cancer, then inoperable lung cancer. She came on my show the night before she died. She must have weighed about sixty-five pounds. It was like looking at death. I actually thought she might die during the show. She could hardly talk, but she wanted to say goodbye. The announcement of her death was held until my show the next evening. I spoke at her memorial service.

It was a soap opera, all right, but it was hard to turn away. I remember asking Ted Koppel, "How do we achieve a balance between tabloid and news on our shows?" Ted said, "I report on Jim Bakker for them. They let me report on the Middle East." It was similar to my situation. Only Ted Turner gave me the end of the Cold War and everything that followed.

I don't know if Ted could have predicted the Bakker scandal when he started CNN. But he certainly wanted to see the end of the Cold War. Relations between the United States and the Soviet Union were not good when CNN was launched. The Soviets had invaded Afghanistan in 1979. As punishment, President Carter refused to allow Americans to go to the Moscow Olympics in 1980. The Soviets returned the favor four years later. They boycotted the Los Angeles games and held back much of the Communist bloc.

Ted got the idea to bring the Soviet Union, the United States, and the rest of the world together. He called it the Goodwill Games. His timing was just right. Mikhail Gorbachev became premier of the Soviet Union in 1985, and brought with him a feeling of openness. A year later, thousands of athletes from around the world showed up in Moscow for the first Goodwill Games. Ted met Gorbachev. A Soviet band played the American national anthem. Rowers for the Soviet Union and the United States exchanged places in each other's boats. It was so simple to Ted. He came back and said, "Communists eat like we do. They walk like we do. They've got two eyes like we do. You can talk to them. You don't have to agree with them. But you can talk to them." How could anyone disagree with that? A year later, Ronald Reagan was in Berlin asking Gorbachev to "tear down this wall." CNN viewers would watch as the Berlin Wall fell in 1989. That was less than ten years after Ted started to bring people together through satellite broadcasting.

I was never more important to CNN than in 1989. My ratings were going through the roof. I had the world to myself at nine o'clock, and my show was getting a lot of press. Coincidentally, a window in my contract opened. The window gave me thirty days to make a deal with any other station. I had to tell Ted within those thirty days if I was going to leave, and then give him three months' notice.

Bob Woolf negotiated all over the place during this window. He got two great offers. One was from Roone Arledge at ABC. Roone's idea was that I would follow *Nightline*. Ted Koppel would be on until midnight, and I would be on from midnight to one.

The other offer was from the brothers who ran King World—the same guys who started *The Oprah Winfrey Show* and do a lot of quiz shows. They were really nice guys, crazy guys. Their concept was for a show called "Larry King Wired." We were going to have two jet planes with reporters who'd fly to the big story of the day and set me up to tackle the story from there.

I was making about eight hundred thousand dollars a year from CNN at the time. Each of the other offers would have nearly doubled my salary. There was a little more prestige to ABC. But King World's offer also included a percentage of profits from the syndicated show.

Bob and I discussed the two options over and over. But we couldn't decide which one to take. I was really nervous as the window began to close. This was heady stuff. I flew out to California. I was seeing Angie Dickinson at the time and she met me at the airport. It was raining. As we drove to the hotel, I told her the whole situation.

I can still see her gorgeous face looking over at me with the rain pelting down outside the car window. "Are you unhappy?" she asked.

"No."

"If you're not unhappy, then why are you leaving?"

"Well, it's more money."

"You've got to have a second reason."

We got to the hotel and fooled around a little. But afterward, I couldn't go to sleep. Bob would be meeting with Ted in the morning in Atlanta to tell him I'd be leaving for one of the two offers. I lay in bed all night thinking about what Angie had said. It was complicated. It's very hard for me to leave a place that feels like home. But it was also nice to be courted. Plus, Bob had worked really hard lining up the two offers. He wouldn't make a penny more if I stayed at CNN. But he'd make a lot more if I left.

At six in the morning, the phone rang.

"Larry, it's Ted. I'm on a speakerphone. Bob is right here, and he tells me you're leaving."

I heard Bob yelling, "This is unethical. It's unethical!"

"The hell with ethics," Ted said. "This has nothing to do with ethics! Larry, listen to me. Here's what I want you to do. It's simple. Just say, 'Goodbye, Ted.' You say 'Goodbye Ted,' and we're friends. You start your new job in three months— whatever job you take—and nobody's angry. The reason I'm calling is, I want you to say it to me. 'Goodbye, Ted.' I want to hear you say goodbye."

I stood there in my underwear with the telephone at my ear. Nothing would come out of my mouth.

Ted waited and waited and waited. The room filled with silence.

"You can't say it!" Ted said. "You *can't* say it!"

I could hear Bob in the background, screaming, "This is crazy!"

But there was no stopping Ted. "Here's what I'm going to do," he said. "Because you're loyal to me, I'm going to give you the same money you'd get from ABC one year from today. I don't pay anyone that kind of money. I'm expanding right now and I don't have the money to give you today. But I'm going to pay you $1.5 million one year from today. Write the date down. You're stayin' with me."

Afterward, when things calmed down, Ted said something I'll never forget—a little wisdom that I'm happy to pass on. "Never go someplace else if it's just for money. Because if it's just for money, the first day you're unhappy, you're going to be upset with everyone who told you to go."

Ted had reinvented television, and soon he would be able to afford my raise. Even when people were sleeping, they were paying to watch CNN through their monthly cable bills. ABC didn't have that same revenue coming in. It was dependent on advertising. The viewer doesn't pay ABC anything. Ted was also bringing in money from advertising. The power of CNN became even more evident when the next big news event hit: the Gulf War.

When Saddam Hussein invaded Kuwait, people wanted to know how the world would respond. Developments could break on CNN at any minute. The news division at CBS couldn't compete with that. CBS would be in upheaval. *Cancel the show? What about the advertisers?* To make a preemptive decision at a regular broadcast network, you've got to move mountains. Ted and his network made decisions in the blink of an eye.

One of the CNN anchors, Bernard Shaw, was over in Baghdad to interview Saddam. He was talking to me on the air when Iraqi authorities moved in. Bernie said, "I think they're going to shut—" and the screen went blank. This was not happening on other networks. I don't think there was ever a time before this when a war was broadcast live from behind enemy lines. Peter Arnett, Bernie Shaw and John Holliman reported courageously for countless hours. The three of them were ducking for cover when bombs dropped on Baghdad, and no one was calling CNN the Chicken Noodle News any longer. There were days when more people were watching news on cable than they were on any one of the three major networks.

The whole nature of politics and television was changing. I saw the shift right on my show. We became part of the political scene when Ross Perot came on during the 1992 presidential campaign. Perot was a wealthy Texan, and he had a lot to say about budget issues. He'd opposed the Gulf War and he had solid reasons even though the conflict ended in a hundred days and worked out well for the United States. The topic on my show that night was the difficult economy. But a friend of mine had put a thought in my head beforehand: "Ask Ross if he'd run for president."

"Why?" I asked.

"I was with him at a party and I just got the feeling he would."

At the beginning of the show, I asked if he'd run.

"Oh, no," he said. "I really wouldn't be interested."

We talked about a lot of things. Then an instinct took over. I said, "I don't like to revisit things, but are you sure you wouldn't run for president? Is it absolute?"

He said, "Yeah."

Just before the end of the show, I couldn't help but come back to it again. "Under what circumstances would you run?"

He said, "Well, I'll tell you. If the people put me on the
ballot as an independent in all fifty states, I'll run."

It didn't strike me as a big deal when the show ended and
we said goodbye. It didn't hit me until my Mutual radio show
later that night. The first caller asked, "How do I help Ross
Perot?" A flood of calls about Perot followed. I later learned
that when Ross got back to the hotel after the show, he found
a ten-dollar contribution to his campaign. It had been left by
a bellhop. Soon Dan Rather was reporting the story. A week
later, we realized how monumental the show had been.

George Bush, the incumbent, couldn't understand. "What
does Ross have against me?" he once asked me. "We're fellow
Texans. I thought he liked me."

Everything seemed to change around the time of that election. I had Bush on, and one of Clinton's people, George
Stephanopoulos, called in with questions that infuriated the
president. One of Bush's friends, Robert Mosbacher, called in
while Perot was on and blasted Ross. Interaction like this had
never happened on television before.

At one point, Perot even led in the polls. The economy
had gone sour and Clinton was navigating his way through
questions about his marital fidelity. But Perot made a couple
of mistakes. He spoke to the NAACP and addressed his audience as "you people." He didn't mean it disparagingly. But
that's the way it came out. Then his vice presidential choice,
Admiral James Stockdale, was mocked after a debate with
Quayle and Al Gore. Stockdale stammered and wondered
aloud what he was doing on the same stage. It was sad because Stockdale was a good man—a former prisoner of war
who'd taught at Stanford.

Ross unexpectedly dropped out of the race, claiming the
Republicans were trying to sabotage him. The singer Cher
called in to my show crying about it. Later Ross got back in,

but his candidacy was damaged. The week before the election I had Bush on Wednesday night, Clinton on Thursday night, and Perot on Friday.

It wasn't a conventional presidential debate. But at the time, it didn't get any better.

ANOTHER POINT OF VIEW

Marty Zeiger

It was during this time period—the late '80s—that Larry married Julie. I was the best man at that wedding. My recollection of that marriage is that I thought it happened too quickly and they really didn't know each other. In fact, I can link the way I felt to a specific moment at a dinner in New York. Larry and Julie had just gotten engaged. At this dinner there were five people. Larry and Julie. My wife, Ellen, and I. And Angie Dickinson. Angie was sitting next to me. At one point in the conversation, it came up that Julie could speak French fluently. Larry said, "I didn't know you spoke French."

Angie leaned over to me and whispered, "Do they have a prenup?"

Chapter 14

O.J.

M Y EIGHT- AND NINE-YEAR-OLD SONS may hear the O.J. Simpson murder case described as the trial of the century. But they live in a different century. Now nobody cares about O.J. It would be hard for me to explain to my sons just how big that trial was at the time. The best I can do is this. Bill Clinton told me that when he went to greet Boris Yeltsin on a state visit, the Russian president whispered into his ear, "Did he do it?"

O.J. was the most famous person ever charged with murder—anywhere. For years, he'd been an all-American hero to millions. He had speed, instincts on a football field that couldn't be taught, and matinee-idol looks. You can argue all day about whether a sports star is heroic. O.J. didn't save lives. When you got up on Monday morning, had he changed your life? No. Yet he did. He made you feel better. When O.J. ran down the field, you were with him all the way. When O.J. hurdled a luggage cart in an airport, you smiled and wanted to rent from Hertz. O.J. was one of the first crossover stars. Jackie Robinson was black. Muhammad Ali was black. O.J. was black and white. O.J. had a white life and a white wife.

When I was broadcasting the Miami Dolphins I can remember a particular coach around the league being shocked
when he learned that a black player for the New England Pa-
triots was married to a white woman. It wasn't prejudice. It was
just rare to see a black man and a white woman together in the
early '70s. But O.J. Simpson could date anybody's sister. He set
the stage for Michael Jordan. Derek Jeter. Tiger Woods. These
guys were no longer men of color. They were seen as gods.

I didn't even suspect O.J. when reports came in about the
murder of Nicole Brown Simpson. Not only did it seem crazy,
it appeared impossible. The first story we heard was that O.J.
got word of the murder while he was in Chicago. How could
he stab his ex-wife and a waiter, who'd come by her place to
drop off a pair of glasses, when they were two thousand miles
away? It was only later that we learned that O.J. had boarded
a plane for Chicago after Nicole and Ron Goldman were
found dead outside Nicole's condominium.

Very few people knew that there were two O.J.s. The O.J.
I met on a television set always had a smile. A childhood friend
of his told me that O.J. was the captain of every team he played
on, the guy a teammate would go to with a problem. He never
argued with a referee, never lost his temper on the field. People
who filmed the Hertz commercials said they'd never worked
with a more cooperative star. The shooting was done in airports
at 2 a.m., but O.J. never complained. *Need another take? No
problem.* O.J.'s secretary said she never heard him swear.

After the murder, you started to hear about the other O.J.
There were whispers about drugs, his temper, and his jealousy
over his ex-wife's lovers. When the name of a certain friend of his
was mentioned, you got an idea why he might be jealous. There
was talk of a 911 call made by Nicole and domestic violence.

It's not hard for me to see how all these different charac-
teristics and complications fit inside one person. Slobodan

Milošević was known as the Butcher of the Balkans. He died while on trial for crimes against humanity. I interviewed him once. A few years afterward, the same guy who'd been a symbol of murder and ethnic cleansing had a diplomat go out of his way to wish me well and ask how my kids were doing. Any person who excels is going to have many facets to them; "ordinary" usually isn't one of them. Unfortunately, most people have a hard time seeing the complications and depth in others. They see in terms of black and white. Which is exactly how the O.J. trial played out.

We knew something was up on the afternoon when O.J. promised to turn himself in to the police but didn't show. Instead, he left a suicide note that was read aloud on television by his close friend Robert Kardashian. The words "I can't go on . . ." made me shiver.

I was dating Cindy Garvey at the time. Cindy was once married to Steve Garvey, who'd played with the Dodgers. She'd been a friend of Nicole's. She hated O.J., and she thought he'd done it. I had her on the air that night along with a representative from the NAACP. From the very start, this story was about more than murder. You knew that no matter what happened, it was going to play out in black and white.

The stage had been set in Los Angeles during the previous four years. First, there was the beating of Rodney King. That was in 1991. King was a black guy who'd been stopped after a high-speed car chase by white policemen. For years, blacks had complained about police brutality. This time, however, everyone in the world could see it because the scene had been secretly videotaped. It was a huge story. The biggest stories are always about one person. It's hard to take in the overwhelming horror of a catastrophe like Hurricane Katrina. But we can all feel for the guy holding a cat on the roof as the water rises. The Rodney King video was horrific. It was one guy on the ground in the darkness being kicked and clubbed long past the point of resistance. That video changed journalism forever. From that moment on, everybody could be a reporter. Anybody could film an event and have it beamed around the world on satellite.

Without that footage, who would have known the beating had occurred? There was a public outcry and the officers were charged with excessive force. But it was determined that they couldn't get a fair trial in Los Angeles after all the media attention, and the case was moved to Simi Valley. The jury there was made up of ten whites, one Asian, and one Latino— and the officers were acquitted. What a travesty that was. Riots erupted all over Los Angeles. More than seven thousand fires were set. More than fifty people died. More than two thousand people were injured. There was a billion dollars in damages in Los Angeles alone—and the rioting spread to other cities. Numbers can tell a story. But the one sickening image we were all left with was of a white truck driver being pulled out of the driver's seat and beaten by a bunch of blacks with a claw hammer and a chunk of concrete. Reginald Denny, his name was. I would later interview him. The beating he'd taken was filmed from a helicopter.

One thing I've always tried to do is allow viewers to see a situation from different angles. The Reginald Denny who came on my show did not sue the people who beat him. He hugged the mother of one of those men after they were convicted. Denny sued the city of Los Angeles for not responding to his emergency after repeated 911 calls were made, and he was represented by a prominent black attorney whom we all came to know—Johnnie Cochran. Johnnie had worked as an assistant prosecuting attorney for many years and he knew about problems in the police department. So here was a white guy coming on my show, expressing no anger at the black men who'd beaten him, and hiring a black attorney to file his case against the city. It's important for journalism to offer that kind of depth. Without it, people's minds are left with only the raw memory of a beating they've seen replayed over and over.

The O.J. trial would have been huge in any case. But it was even bigger because everybody watching had fresh memories of Rodney King and Reginald Denny.

A live feed of the white Bronco flashed on the screen toward the end of my show with Cindy Garvey and the guy from the NAACP. Helicopter footage showed police cars in orderly pursuit. At first, I didn't even know if O.J. was in the white Bronco. I was in new territory. I had never done a show like this. I had none of my usual control over this show, because I had no control over the events unfolding before me. It was wild. When the show started, I was hoping that O.J. wouldn't follow through on his threat to kill himself. Fifty minutes later, I was wishing I knew which way he was headed on I-5. We stayed on the air. A producer brought over a road map so I could get a grip on the scene I was describing. We got word that O.J.'s friend, Al Cowlings, was driving and that O.J. was in the back. Crowds lined the road with signs that read: "Go, O.J., go!" They didn't want to let go of the O.J. in the Hertz commercial. Finally, the Bronco reached O.J.'s home and he gave up. We were on for three hours that night.

Events change lives. But this one took my personal life in a direction I never could have predicted: it brought me out to Los Angeles to cover the trial. I'd visited Los Angeles prior to O.J., but I didn't know it well before then. What I knew was the Nate 'n Al Deli in Beverly Hills. I first walked through the door in 1985. Whitefish, corned beef, and pastrami were behind the glass counter to the left—just as they are today. The halvah was by the cash register. Sid Yallowitz was sitting in the second booth—the same Sid whose all-star basketball picture is still in the glass case downstairs at the Jewish Community House in Bensonhurst. I slid into the seat across from him and said, "Hey, Yallowitz." We could have been in Maltz's candy store. Sid had been friends with Asher Dan since kindergarten. I remembered Asher from Brooklyn. But I didn't know that Asher had married Iris Siegel, the girl who refused to walk down the steps of Lafayette High with me. Asher was now selling real estate in Los Angeles and eating breakfast at Nate 'n Al. I sat with Sid and Asher and said to myself, *You* can *go home again*. There was a lot more than Brooklyn at Nate 'n Al. A waitress named Kaye Coleman became your friend for life the day you met her. What a character she was. She could have been the mayor of Beverly Hills. The kindest woman you'd ever know. But don't leave her a lousy tip. I once saw her throw a dollar back at a guy and say, "Hey, fella, you need this more than I do." It's hard to know exactly when it happened, but during the O.J. trial, something inside me began to feel right in the city the Dodgers now called home.

I can remember asking the TV detective actor Peter Falk about the Simpson case. "Ah," he said, "it's a ten-minute *Columbo*." That's how long he figured it would take to solve the crime. That ten-minute *Columbo* riveted America for months. I was at the center of it all, right there at Nate 'n Al.

It turned out that Sid had played tennis with O.J. One of O.J.'s lawyers, Robert Shapiro, occasionally came in for breakfast. So did Rosey Grier, O.J.'s minister. There was a big rumor at the time that O.J. had confessed to him—which Grier denied. It was the same Rosey who was guarding Bobby Kennedy's wife when Bobby was assassinated and who succeeded in seizing Sirhan Sirhan's gun. I can still remember hearing the tape: "Rosey, get the gun!" Rosey was a friend of the book publisher Michael Viner, who took a seat at our table. Michael was publishing a tell-all by a fashion designer named Faye

Resnick, who claimed she was Nicole's best friend and that O.J. had been stalking Nicole. When we set up an interview with Faye for my show, the judge, Lance Ito, asked us to hold off while the jury was still being selected. We did, and Judge Ito invited me into his chambers to say thanks. I don't know why, but I've never been very close to guys named Lance. But Judge Ito and I got along quite well. We talked for almost an hour. When it was time to leave, I walked out the wrong door, straight into the courtroom. The first thing I heard was, "Hey, Larrrrrrrrrry!" It was O.J. saying hello. The cameras were on because they were about to resume the trial. I was really embarrassed. "Hey, Juice," I said. I said hello to Bob Shapiro, then I made sure to greet everyone at the prosecution bench. I didn't want anybody to see me leaning one way or the other. That wasn't easy. When I walked out of the courthouse, I found myself surrounded by a crowd of reporters, with questions coming from all sides. "Larry, is it true you are a character witness for O.J.?" I must have said "No comment" about eleven times before I could get away.

As it turned out, I ended up getting very much in the middle of things. I was single at the time, and I began to date the woman who was the jury consultant for the defense team and another who was the publicist for the prosecution. I don't think either one of them knew about the other. But my table at Nate 'n Al did. I'd come in the morning and everyone would want to know what new tidbit I'd learned the night before. As I look back on those days, I don't think, "I was dating women on both sides of the case. What was I doing?" Instead, I think about Bill Clinton's reaction when he found out. "I admire your flexibility in women," he said. It was fun, and I have to admit, it came in handy. We were able to get notes to O.J. through the jury consultant asking him if he'd like to call in to the show after the trial.

Before the trial started, I had breakfast with the Los Angeles district attorney, Gil Garcetti. My friend Asher remembers that breakfast well. "We got him nailed," Garcetti said.

Garcetti was right. O.J.'s glove and blood had been found at the scene. The evidence was overwhelming and the prosecution had an open-and-shut case. But they lost it. They had some bad witnesses. Remember the prosecution's DNA witness? Poor guy. Dennis Fung. He was out of his league against the expert defense attorney Barry Scheck, and he got hung out to dry. Then there was Mark Fuhrman—one of the first cops at the scene of the crime to collect evidence. He was made out to be a racist who might have manipulated the evidence. It was great drama when F. Lee Bailey cross-examined Fuhrman, "marine to marine." When Bailey asked Fuhrman if he had used the word *nigger* in the past ten years, Fuhrman denied doing so. He obviously wasn't aware the defense had a tape on which he'd made racial slurs something like forty-one times. Bailey believed O.J. At least he convinced me that he believed him. Bailey and Johnnie Cochran suckered the assistant prosecutor, Christopher Darden, into making O.J. try on the bloody glove that had been left behind at the scene. O.J. had told Bailey that it wasn't going to fit. It was a huge mistake for the prosecution. The glove had been frozen and unfrozen several times during testing. And O.J. was wearing a rubber glove on his hand to avoid contaminating the evidence when he tried it on. When the glove didn't fit, it opened the door for Johnnie Cochran's famous line to the jury, "If it doesn't fit, you must acquit."

Cochran and Shapiro weren't speaking by the end of the trial. Shapiro didn't like that Cochran played the race card in his closing argument. I became very friendly with Shapiro. If I had to bet, I'd say that Bob thinks O.J. was guilty. He'd never say. If he did, he'd violate every tenet of legal ethics. You can sense it in his body language, though.

One of the biggest surprises for me was how quickly the
jury reached a verdict. After an eight-month trial, it was hard
to believe that the jury could come to a decision after only a
few hours of deliberation. I thought it might take weeks just
to go over all the evidence . . . and then another hundred years
to decide. I remember waiting for the verdict in my hotel room.
I looked out the window. Nobody was walking down the side-
walks. No cars were going down the street. Everybody was in
front of a TV.

Sid was with me. So was my executive producer, Wendy
Walker. We all held hands as the verdict was announced. There
was never another moment in my life when I held hands like
that. But there never was a trial like that.

When I heard the words *not guilty*, my first thought was
disbelief. My second thought took me by surprise. It was, *Oh,
shit. The trial is over. I've got to go back to Washington.* Then
came all the images of the black viewers celebrating and white
audiences in shock.

It's hard to believe America now has a black president
when I think about my show on the night of the verdict in
1995. The writer Dominick Dunne was my guest for that show.
He believed that the nation was so polarized that day that all
the civil rights advancements made over thirty years had been
washed away.

There's a guy I know who comes up with some crazy theories. One of his wilder ones is that Barack Obama would never
have been elected president if there had been no O.J. trial. His
theory is that America was forced to see its own reflection on
the television screen when that verdict was announced, and it
didn't like the divide that it saw. Johnnie Cochran talked about
holding up a mirror to society in order to understand our differences. But it still seems like a stretch to me. Obama certainly
wouldn't have been elected right after that trial. But maybe the

Simpson trial was another event in a long continuum that led to the change.

The night after the verdict, as we were finishing our show, O.J. called in. He hadn't testified at the trial. Nobody had heard from him in eight months. Everyone wanted to hear what he had to say. He was given a number with a special password so that we would know it was really O.J. The strangest part about our conversation is that CNN wanted to cut the show off at its scheduled end even though O.J. had just begun to speak. A taped O.J. special was all set to run. Wendy had to tell them, "You may have a taped O.J. special. But we have O.J."

After all this time, I can't help but wonder what the outcome would have been if O.J. had stayed in the driveway after the murders and screamed for the police. What if he'd stayed there with the knife in his hand until the police arrived and admitted that he'd killed his wife and the waiter? If he'd just said, "I was in a rage and I lost it! I'm guilty. Punish me. I deserve to die." My theory on Americans and forgiveness is that if he'd done that, he'd be out of jail by now. He'd have done a few years, written a book on rage, and gone on all the talk shows. O.J. would have become the number one rage expert and been forgiven. He just wouldn't have been able to smile ever again.

O.J. was never forgiven. He lost a civil suit to the families of the victims. And as I write this he sits in a jail about ninety miles from Reno for forcibly trying to get back some of his sports memorabilia. He could serve up to thirty-three years. Certainly, the punishment doesn't fit the crime. It was his property. Nobody was killed. He was convicted of kidnapping only because in Nevada it's kidnapping if you lock the door while you commit a crime. O.J.'s in jail for the wrong reason. But maybe it's the right reason if you go back in time and look at the big picture. The bottom line is, nobody cares.

It's amazing how someone can be so important, then fade right before our eyes. For me, the trial became even more important over the years than it was at the time. No O.J., and I might not have thought about moving to Los Angeles. You could even make a case that I wouldn't have my two youngest sons if it weren't for O.J. That's because I met the woman who would become their mother in L.A.

Before Chance and Cannon arrived, though, there was a little surprise.

Chapter 15

Jr.

I T WAS SO INNOCENT. I was at CNN, sitting at my desk in Washington late one afternoon. I got a message: "Larry, a lady from Miami named Annette is on the phone."

I knew right away who that was. I'd never told anybody that I'd been married to Annette. Not even my brother. The only record of the wedding was a document at Broward City Hall. I didn't see her much after the wedding—maybe a couple of times. The point is, I hadn't spoken to her in what—thirty years? So I had no idea what this would be about. I picked up the phone and started in on one of those "How are you?" conversations. But Annette was very direct.

"I have lung cancer," she said. Annette was a big smoker. She used to outsmoke me. But I didn't have time to react. Her words began hitting me all at once. "You have a son. He's getting married. I want you to know him before I die. No, I *insist* that you know him before I die."

There's always a possibility that any woman you've been with has gotten pregnant. But more than three decades had passed since we'd been together. I sat there, blindingly amazed. That's the only way I can describe it. I can't tell you much more about the early part of the story because I wasn't there for the first thirty-three years of it. So I'm going to have Larry King Jr. fill in what I never knew.

Larry King Jr.

SON

Unless someone directly asked me, "Is Larry King your father?" I never told anyone who my father was.

I'm that way to this day. Not long ago, I was checking out at Hertz when the guy behind the counter looked at my driver's license and said, "Larry King?"

I said, "Yeah, no suspenders today."

He just laughed.

I always remember the teachings of my mother. She said, "Be your own man. The minute you sell yourself as your father and try to live off that, you'll no longer be a man." It was drilled in. She said, "I named you Larry King Jr. because it was the right thing to do. You know who you are. There's no disputing who you are. Your father may not be there or recognize you when you want to be recognized. But deep down he loves you. There'll be a day when he's there for you. It's my job to bring you up."

My mother and father met in 1958—about a year after my father came to Miami. She was in a bowling alley while he was doing man-on-the-street interviews there.

She was nuts about my father. My mother used to love going to the movies. I guess they went to the movies a lot together. So my dad, he made a bet with her. He was probably just kidding. He said, "I'll bet you can't go a week without a movie." It must have been around the time that their relationship ended, because she never went to a movie theater again. Never. Wouldn't set foot in one. Even later in life, when I said, "Mom, c'mon. Let's just go to a movie," she refused.

Isn't that crazy—that kind of love? It was so strong that from the day they started dating to the time of her death, anytime his name was in the newspaper she'd cut out the article and save it. I have huge boxes filled with clippings. When I asked her why she did it, she said, "It was the best way for you to know what your dad was up to."

Their relationship was over when I came around. I was born November 7, 1961. The divorce was official in 1962. My father married again a year later.

My mom had three kids of her own when she met my dad. It must have been tough on her bringing up four kids by herself. She worked two jobs. One at a cleaner's. The other at a liquor store. I admired what she was able to pull off. My older sisters helped raise me. As I grew up, my older brother went into the military, so I didn't see much of him.

I never saw my dad, but I don't think there was ever a time when his name didn't come up. Today, he's known around the world, but in the late '60s, he was Mr. Miami. I was a huge Dolphins fan and I would tune in to his sports show in the afternoons. I'd listen to him announce the games on a transistor radio from my seat in the Orange Bowl and look up at him in the booth.

This may sound weird, but I think that was my connection to him. Did I wish I could sit in the booth with him? Did I wish I could talk to him? Yeah. But as I listened, I felt like he was talking right to me. I put it in my head: *He knows I'm here.* Even though he didn't.

When I was about nine, my mother remarried.

She's no longer here to talk about it. But I think she did it to give me a male presence. Richard Love, whom

she married, a really, really nice guy, never tried to get in
the middle. He would always say, "Your dad will be there
for you one day."

Then my dad's life spun out of control. Front page
of the *Miami News*: LARRY KING ARRESTED.

I was in fifth grade. Parents of kids at school were
talking about it. As I grew older, the razzing started. Other
kids would say, "Your dad owes all this money. Why don't
you give the money back?" I wanted to defend him. But
I didn't know what to defend. Here I'd grown up not understanding why we didn't have a relationship, and now
suddenly I was taking the heat for his difficulties. A lot
was running through my mind. I didn't even know if he
was thinking about me.

I had my birth certificate. I also had a letter that my
mom had given to me, saying it was from my father. It was
typed on letterhead from the radio station he worked at.
I don't know if my father wrote it or not. My mom probably wrote it, because it was typed. But the letter held me
together in moments when I wondered, *Who am I?*

It basically said, "I've made mistakes in my life. But
you were not a mistake. I may not be with you, but you'll
always be my son. Be good to your mother." I'd reach for
that letter in tough times.

Things got real bad at one point after the arrest, and
my mother went to incredible lengths to protect me. She
said, "Use the name Larry Love for a while. When it
calms down, you can go back to saying you're Larry
King." My dad left town, and I called myself Larry Love
for several years. It seems crazy now, but my mom saw the
world crashing down on me, and that was her best plan.

When I reached an age when I could apply for my
own credit card, I was turned down because of my dad's

credit problems. I had to go to an office with my mom and say, "But I'm Larry King Jr., different Social Security number. That's not me." I hadn't tried to live off my dad, and I didn't deserve the negativity off him.

I remember being told that I acted older than my age. Looking back on it, I probably didn't have a choice. My mom was tough on me, harder than some moms are with their children. But I don't think I would have survived in business if not for my mother. She built in me a heck of a foundation.

The first job I got was at McDonald's. I made the sauce. The Filet-O-Fish. Moved to the fryer. Worked myself up to grill chief. Handled the cash register. Then I got promoted to store assistant manager—which was huge. I got to wear a tie. My mother used to come on Sundays. She'd sit for hours watching me work, beaming with pride. Her son was assistant manager.

Later on, McDonald's put out an advertising campaign. They'd show a guy who was CEO of a company and he'd say, "My first job was at McDonald's." I'm a classic example of that commercial. I can walk into a McDonald's now, hear a certain beep, and know they're behind in Big Macs.

I was getting set to go to college in 1979. I wanted to go to the University of Miami. I'd always wanted to be a Hurricane. I sat down with my mom and she said, "I just don't have enough money to get you into Miami. But if you start at Miami Dade Community College, and you can get your grades high, you can get a scholarship and then I'll do everything I can." I didn't know it until afterward, but she took out a second mortgage on our house to help me get into the University of Miami.

By this time, my dad had come back to town. I remember on New Year's Eve I went out with a girl. We went to a restaurant and danced. As we were driving home, I clicked on the radio and heard my dad say, "I'll be here at the Dupont doing my show for four more hours." I drove the girl home, swung around, and went to the Dupont. I sat and watched him for the rest of the night. Never approached him. Just watched him.

Part of me wanted to go up to him while he was on break and introduce myself. But I had such respect for my mother. She always said he'd be there for me when the time came. That moment, it just didn't feel like the right time. *I'm not prepared for this,* I thought. *He's not prepared for this.* I just needed to be close. It was sort of like going to the Orange Bowl, listening to the game on the transistor, and looking at him. It gave me that same comfort. Live from the lobby of the Dupont Plaza—that was the closest I'd gotten to my father up to that point.

When I started school at Miami Dade, people said, "Why don't you try out for the radio station?" I was outgoing and easy to talk with. So I went in and tried out for a deejay spot on WMDS. I was told, "Kid, you've got what your dad has." I never really thought of it as a career move. I guess it kept me close to my dad. But it also put me in a direct line of questioning. Now I was hearing, "Why doesn't your dad talk about you?"

After two years at Miami Dade, I got my opportunity to go to the University of Miami. I announced the football games on the campus station. Then, after an internship, I got a job at a local talk/news station—WNWS. My mom used to listen to me on the air and take notes. She said she used to do the same thing with my father. She'd tell me to stop saying, "Uhhhhh," watch how you cut into the breaks, that sort of thing. Some of the people at the sta-

tion knew my dad. I sensed it wasn't going to be long before we ran into each other. Then I got an all-night radio
show. My dad was on Mutual at the time. So we were com-
petitors for about three months.

My mom said, "You know, it's not fair that you're in-
troducing yourself as Larry King Jr. If you're going to do
this, you can't live off his name. You need to know you can
make it on your own merits, not because you're a Jr. Go
back to the name your father had before he started." So
I went on the air as Larry Zeiger.

I was just finishing up school when the television station where my dad's career took off—WTVJ—offered me
a job working behind the scenes.

"How's your dad doing?" people who'd known him
would ask.

"He's fine," I'd say.

I was very good at deflecting. If someone said, "I
know your brother, Andy," I'd say, "Great, tell him I said,
hi." Where was I going to go with that?

I was making eight dollars an hour at the television
station, working my butt off, working weekends. I started
asking myself, "Do I really love this? Or am I doing this
because I'm chasing something?"

I got offered a job at Southeast Bank, supervising a
team of people. I thought, *Let me try management. This
may be my path.* I was at Southeast when I got a phone
call from my mother. She said, "You're going to get a lot
of questions today."

"What's going on?"

"Your father's had a heart attack."

"Is he alive?"

"From everything I can tell, yes."

"I think I should go see him."

"Your father's just gone through a heart attack," she said. "The last thing you want to do right now is pop up in front of him."

I did send a card to the hospital. I have no clue if he ever got it. It probably never reached him among all the other notes from well-wishers. I just needed to do that.

I took a job with American Express in 1989. A big article came out in the *Miami Herald* about my father around that time. He mentioned all his children—but not me. It was like when my dad's books were published. I would immediately turn to the dedication page to see who he'd dedicated the book to. I wanted to see if I'd been mentioned. But I never was. Those were private moments, but the story in the *Miami Herald* was public. It made me see how my life had changed. I was now working at a Fortune 500 company and stories like this affected my credibility. When it appeared, coworkers at American Express started questioning if he was my father. When I said yes, they wondered why I wasn't in the article. I think by this time my mom was starting to get a little worried.

In 1992, before I got married, my fiancée, Shannon, and I put a wedding announcement in the paper. You know, father of the groom is Larry King. Mother is Annette Kaye Love. A few days later, a letter came in the mail. Shannon opened it. The letter was written in cut-out letters pasted on the page. It looked like a ransom note. It said, WHO ARE YOU, REALLY?

"How long have you had to deal with stuff like this?" Shannon asked.

"All my life."

Then my mom found out that she was ill. She didn't tell me at that point. But she had cancer, and I think she knew she didn't have much time left. It's so clear to me now that her dying wish was to make good on the promise she had made to me when I was a kid. *When the time is right, he'll be there for you.*

She reached out to my father and got hold of him. I'd love to know what that conversation was like.

Larry King

I hung up the phone, and some things started to make sense. When I was in Miami, people would sometimes come up to me and say, "You've got a son who's a great golfer." I knew Andy didn't golf. So it didn't make sense. I would think for a second, *Do I have a missing son?* But then I'd dismiss it. The most amazing thing to me is that as well known as I was in Miami, nobody ever came to me directly to ask about Larry King Jr. I never saw an article ever written about him. Never heard him on the radio. How was it that not one person said to me, "Who's this kid named Larry King Jr.?"

Who could it be? Did I have a missing son?

I called up Mark Barondess, my lawyer. Now, you know what the first thought of any lawyer is going to be. *What do they want? Is he really your kid? If he is your kid, he's got a right to be in your will.* My lawyer wasn't the only one thinking that way. I was dating Cindy Garvey at the time. She said, "Oh, they're out to get you. They're gonna grab you for big money. Watch out!"

So Mark flew down to meet with Annette. Then he met with Larry Jr. Afterward, he called me up and said, "Look, if you want to spend $750 on a DNA test, you're welcome to it. But this is your kid. He talks like you. He laughs like you. He's just like you."

So I called my friend Herbie. And, of course, Herbie said, "Let me handle this . . ."

Larry King Jr.

In business, we do something called "on-boarding." It's the process of getting a new employee accustomed to your environment so that he or she is ready to go as soon as they officially start. Herbie was on-boarding me. We met at the Watergate Hotel.

He did a great job of grounding me, saying, "Here's your father. Here's the pluses, here's the minuses. Look, everybody makes mistakes. There are times when things don't work out." Herbie was on-boarding me to help me understand my dad. At the same time, he was checking me out so he could help my dad ease me into the family.

Unfortunately, in this day and age, many people would use a situation like this to get money from someone in my father's position. My mom wanted nothing from my father but for him to love me. My father couldn't possibly have known that all my life my mother had said to me, "Make your own money and never take a dime from your father." He couldn't have known that I had great mentors at American Express and Intuit, and that my career was starting to rocket. But the fact that my mom was ill must have made it easier for him to understand. There isn't any amount of money that could resolve what drove my mother. My mom had poured herself into me, and she wanted to know that my dad would be there for me now.

Looking back on it, there were things that I didn't connect. My mom knew she was dying. But at that point, I didn't. I didn't know why she was pushing this thing all of a sudden, after all these years. But as it unfolded, it seemed like the timing was right. The reality is that my mother was just not going to die without this matter being resolved.

Larry King

What must it have been like for him? I can still remember the night I was doing a radio show on a boat called the *Surfside Six* when Joe DiMaggio Jr. wandered by, and I asked him if he'd like to come on the air.

He said, OK, and it was unbelievable. He started talking about a father he never knew. He remembered being flown out as a little kid to photograph a *Sport* magazine cover with his dad and then being flown straight back. His father was very remote. Joe DiMaggio was the first guy on the Yankees not to have a roommate. The son decided to play football instead of baseball because he felt cursed by the name DiMaggio. When he enlisted in the Marines, he called his father to tell him. His father said, "Good luck." That was it.

Joe Jr. became very close to Marilyn Monroe. She took a liking to him. Marilyn became the tie between him and his father. In the limo as they drove to her funeral, his father took his hand. It was the only time he ever remembered touching his dad.

I couldn't believe that a father could be so remote. Yet in thirty-three years, I had never touched my son. What must it have been like to be Larry Jr., to have this famous father who doesn't acknowledge you? And a mother who kept everything under wraps and floating along? That was Annette. Always in control.

If it was blindingly amazing to me, I can't imagine what it was like for Larry Jr. His mother was gravely ill, he was about to get married, and he was going to meet the father who never knew about him.

Larry King Jr.

I went with my wife to meet him at my sister Chaia's graduation from American University in Washington, D.C. It was just before my mother's death. That was a safe environment. There were a lot of people around. I didn't know what to expect. I didn't know if we'd have this one interaction and that would be it. I didn't know if it would end with us talking once in a while. Or if it would be, "See you later."

We hugged, and stepped back. He said, "How's Annette?" It was like a time warp. The black hole was gone. You've got to remember, even though I knew who he was, it was all from my mom's perspective. I had never heard him say, "Annette."

He asked about my brother and sisters. I had never heard him say the names Candy, Pamie, Ronnie. He told me about times he had spent with them and asked me what they were like now. It just collapsed that whole thirty-three years of separation. It validated me. Even though I knew about my father from my mom, I still needed to see him and hear him for myself. Up to that moment, I'd lived my entire life clinging to a letter I believed my dad had written. But I had never heard the words come from his mouth. It's impossible to describe what it felt like when they did. All I can say is, I could feel my mother smiling.

Larry King

Time disappeared, and I liked him right away. Annette had done a great job raising him. There is also a quality about Larry, he's so likable. You can't *not* like him.

Larry King Jr.

We got into a comfortable conversation about sports. It was like a lot of conversations about sports, but it was amazing because now that we were up close I was seeing many of my mannerisms. When we're really laughing hard we have a similar laugh. Our body types are similar—our walk. Our legs. It all came from him.

It was surreal. Because I wasn't just meeting my father. I was being opened up to another side of my family. I now had a very caring and loving sister. She would fill in blanks about what it was like growing up around my dad. Filling in the blanks in what I assumed must have been perfection, but in reality wasn't always perfection. I had a brother. I had an uncle who was blown away. He'd never heard about me, and he was trying to put pieces together. It was wild.

Some people wonder why I don't seem to have negative thoughts about what happened. The way I look at it, I wouldn't exist if it weren't for my father. So why be mad at him? OK, it wasn't the perfect family situation. But I had a good childhood. I know other people have other stories. You read about Tim McGraw not knowing about his father, Tug, until he read his birth certificate. I feel blessed that I was balanced and comfortable in my own skin when we finally met.

When the night was over, I really didn't need anything more. Whatever else that came after that first meeting would be gravy. I was so happy, and I had no idea how good things were going to get.

Chapter 16

The Wife

THE THING IS, I'd never married women who were much younger than me. Apart from Annette, who was older, the biggest age difference was with Sharon, and that was about eight years. I was never attracted to young girls. Herbie had a funny line about that. He said, "I could not wake up in the morning with someone who didn't know who Adlai Stevenson was."

One time I met a young girl who was doing makeup for a television shoot in Washington. She was very pretty. I said, "Hey, you wanna go out? We'll go to the Palm." She was a modern girl and she offered to drive over and pick me up. It made more sense because of where we each lived.

Chaia was staying with me at that point. She must have been eighteen at the time. I was in my fifties. When the girl got to the apartment, I said, "Chaia, I'm just finishing getting dressed. Talk to her for a minute."

Chaia came back gritting her teeth. "Are you crazy?" she said. "She's twenty-two! She could be my friend!"

So the girl and I went to the Palm and were seated. It was around November 22, the anniversary of Kennedy's assassina-

tion. I told her how I heard the news on the radio and nearly
got into an accident making a U-turn to get back to my radio
station. Then I asked, "Where were you?"

And she said, "I wasn't born."

"Weren't born?"

Now I look at Shawn: Shawn was four at the time of
Kennedy's assassination. When she was four, I wouldn't have
given her a second look. But she definitely caught my eye when
I was going to pick up a birthday present for Chaia at Tiffany's
in Beverly Hills. This was around Christmas of 1996. The way
I tell the story for large groups is, "Shawn and I bumped into
each other in front of Tiffany's, and it's cost me a lot. Why
couldn't it have been Target?"

I'll let her pick up the story from here. When it comes to
describing what it's like to be married to me, she's definitely
more qualified than I am.

Shawn Southwick-King

WIFE

I was walking out of Tiffany's. Larry was coming across
the street from the Beverly Wilshire. We headed straight
for each other. I looked up and he looked up. He gave me
one of those grunting acknowledgments. I took a few
steps and kind of grunted back. Neither one of us said
anything, and we kept going.

Of course, I knew who he was. I had watched him
during the O.J. trial. I wouldn't say I was a falling-down
Larry King fan. But when there were important news
events, I would tune in to Larry. His celebrity wasn't a big
deal to me. From the time I was a kid I was around people
who were famous. My dad worked at Warner Brothers and

Arista and Capitol Records and we often had celebrities in our home. The Beach Boys would sit at our piano and play songs. I can remember going to school in the car with Glen Campbell. When a Glen Campbell song came over the radio, Glen started clapping and saying, "Go, Glen, go!" That was normal to me.

My dad was managing Donny and Marie Osmond when they became big, and they asked me to go with them on tour as a backup singer. Oceans of people were always there when we got off the plane. It didn't matter what time we arrived. If we landed at three in the morning in some foreign country there'd be thousands of people with banners waiting for us. They'd try to tear our hair out, I kid you not.

After that, I got married, had a son, and divorced. I was in a lot of sitcoms. Comedy was my favorite thing. I was on the very first episode of *It's Garry Shandling's Show*. The part I played made me look like a ditz. I was the cable girl on a date with Garry, singing the entire theme song to *Gilligan's Island*. I also interviewed movie stars and rock stars for seven years as host of *Hollywood Insider*. So bumping into a celebrity was not uncommon.

I kept walking toward the elevator to get to my car. By the time I got to my car, Larry was coming out the back door of Tiffany's and we bumped into each other again. That's when he said, "You better get out of here right away or else we're going to be all over the tabloids."

That made me laugh. It hooked me pretty quick. He has great timing. My family has always been big on telling funny stories over and over. Larry loves to do that too, so it was very familiar to me.

We had a quick conversation. During the conversation I told him I had just broken up with somebody and I wasn't much up for a relationship, but that it would be great to be friends. I didn't know it at the time, but telling Larry that you're not up for a relationship is like waving a red flag in front of a bull. If you tell him he can't, he's going to think, *Oh yes I can.*

Larry King

Shawn was very mature. And she was very striking. I immediately fell for her . . . and that was before I knew that she was the quarterback on her powder-puff football team in high school. Almost every girl I've been with since I've been in broadcasting has been very pretty. It's a turn-on to me to be liked by a beautiful woman. I'd have beautiful girls say, "You're really funny. You have a great voice." I never thought of myself as being in that kind of league.

Not only was Shawn beautiful, but she was smart, talented and she had a close-knit family. On top of that, she was a fantastic businesswoman. She had invented clip-in hair extensions and then marketed them with an infomercial that did millions in business in a single quarter. Just looking at Shawn made me feel like I was hitting the jackpot on the back nine. What could be better?

Of course, I had to convince Shawn that I was right for *her.* It became a quest. Shawn had just broken up with this guy who was still after her. That spurred me on. I'm very competitive in that regard. Sometimes I don't even know what it is that's driving me—the girl or the challenge.

Shawn Southwick-King

So, he said, "I don't have a pen. I'm at the Wilshire. Give me a call."

I was the hall monitor in fifth grade at Colfax Elementary School. I was the one who raised my hand every time there was a task that needed to be done. Larry would be the school traffic monitor on purpose because he and his friends liked to wave cars into each other and create chaos. But I was the rule keeper. If I told you I was going to call you back, I put you on my to do list and called you back. I was getting ready to go to Utah to celebrate Christmas with family. I was checking off my things to do. One of those things was to return phone calls. I was at the corner of Riverside and Woodman, waiting for the light to change so I could make a left turn. I had a minute, and that's when I called him. We had a short conversation, and I gave him my phone numbers.

Larry King

She went to Utah; it was right before Christmas. We had met on December 21, but I didn't go out with her until she came back. That was around January 8. In between, I called her every day. But I was really spurred on when she told me that her ex-boyfriend was trying to get back with her. That drove me nuts.

I ran into Al Pacino shortly before Shawn was supposed to meet me once in New York. He asked me what I was up to, and I told him that I'd met this girl and really liked her.

He said, "Can I help?"

"Well, I'm having dinner with her tomorrow—"

"I got it!" Al said. "I'll drop by the restaurant and act like I've known you all my life. Give you the full treatment."

I'd never mentioned Al Pacino to her.

The next night, Shawn and I were having dinner. In he came with a big hug. "Hey, Larry! Jeez, where you been?"

It didn't hurt.

I was completely smitten. I remember a time when Shawn was recording a segment in Nashville. I was in Philadelphia with Colin Powell at his volunteer organization. I was trying to reach Shawn all day while she was in the studio. No answer. I was leaving messages on her cell phone. There was no return call. Then I had to go on the air with Colin.

Colin said, "What's the matter?"

I said, "I'm with this girl."

He gave me a look. That *Oh, I get it* look. Finally, I got a message that Shawn was calling. I remember how excited I was. Colin picked up the phone and said to her, "Listen, you're going to ruin this man. You're going to ruin his career. It may cramp your style, but you've got to call him."

Shawn Southwick-King

As time passed, we got to know each other. In some ways, we're polar opposites. But we also had a lot in common. I'd be lying if I said the age difference didn't come up. Larry is almost thirty years older than I am. But I remember my dad working on the Glenn Miller big band project. He blasted the music on speakers at the house and taught us how to dance the jitterbug. Early on in our relationship, Larry and I were dancing the jitterbug and he said, "Whoa! How did you learn?"

Larry King

Our song is "The Way You Look Tonight." Frank Sinatra. It's one of my favorite Sinatra records. It's right up there with Frank singing "There Used to Be a Ballpark Right Here."

Shawn Southwick-King

As we got closer, my parents were up in arms. "He's been married a hundred times!" they said. I don't know how I explained it to my parents. To be honest, I don't know how Larry explained it to me. He must have felt me wavering a bit at one point. Because one night I got a call at about three in the morning from somebody very close to him. She said, "Shawn, Larry asked me to tell you that he was only really married three times."

As if I would buy that! It's obvious that he was sensitive about it. He's been married eight times, but for years he managed to keep it to seven in the media. I guess when you compare it to seven or eight, three marriages doesn't seem so bad. What happened in the past, for me, is in the past. I was just thinking about us in the present.

The big issue for me was faith. I'm Mormon, and my faith is strong. If we did get married, and have children, my faith would have to prevail, because there was no religious faith on his side. He was OK with that. It probably bugs him every once in a while. It would bug me. But I don't know. If I wasn't religious, maybe it wouldn't bug me.

I knew I would raise the kids so that they'd know about their Jewish ancestry and traditions. It was the Mormon Church's genealogical records that told Larry all about his background. He didn't know where his father really came from until he saw those records.

We weren't engaged yet when we went to do a book signing with Chaia. Larry and Chaia had written a children's book. We were in the back of a limo, and Larry started to get sweaty. His mouth was really dry. He said, "There's something I need to tell you that I haven't told you. You know about Chaia and Andy. I have another child. The reason I'm telling you now is that you're going to meet him today."

It didn't matter to me if he had three kids or ten. My son Danny is from a previous marriage. Maybe Larry thought I would have a bad reaction. I don't see why having another child is a bad thing. It's what a person does and says when he's with me that's important. So I was thinking, *Why didn't you tell me?* But that was Larry, trying to minimize. Larry had a way—and still has a way—of making things the way he wants them to be.

It may all go back to the fact that his dad was taken from him when he was so young. Larry has had so much pain in his life. I see decisions he makes now that I think are affected by his father's death. It's as if he'd been abandoned. It's not easy to talk about. If he heard me talking about it, he'd probably tear up.

I met Larry Jr. and his wife that day. We all had lunch. It was surreal; partly because Larry hadn't told me, but maybe also because of the guilt Larry felt for all those years he wasn't there for Larry Jr. In the end, I guess I did what I always do. I protected Larry. I'll protect him to the end. I'll take as many bullets for Larry as I need to take.

Larry King

I proposed when Shawn was in the hospital. But I was afraid to hear no.

Shawn Southwick-King

I had just had a procedure and I was a little woozy. He was at my bedside, and he said, "This would be a knife in my heart should you refuse. So, I'm not gonna ask. I'm just gonna put it out there. The offer is on the table. Should you decide that you want to accept, just give me some sort of signal." As he said it, his hand moved like a slap, a twirl, and a bird flying away. That became the signal.

Larry King

We went to tell Shawn's parents. When we told her mother, she nearly fainted. The day we officially got engaged, when I got Shawn her ring, was also the day I got my star on the Hollywood Walk of Fame. We didn't say anything about it because my attorney Mark Barondess also got engaged the same day and we didn't want to take away from his big day. It was a funny time. Warren Beatty, who'd directed me in *Bulworth*, wanted to do some extra shooting for the film. So he came to CNN to shoot. Mark Barondess brought Rose, his girlfriend, that night. So when Warren came in, I said, "I got an idea. What if you came on to Rose?"

As everybody knows, Warren Beatty is a good-looking guy. He walked by Rose and said, "Hey, what are you doing later?"

She started getting all flustered.

The more flustered she got, the more he kept going around to her and whispering things.

Finally, at the end of the shoot, she went by the set. He walked over to her and got down on his knee. Now she was totally frightened. She didn't know what he was going to do.

He pulled out a ring. You should have seen her face.

And then he said, "Will you marry him?" And then nodded to Mark.

That was fun.

Shawn Southwick-King

We planned for our wedding to be at a friend's home, a giant estate. The ceremony would take place on a tennis court draped in beautiful fabric. There were going to be chandeliers on clear wire so it would look like they were hanging in midair. Vic Damone was going to sing. Billy Graham was flying in. It was going to be great.

That week, I found out that Larry had another daughter—a daughter that he was distant from. It came out in a big magazine profile. I knew that I loved Larry. I knew that I wanted to marry him. But I was definitely going to talk about it with him before the wedding. It's just that there were so many things going on at the time. People were flying in from all over. I was trying to make sure that everything was just right. Then, when I was getting shoes for the wedding dress, the phone rang. It was Larry. He started talking about how his shoulder was hurting and how he was feeling chest pain.

Larry King

I went to the hospital and failed a stress test. An artery was closed. If I had left the hospital then, I could have had a heart attack and died. It was bizarre. The doctors at UCLA wanted to do another bypass surgery as the clock to the wedding was ticking. Herbie insisted on bringing in the New York doctors.

Wendy Walker

EXECUTIVE PRODUCER, LARRY KING LIVE

People were coming in from all over for the wedding. I had to set up a situation room at the Wilshire to call everyone and tell them this formal affair wasn't going to happen.

Shawn Southwick-King

We decided to get married in the hospital room the day the doctors arrived from New York.

Larry King

I suppose if you can propose marriage with one of you in a hospital bed you can certainly get married with the other one in a hospital bed.

Shawn Southwick-King

It was crazy. I was feeling vibes from some of his friends. Some of Larry's friends were skeptical of me. Not so much Sid and Asher. But his attorney was giving off this vibe: *Who does this girl think she is, marrying Larry without a prenup?* It felt like he thought, *Here's this young chick who's going to say "Boo!" to Larry, give him a heart attack, and get his money.* But if Larry had died, I wouldn't have taken anything. I was doing very well when we first crossed paths. I had my own money. I just knew that this marriage was right. It may sound strange when I describe the wedding. But I wouldn't change anything about it.

Larry was lying in the bed. Monitors were hooked up to his heart. I was standing by his side with not a lot of makeup on. Herbie was dressed in shorts and black socks. Chaia was there. My parents were there. By then, they weren't up in arms. They knew I was in love. The whole thing was silly. Larry's hair was all skattywampus. My mom and dad have pictures. Those pictures would probably be humorous to look at now.

Larry King

I thought I'd married Herbie because Herbie was right next to me. Shawn was like two feet away.

Shawn Southwick-King

I kept thinking, *I hope he lives.*

Wendy Walker

That hospital room was packed. There were so many people that I thought Larry and Shawn wouldn't even remember who were there. We didn't have cellphones with cameras in those days. So I wrote the names of all the people who were in the room on a yellow legal pad just so Larry and Shawn could remember. I framed it and sent it to them.

It sounds crazy, but I wasn't surprised the wedding happened like it did. Larry really wanted to get married and there was a lot of stress when it got called off. Getting married made him feel better.

Larry King

The whole thing was nuts. It's not only crazy talking about it now, it was crazy while it was happening. I was in a swirl. At any second I might have another bypass surgery. Or else I was going to fly to New York for a different procedure.

Dr. Isom arrived with a Russian specialist named Shaknovich on a medevac. I'll never forget. Shawn was crying. And Shaknovich said, "Please, tears are premature."

What a great line! Talk about eloquence. It made me trust him. Shaknovich said he could open the artery through angioplasty. I signed a waiver saying that UCLA would not be held responsible if anything happened to me. Then Shawn and I made plans to fly back to New York on the medevac with Isom and Shaknovich.

Shawn Southwick-King

I get post-event migraines—they always hit after tension. I got a hideous migraine that day. So I got the bed on the medevac. Larry was sitting in the seat.

Larry King

We got to New York, and they opened the artery through angioplasty. It's not an extremely invasive procedure. They go through the groin. I was released a day or two afterward.

Shawn Southwick-King

When we got back to L.A., we had a second wedding. Ted Turner was best man. Jane Fonda was a bridesmaid. We went through the ceremony again. Then we had a fun party. Al Pacino recited an E. E. Cummings poem.

Larry King

It's called "Somewhere I Have Never Travelled, Gladly Beyond." Al did it by heart. We have it framed in our living room.

somewhere i have never travelled, gladly beyond
any experience, your eyes have their silence:
in your most frail gesture are things which enclose me,
or which i cannot touch because they are too near

your slightest look easily will unclose me
though i have closed myself as fingers,
you open always petal by petal myself as Spring opens
(touching skillfully, mysteriously) her first rose

or if your wish be to close me, i and
my life will shut very beautifully, suddenly,
as when the heart of this flower imagines
the snow carefully everywhere descending;

nothing which we are to perceive in this world equals
the power of your intense fragility: whose texture
compels me with the color of its countries,
rendering death and forever with each breathing

(i do not know what it is about you that closes
and opens; only something in me understands
the voice of your eyes is deeper than all roses)
nobody, not even the rain, has such small hands

We also had Don Rickles do a bit. He was really funny. We had Mormons and Jews. Rickles said the Mormons had arrived by covered wagon. It's a good thing Mormons have a great sense of humor.

Chapter 17

Sex & Birth

THERE'S ANOTHER THING I never understood about God: His rules concerning sex.

Mark Twain had it dead on when he summed up the problem in *Letters from the Earth*. God gave you all this desire, aptitude, and biological need. And then he said, *You can only do it with one person your entire life.*

Makes no sense.

Lenny Bruce had it right, too. Lenny used to say, "What if you raised kids with the rule that elbows cannot be touched by anyone except your spouse. Only married people can touch elbows. The genitals would never even be mentioned. You could do anything you wanted with genitals. But when you go out, you've got to cover your elbows. A guy would come home one day, find his wife touching elbows with another man and kill him. Why? Because that's how he's been taught to react. It's the same as prejudice."

I wonder how kids would see sex if they weren't told anything about it. When I started in radio, every Saturday was children's day at Pumpernik's. People brought their kids in and I would interview them. It was sort of like the show Art

Linkletter had: *Kids Say the Darndest Things*. One day, we had a genius on. He must have been about eleven. I think he was already at Michigan State University tutoring the football players. The kid was amazing. I asked him, "What do you wonder about the most?"

He said, "Sex."

I said, "What do you mean?"

He said, "I know that my mother and father have sex. And I know when they're going to have it because they look at each other in a certain way, and then I go into my bedroom, and they go into their bedroom. But I don't know what's exciting about it."

He was smart enough to know about it, but not old enough to know what it really was. His mother was a teacher. She told me that when he asked what an orgasm was, she had to tell him, because he knew such a thing existed. She said it's like having to sneeze and then sneezing. In fact, that's exactly what it is. There's all that preliminary sound and buildup. I think about that a lot when I sneeze.

It's amazing to me how hung up we are on sex. I think it stems back to the Puritans. I've always felt sex is a private matter. I just don't see its relevance in public life. Why should it matter if the man who replaced Eliot Spitzer as governor of New York had other women, and his wife had seen other men, if they had an agreement about it? Why should it matter if the married governor of New Jersey is gay? That's between him and his wife. What does it have to do with the way he governs?

When the news broke about Bill Clinton's affair with an intern in January of 1998, I knew we were in new territory. Then I heard the name and saw the picture. Monica Lewinsky. Monica's parents were mentioned. And I started thinking, *I know her, I know her*. Then I made the connection. I had gone out with Monica's aunt—her mother's sister. My thoughts went from *I know her, I know her,* to *I really* knew *her*.

I didn't want to talk on the air about what might have gone on between Bill Clinton and Monica Lewinsky. I don't care who people have sex with, and it was really none of my business. The way I saw it, it was a matter between Bill and Hillary and their daughter. But there was no getting around the fact that it would be the topic on my show for a long time to come.

I can remember the president of CNN once asking me to write down questions that might be appropriate to ask about the private lives of candidates. I told him I couldn't do it. There are no rules. The situation surrounding every interview is different. While I generally don't like to talk on the air about who's having sex with whom, the topic of Clinton and Monica Lewinsky was certainly not the first time I'd gotten into sex on the show. There was the Jim Bakker–Jessica Hahn scandal. There was the 1988 presidential campaign when Gary Hart dared reporters to follow him around if they didn't believe his denials of an extramarital affair. Not long after, photos of him with the model Donna Rice, onboard a boat called *Monkey Business*, appeared in the *Miami Herald*, and Hart was forced out of the campaign. I spent an hour interviewing Judith Exner about her relationship with John F. Kennedy. She was in her fifties at the time, fighting cancer, and she wanted to go on the record to separate fact from fiction.

She mentioned times and places. But to me, that interview wasn't about sex. It was about what a different country we had become. I was fascinated by Judith Exner. I was fascinated by how public she and Kennedy were, yet their meetings were never reported. The name Judith Exner never appeared in the media when Kennedy was alive. Writers wouldn't even mention that Franklin Roosevelt was in a wheelchair when he was president. David Brinkley told me that when he was young, he got assigned to the Washington pool of reporters working the White House. The first time Roosevelt came into the room in a wheelchair, he was shocked. *What? Our president is in a wheelchair?* Roosevelt was paralyzed from the waist down, and he was lifted up so he could stand behind the podium when he gave speeches. "Why don't we write about this?" Brinkley asked a few reporters. The other journalists all said the same thing. "Why? What does it have to do with the decisions he makes as a president?"

Exner told me she would sit with President Kennedy for lunch, then he'd get up, do a press conference, and walk back to her. Nobody asked, "Who's that?" While he was senator, before he announced his candidacy, he brought her to the home he shared with Jacqueline Kennedy in Georgetown—which really unnerved her. I asked Ben Bradlee about some of this. Ben was a close friend of Kennedy's before Bradlee became the editor of the *Washington Post*. He said he didn't know, and he didn't care. We were a different society back then. In that realm, we've taken an enormous step backward. When tabloids started selling sex stories, we began to go in reverse.

Once you start broadcasting what's appearing in the tabloids, you're swimming in the same water. Gennifer Flowers provided a few more details than I wanted to know when she said on the air that she had sex with Bill Clinton while he was the governor of Arkansas. It was relevant to Flowers because it was spicy and she was trying to sell a book. But I would try to keep the conversation on a higher level. Sometimes it wasn't easy.

I once asked Flowers how she might explain why such a bright person and brilliant politician would get into situations like this. You know, why do bad things happen to good people?

"I think," she said, "he was thinking with another head instead of this one."

We had Linda Tripp on the show. You had to have Linda Tripp on. Without Linda Tripp, there was no story. I didn't like Linda Tripp because I thought she was pretending to be Mon-

ica's friend, but actually trying to destroy the president. That
probably showed in my questioning. She's the one who encouraged Monica to save the blue dress with the semen stains. She's
the one who taped her phone conversations with Monica without Monica knowing—although she wouldn't use the word
taped when she came on my show. She was facing a criminal
proceeding in Maryland for making the recordings, and so she
had to use the word "document" to avoid incriminating herself.

I suppose that since Bill Clinton was saying that oral sex
wasn't included in his definition of sex, I guess Tripp could turn
the word *taped* into *documented*.

Monica looked like a victim to me. She was an intern, and
the power of the presidency is enormous. How must he have
appeared to a twenty-two-year-old kid? I can remember when
Monica showed up at a book party I had in Washington in the
midst of the scandal. I thought Tim Russert would faint. Pa-
parazzi were running down the street. Monica was probably
the most famous woman in the world at that point. Wolf Blitzer
came over to talk to her. She said to Wolf, "When you were at
the White House, you never noticed me."

There must have been incredible pressure on her. She was
out of her league, just like I didn't belong in Lou Wolfson's
league. When you step out of your league, what do you do? You
get in trouble. One minute, she was an intern. The next, she
was at the center of an investigation and being watched by
everyone in America. I've got to come out and say it. I think
Kenneth Starr created more of a mess with his investigation
than Clinton did.

What should Clinton have done? All he had to do was say
it was a private matter between his wife and himself. The story
would have continued, but he could have deflated it. He got
in trouble when he said, "I never had sex with that woman."
He got in trouble when he said that oral sex isn't sex. I guess

it's open to interpretation whether oral sex is sex. Maybe it's sort of like what Justice Potter Stewart of the Supreme Court said about pornography: "I can't define it, but I know it when I see it."

Martin Luther King Jr. once told me that he'd preach about many things, but marital fidelity was not one of them. This was so he could not be seen as a hypocrite. In Clinton's case, the denials opened the door for all the Republicans who wanted to get him. Bob Barr, the congressman from Georgia who led the drive to impeach Clinton, came on my show and said he didn't care about the improper relationship at all. What bothered him, he said, was obstruction of justice, tampering with witnesses, subornation of perjury, and the possible destruction of evidence.

I tried to keep my show focused on how the scandal affected impeachment. I just did not see this as an impeachable offense. There were a lot of people out to get Clinton, though, and the House voted to impeach. That meant it was up to the Senate to decide if Clinton would finish his term. I phoned the president that day to wish him well, and let him know that he could come on my show anytime to get his feelings across. I left a message with his secretary. The Washington Redskins were playing Tampa Bay that day. I was watching when Clinton called back, and he heard it in the background.

"Is that the Redskins game?" he asked.

"It sure is."

"Who's winning?"

"Tampa Bay is ahead, 16–7, but the Skins are driving."

"Yeah? Who won the Jets game? I've been distracted all day."

Talk about a guy who can compartmentalize. We spoke a little about the impeachment. I remember him talking about the affection he had for a Republican congressman named Peter

King, who stood up to make a speech against the impeachment. "This is all such a crock," Clinton said. "But I ain't going down."

He didn't go down. After his presidency ended, after he had written his autobiography, Clinton came on my show and said that he might have been fortunate to have had tormentors. He believed that it was the people who tried to destroy him who ultimately helped save him. Hillary got so mad at the people trying to take Bill down that they were the only people who could make him look good to her again.

The day after Bill Clinton went in front of the nation to admit his relationship with Monica, he flew off to Martha's Vineyard with Hillary and Chelsea to try to bring the family back together. I couldn't help but remember being in the White House watching a movie with the president. The movie was *Rudy*—about the inspirational Notre Dame football player. Rudy Ruettiger was there for the showing. Chelsea brought in popcorn. She sat next to her father. He put his arm around her. It was a wonderful time. It would be beyond sad for a father to lose moments like that. Clinton later told me that he feared that he'd hurt Hillary and Chelsea irrevocably and that he might not be able to make it all right again. I remember them walking toward Marine One on television. Chelsea was leaning toward her mother and the president reached out to bring her closer to him. It was one of those private moments that I felt I shouldn't be in on. But I watched until the helicopter took off.

It's hard enough to tell your wife. But what do you say to your daughter? Your wife is an adult. She can call you a son of a bitch. She can divorce you. Your wife may not always be your wife. But your daughter is always going to be your daughter.

I felt so sad for what Bill Clinton and his family had to go through. A lot of people didn't like him politically and said he deserved what he got. I don't think so. I may not be a Bible man, but I do appreciate that great line, "He who is without sin, cast the first stone." We all have weaknesses. Some you can't help falling prey to. I relate weaknesses to smoking. I couldn't stop smoking. You could have pinned all the statistics on the wall for me, but I loved that cigarette. It owned me. If it's one thing I understand it's weakness. That's why I could empathize with the president as well as feel for his family.

Wendy Walker

It was very difficult to report the Clinton-Lewinsky story. But the reason why you see Bill Clinton coming on the show to this day is that Larry never did anything that would have made Clinton feel like he was being treated unfairly.

Larry asked questions. The answers came out. And the viewer was left to draw his or her own conclusions. That's a lot different from other interviewers who are calculating, How can I get this guy?

It's why, when an interview is over, someone watching will say, "That guy looked great." And another viewer will say, "Are you kidding? I didn't think so."

The viewers will judge you. But Larry is not going to judge you. That's a big difference.

I really admire the Clintons for having the strength to bring their family back together. I don't usually psychoanalyze my own life. But when I look back now I can see that a lot of things started to play out around that time—things that made me aware of the impact I have on my children. Larry Jr. came into my life around then. Then Shawn became pregnant. It was almost simultaneous. It was one joy after the next. When I met Shawn, I was about sixty-three. I never thought I'd have children again.

Shawn Southwick-King

I got pregnant about ten months after the wedding party. I was trying to keep Larry calm in the delivery room the whole time I was trying to give birth. He was furious that the baby hadn't come by six o'clock because his show was on at six. He wanted to announce that we had had that baby.

Larry King

I'm always so in a rush for things. Would you get this done? *Come-mahhhhn!*

Shawn Southwick-King

I was hard-pressed to get that baby out. Larry was making the doctor sweat like crazy. Our son was born at 6:31 p.m. and Greta Van Susteren, who was with CNN back then, announced it at 6:36.

Larry King

It was the first time I'd seen a birth. The father was kept outside the room back in the '60s. He was not allowed to watch. I cut the umbilical cord. We named our son Chance because Shawn and I met by chance.

Chance was four months old when we went to the White House to see Bill Clinton. We thought our appointment with Clinton would be canceled because the war in Bosnia had ended that day—but it wasn't.

Clinton took Chance in his arms in the Oval Office. He was standing there with the paper in his hand announcing the end of the war. He posed with Chance for a picture. He looked down at him and said, "You don't know what's happening here. But someday, little man, you're going to be in history class. And the teacher is going to say, "Today, we're going to talk about Bosnia, and when she does, *raise your hand*! You were there. You bring this picture to class. You were there!""

Shawn Southwick-King

Chance was five months old when I got pregnant with Cannon. We went into the hospital early in the morning for Cannon. I think he was born midday. He came out really fast. That's Cannon.

Larry King

We gave him the name Cannon because he was conceived on a street by that name. I don't know what we would have done if he'd been conceived on Elevado.

The thing I remember about Cannon's birth was that I noticed him having problems breathing. Everyone was talking, and I pointed it out to the doctors. It was a bronchial condition that lasted for a few days. But I was the one who heard it first.

Chapter 18

The Presidents

Y EARS AGO, a university asked if I'd like to teach a course on interviewing.

"Can you give us a syllabus?"

I never went to college, so I'd never seen one.

"Well, just tell us what you'd teach the first week, what you'd teach the second week, and so on."

As if, on the third week, I could teach the class how to interview presidents.

The thing is, I don't think I'd have anything different to say on the third week than I would on the first. The lesson's the same: just be yourself. I look at the president with the same curiosity that I have for the plumber. I think that's what has separated me from everyone else. I don't sit for hours thinking up six hundred questions because I'm going to interview the president. It's not my style, and it's not what got me to where I am.

Sometimes when a major interview comes up, I'll hear, "Hey, you've got to be at the top of your game tonight." You know, put a little something extra into the show. People say it because they're juiced. But it always offends me. Does that mean I shouldn't put in a little something extra when I'm talking to the plumber? Of course, when I go to interview the president, I'm aware that I'm with the president. But if I treated him differently from the way I treat anyone else, I'd lose being me.

I've become friendly with every president since Richard Nixon. The more time I've spent with them, the more human they appear—especially after they leave office. Gerald Ford once started slurring while I was interviewing him. We had to cut the interview short, and he had a stroke later in the day. George H. W. Bush became teary while opening up about the loss of his daughter. My son Chance was imitating one of the Power Rangers at CNN headquarters in New York once when he was about four, and he karate-chopped Bill Clinton in the groin. Bill pulled through it well.

So I wouldn't rate each president the way a historian would. I've seen their strengths. I've seen their weaknesses. And I know that nobody can control world events. Some events presidents screw up, just like we all screw up in life. Some events presidents bring on, just like Lincoln brought on the Civil War. And some events are beyond a president's control and simply can't be stopped. One thing George W. Bush said was very true. When he was asked, "What will history think of you?" he replied, "I don't know. I'll be dead."

I can only tell you what it's like to know the presidents while they were alive.

RICHARD NIXON

I was out of work when Nixon resigned. I had fallen, through my own fault—just like Nixon. There was no reason for me to lose my job, and there was no reason for Nixon to lose his. What possible reason could there be to break into the Democratic Party headquarters at the Watergate before the '72 election? Nixon went on to win forty-nine states. His victory over George

McGovern was one of the biggest landslides in presidential history. He could easily have won that election without the aid of a single document in those headquarters.

I understand people who have taken a tumble. So I understood what Nixon went through. I think that helped when I interviewed him years later. Nixon could sense my sympathetic tone. When I asked him about the Watergate, he said he'd never been in the hotel and he wouldn't even look at it when he drove by.

The most amazing thing about Nixon to me was how a politician could rise to the greatest heights without being likable. You can't make yourself likable. There were all kinds of stories about Nixon being brusque to people on planes during campaign trips. Not only was he not likable, I really don't think he liked other people, either. I think he liked situations.

If I owned a network, I would have hired Nixon to do analysis. Nobody could tell you how a situation got to be a situation as well as Nixon. Whether he could solve the problems in those situations is a different subject. But he was a terrific historian with a steel-trap mind.

He was fascinated with things foreign. Nixon was the type of guy who'd rather sit down with Premier Brezhnev than with the governor of Pennsylvania. That's one of the reasons why so many domestic liberal changes came about during his administration—he didn't care about them. Nixon cared about opening the door to China.

It was his insecurities that did him in. Once I had him on the radio in Miami. He was the lead guest. We had four men from the men's fashion guild scheduled for the following segment. They were in town for a convention, and they were watching Nixon and me do the show as they waited to go on.

During a break, Nixon said to me, "See those guys?" He said it very suspiciously. "You know, they're talking about me."

I said, "How do you know?"

He said, "I know."

They could have been talking about his tie. But Nixon thought everybody was out to get him. He was complicated. But nearly everybody who excels in his field is complicated. Here you had this guy who wasn't really likable. Yet Hubert Humphrey told me a story about him that made me see a different side.

Humphrey and Nixon had fought out what was then the closest election in history in '68. Years later, on Christmas Eve, Humphrey was in Memorial Sloan-Kettering hospital. He had cancer, and he was about to start chemotherapy. His wife was spending the holiday evening with the family, and he told the switchboard operator that he didn't want any calls put through to his room. The phone rang. *Damnit!* Humphrey was thinking, *I told the switchboard . . .*

It was Nixon. One man was dying, the other was in disgrace. They talked through Christmas Eve. I always remember that story because Nixon's first trip to Washington after his resignation was for Humphrey's funeral.

In the end, Nixon's legacy is mixed. He opened the door to China. Humphrey couldn't have done that. Republicans would have jumped all over a Democratic president who visited Communist China. But Nixon will always be primarily associated with Watergate and the resignation.

One of the lasting memories I have of Nixon concerns the Nixon Library. On display the last time I was there was his desk pad. The last thing on his pad was "9 p.m. Tuesday, Larry King Live." He had just agreed to do our show before he was taken to the hospital with a stroke. A few days later, he died.

GERALD FORD

The Ford Museum in Grand Rapids, Michigan, is a beautiful three-sided building. When the comedian Mark Russell was asked what he thought of it he replied, "Well, Ford only served three years."

Ford took office at a pivotal time, though. Watergate was an incomparable event—the president breaking the law. Ford gave Nixon a full pardon a month after he assumed office. I'll never forget his line. "Our long national nightmare is over . . ." The pardon came with a cost. The country was divided. It was such an intense time. Ford's own press secretary quit over the pardon. There were people who believed the pardon was one of the reasons Ford lost the election in 1976.

But when I asked him about it years later, Ford said that he was even more convinced that it was the right thing to do. The way he explained it certainly made sense. If he wanted to spend 100 percent of his time working on the country's problems, he needed to get the Nixon problem off his desk. He believed the public came to understand that as the years passed.

Ford was the most regular guy ever to be president in my lifetime. He never would have had the ambition to run for president. He was a true congressman—the kind of guy you wanted to call if your Social Security check hadn't arrived. Gerald Ford would make sure you got it.

He was parodied as an uncoordinated bumpkin after he fell down steps coming off an airplane. The famous line was that he had played football without a helmet. But he had high grades in school. He was very likable, an easy guy to be around. He was much less conservative in the White House than he'd been in Congress. But that happens to a lot of people when they become president. The country takes them to the center. When you're the representative from Michigan, you're the representative of the people of Michigan. When you're the president, you're the representative of everybody.

Ford was hurt when Ronald Reagan tried to get the nomination from him in 1980. But his big blunder came in the debate against Jimmy Carter when he said that Eastern Europe wasn't under Soviet domination. That was another reason why he lost.

In the end, the legacy of Ford and his wife, Betty, will be as healers. Ford tried to bring the country together after Nixon's resignation. And I can remember him talking about the family intervention at Betty's bedside to stop her addiction to alcohol and painkillers. Betty became synonymous with rehabilitation. When you think about rehab, you think about the Betty Ford Center. It's as if there weren't any rehab centers before it. The comedian Albert Brooks had a great line. He said, "Where did Betty Ford go?"

Gerald Ford became very friendly with Jimmy Carter after they were both out of office. They were both sent by Ronald Reagan to represent the United States at Anwar Sadat's funeral. Richard Nixon went, too. Nixon came home quickly afterward. Ford and Carter flew back together and they really bonded.

It was a little sad for Ford to watch the Republican Party move toward the extreme right as time passed. I was at the Republican Convention in '92 when George Bush was renominated. Rush Limbaugh had an honored box at that convention. Pat Buchanan made a prime-time speech. Ford turned to me and said, "What happened to my party?"

JIMMY CARTER

Jimmy Carter was a guy who was ahead of his time. He saw the possibility of peace in the Middle East. I didn't know this until recently, but he had solar panels installed on the White House back in the '70s. It may sound trivial, but there are women in the Alfalfa Club now because of Jimmy Carter.

The Alfalfa Club was named for the alfalfa plant. The plant doesn't do anything and neither does the club. It doesn't do charity work. It has a dinner. That's it. The Alfalfa Club goes back to something like 1913. At the annual dinner, you're in a room filled with unbelievable power. Presidents, the top cabinet members, Supreme Court justices, ambassadors, captains of industry. I remember one dinner, talking to David Rockefeller. *David Rockefeller* said to me, "Do you believe the people in this room? This is really something." When he was president, Jimmy Carter would not attend an Alfalfa Club dinner because women were not permitted. It's because of Jimmy Carter that women are now allowed.

Carter could come off very moral—he was a lay preacher—even boring. My friend Herbie used to joke about the peace agreement that Carter made between Egypt and Israel. He said, "You know the reason Carter succeeded with Sadat and Begin during those talks. He bored them to death. They stayed in two different cabins at Camp David. And Carter would say, 'Why don't we take another six hours to discuss this?' And these guys would say, 'Another six hours. Oy! I'll sign anything, bring it over.'"

The reality was quite different. It was painstaking to work that agreement out. Menachem Begin was a very tough guy to deal with. Anwar Sadat was much easier. Begin dotted every *i* and crossed every *t*. He read everything over and over and over because he was mistrustful. He'd say to Carter, "Wait a minute. Wait a minute. What exactly does this mean? Let's change this *the* to *a*."

Carter told me, "Every time I got frustrated with him, I thought to myself, *Was my family killed in the Holocaust? I'm supposed to tell him he shouldn't be so methodical? I'm telling him to trust?"* There were tears in his eyes when he said that. In the end, the accord between Egypt and Israel has held up. People can travel back and forth to this day.

Someone once said that Carter would be great as a saint, but he was lousy as a president. I don't think *lousy* is the right term. Events took over. The hostages were taken by Iran and he just handled it poorly. He was not weak, and he was not naive. People tend to forget that Carter graduated from the Naval Academy and commanded a nuclear submarine.

It's just that his skills played out better postpresidency. He's had a great postpresidency. I've never seen a postpresidency quite like it. He goes all around the world. He oversees elections. He settles peace issues. He writes novels, poems, and children's books. He gives the money from his books to his center. He and Rosalynn build homes for those in need with Habitat for Humanity. He won the Nobel Peace Prize. You may not agree with all his philosophies, but is he a special person? Yes.

RONALD REAGAN

There's a great story about Ronald Reagan that goes back to his Hollywood agents. While he was an actor, Reagan was represented by Sonny Werblin, who would go on to own the New York Jets and run Madison Square Garden, and also by Lew Wasserman. At his presidential inauguration, Reagan said to them, "If you guys had been better at your jobs, I wouldn't be here."

Being an actor helped Reagan when he was in the White House. He was a great communicator. People liked him. That's something money can't buy. There are some people who criticized Reagan for being too much like an actor. But I don't blame him for that. That's what he was. I'm a broadcaster. If I were running, I'd sound like a broadcaster.

So much in life is based on timing. Herbie put it well. He said the reason the Iranians released the hostages in the final moments of the Carter administration was that they saw Reagan coming in on a white horse like the Lone Ranger. They didn't know what to expect. Would Reagan invade? They couldn't be sure.

There were a lot of pluses to Reagan. He befriended Gorbachev and told him to take down the Berlin Wall. That was huge.

Reagan had a simple outlook on things. There was no deep, hidden agenda. My brother liked him because he was able to absorb information from people who were smarter than him on a certain subject and then make the right decision. The thing about Reagan that surprised Marty was how big he was physically. Reagan was six-foot-two, and he was wide. Marty remembers that when Reagan came over to shake his hand, his frame blocked out the window. He gave off the appearance of being large, in body and in spirit, and he had respect for his office. Reagan never took off his jacket when he was in the Oval Office. But a lot of people on the extreme right would be surprised to know that he told dirty jokes.

Another thing about Reagan was that he didn't hold a grudge. Reagan had a great relationship with Tip O'Neill, the speaker of the House. Tip told me this story: "One day, I blasted Reagan on the floor of the House. I went back to my office and the secretary said, 'Telephone call. The president.'"

Oh jeez, Tip was thinking as he reached for the phone. "Hello, Mr. President . . ."

"Tip, did you hear the one about . . ."

You couldn't help but smile around Reagan. He put me on the Council on Physical Fitness when I was twenty pounds overweight and smoking three packs a day. I showed up at a reception in the Rose Room. When Reagan saw me, he said, "Are you the poster boy?"

I didn't agree with Reagan on a lot of issues. I thought trickle-down economics was a terrible idea. I prefer what the guy on the bottom says: "Give it to me now. I'll trickle up."

The Iran-Contra scandal was a minus. That could only have occurred under a president who was not paying attention. Reagan left office tarnished by Iran-Contra. But he remained liked as a guy, and his vice president won the next election.

Right after he left the White House, the president and Nancy invited me to lunch at the Hotel Bel-Air. There was a wedding going on when we arrived. The wedding party invited us in. We all walked down the aisle. Reagan and the father walked with the bride. Funny, the things you remember. Reagan ate an ice cream sundae. He devoured that sundae like my nine-year-old son would have. Whoa, did he love that sundae!

I've gotten to be good friends with Nancy over the years. Many people never knew the real Nancy. Nancy was very important in that administration. Nancy is funny, shy, tough. She's moderate, and she didn't like the fanatics on the far right. If she didn't like you, you were out, because Ronnie was crazy about her.

I first sensed the Alzheimer's setting in on the president when Reagan got the Medal of Freedom. Bush 41 presented it during a reception at the White House. Reagan was standing underneath a painting of Lincoln. I was next to him with George Will and a group of others. Reagan said, "I remember the first time I walked by this painting. Every time I come back and walk through this room I get the same feeling." A few minutes later, Reagan told the same story.

Nancy told me it was really hard at the end. She had to adjust the television to black-and-white. Colors can shock Alzheimer's patients. When they see colors, it's like they're seeing them for the first time.

It's a puzzling disease. Many Alzheimer's patients get angry and throw things for no reason. But Ronald Reagan didn't get angry. Even toward the end, if he was seated when a woman walked into the room, he would stand.

GEORGE BUSH 41

The best way I can describe George H. W. Bush to you is by relating a lunch conversation we had once. He said, "Hey, you know my grandson, the one you had on the air at the convention. Funny kid. He's applying to Georgetown."

I said, "Oh, that's great."

He said, "You know anyone at Georgetown?"

I said, "Hey, *you're* the president."

And he said, "But it would be rude to use the presidency."

I really admired that. That's why so many people like him. I've become very close to George Bush and Bill Clinton over the years, but I'm probably closest to Bush. I was supposed to jump out of a plane with him—go skydiving—but my doctor wouldn't let me.

Bush was an internationalist. I thought he showed strength and sensibility in his handling of the Gulf War. He assembled a coalition, chased Saddam Hussein out of Kuwait, and won the war in a hundred days with minimal casualties. He was wise enough to stay out of Baghdad. He had some great advisers. Brent Scowcroft was strongly opposed to going into Baghdad. I doubt that Bush agrees with the Iraq war his son got us into. I can't tell you for sure. But you can see a lot in his body language. Scowcroft was at the vacation house when I was there. An article about Scowcroft in *The New Yorker* had just appeared, and it was very critical about the war. So I asked Bush what his conversations about the war with Scowcroft were like. He said, "We don't discuss it."

Bush must have had a 90 percent approval rating after the victory in the Gulf War. There were parades when the troops came home. But the economy went into a downward spiral. If there had been no economic problems, the public would have looked at Bush 41 very differently. But he got hurt when he didn't know about electronic scanners at the supermarket checkout counter. That showed his isolation from ordinary people. It's very difficult to win an election when the people see an image like that. Bush had to deal with the ultimate rejection—running for reelection and getting beaten by an upstart. That's tough.

When I think of Bush, I think of a kind and considerate man. And he put me in one of the strangest diplomatic situations I've ever run into when I emceed his eightieth birthday party. It was at Minute Maid Park—where the Astros play. The ceremony was at second base. There was a big crowd. Five former world leaders were on hand to represent Israel, Canada, Mexico, England, and Russia. They were all scheduled to speak.

All the early speakers were going on too long and the program was running really late. I tried to do my best, moving the event along with some laughs. But it became clear to everyone there was no other choice but to cut the program short.

So I said to President Bush, "I'll ask the world leaders to have one speaker represent all of them."

Dan Quayle overheard this and said, "Not a good idea . . ."

But there really was no alternative. President Bush said, "OK, give it a try."

So I gathered all the world leaders together and explained the situation, and they all seemed to understand. Brian Mulroney of Canada was George Bush's close friend. He said, "I'll speak for all of us."

I said, "Fine."

But Mikhail Gorbachev said, *"Nyet! NYET!"*

He said, "I came all the way here for this. I am speaking."

The other four leaders were looking at each other wondering what to do. It was like watching kids on the corner in high school.

So I went back to President Bush and said, "We've got a little problem here . . ."

Quayle said. "I told you!"

I said, "Gorbachev is adamant."

Bush said, "Well, he changed the world."

So I went back to Mulroney and said, "Gorbachev changed the world."

Mulroney said, "OK."

Gorbachev got up to speak. I thought he'd go on forever. But he was funny, spoke well, and finished in a few minutes.

When I think back on it, it's still hard to believe. Little Larry Zeiger from Brooklyn shuttling back and forth like an ambassador between President Bush and Mikhail Gorbachev . . .

BILL CLINTON

Look up *charming* in the dictionary and you'll see Bill Clinton's picture. Clinton's biggest enemy wouldn't last five minutes alone in a room with him. It would take less than that for Bill to win him over.

I remember when his portrait was unveiled in the White House. There was a reception and George Bush 43 was ecstatic, talking about what a wonderful person and great president Clinton was. I saw Bush a few weeks later, and I reminded him of the moment. I asked, "Did you go a little over the top?"

He said, "Are you kidding? Bill's the best. Who wouldn't want to spend time with Bill Clinton?"

Clinton is certainly one of the smartest people you'll ever meet. His knowledge of things is incredible. He met Chaia and they immediately got into a conversation about American

University. She had graduated from American, and he had spoken there once. He recalled the halls and some of the administration by name. His knowledge is mystifying. He understands so many things, from cooking to basketball to heads of state.

I love interviewing Clinton. He's the world's best interview. Some reporters claim to have been frustrated by him, but not me. Well, maybe by his lateness—but that's it.

He has a big heart, a great understanding of black culture, and he's a problem solver. He was able to defuse the situation in the Balkans. He left office with a budget surplus. No Monica, and he would have been seen as a wildly successful president.

There was a good line—I forgot who said it. Maybe it was me. "Don't do anything that you don't want mentioned in the first paragraph of your obituary."

Despite advancements in the war on poverty and in civil rights, the word *Vietnam* appears in the first paragraph of Lyndon Johnson's obit. *Watergate* is in Nixon's first paragraph. Clinton is trying to push Lewinsky down to the second paragraph. Still, the first paragraph will have the word *impeached*.

His obvious weakness is his personal needs. I don't think Clinton himself could explain them.

But what great man doesn't have faults? Churchill was manic. Lincoln was depressive. What did Lincoln call it, his blue period? He'd go into a depression and lock the door. When Lincoln or Churchill would have weak moments, they would remove themselves for three or four days. They would brood and sleep. Clinton's weakness did not prevent him from being a good president. He was and is a hard worker. He was and is relentlessly on top of things.

Even the best presidents are going to have marks against them. Franklin Delano Roosevelt was a giant—the best president of my lifetime. I was twelve years old when he died. I remember walking down the streets and seeing people crying. Roosevelt beat the Depression and he won a world war. I don't think any other president has had to simultaneously face two problems of such magnitude. Yet he didn't bomb the railways leading to the concentration camps. He never pounded his fist for civil rights or stood up for blacks in the South. Eleanor told me he could have done a lot more with Southern Democrats, but he chose not to. I would have liked to have had the chance to ask Franklin Roosevelt about that. But you have to look at each man on the basis of his background, his time, and the complications he was facing.

As it turned out, the people who tried to impeach Clinton are now footnotes in history. And Clinton turned out to be a hell of a president.

GEORGE BUSH 43

I really like George W. Bush. George Bush is a great guy to go to a baseball game with. He's the kind of guy who stays for the whole nine innings. It saddens me to say that by the time he left office, opinion polls rated him as low as I could ever remember a president falling. The problem was that he has no curiosity. He doesn't wonder about things. That's a major failing.

He did a lot of good things. He's done more to combat AIDS in the world than any other president. But when I look back over his presidency, his legacy will be his leadership after 9/11, an unprovoked war in Iraq that was not right at the start and went terribly wrong, an incompetent response to Hurricane Katrina, and the worst economic meltdown since the Great Depression. Nobody could see any of this coming when I moderated a debate between the Republican candidates before the South Carolina primary in 2000. But if you replay that debate now, you can see that trouble was in the air from the start . . .

Chapter 19

Anything Goes

T HAT DEBATE in South Carolina had the energy of a heavy-weight championship fight.

There was no way to know that it would have that sort of electricity when CNN booked the television rights months in advance. The juice came after McCain won the New Hampshire primary. Bush was the favorite. McCain was the upstart. New Hampshire gave McCain a tremendous groundswell. The press was predicting that if McCain won in South Carolina, the nomination might be his. That began an incredible couple of weeks of dirty politics.

There have been nasty campaigns and dramatic ads in the past. One of the most famous was the TV ad that Lyndon Johnson ran during his campaign against Barry Goldwater in 1964. It showed a little girl out in a field picking flowers with a clock ticking in the background. Then, BOOM, a nuclear explosion. The message was that if you voted for Goldwater, the world as we knew it would end. The campaign aired it once, and Johnson cleaned Goldwater's clock in the election.

But the back and forth between Bush and McCain was

largely under the table. There were sordid rumors circulating in South Carolina that McCain had fathered a black baby. McCain was particularly hurt when Bush appeared before a veterans group and claimed that McCain had turned his back on soldiers. You can imagine what that would do to anyone who'd spent more than five years in a POW camp, and McCain fired back with ads questioning Bush's integrity.

When the two arrived backstage for the debate, there was no warm handshake or hello.

"John."

"George."

McCain's fist was balled.

Bush said, "Hey, man, it's politics."

"Anything goes, George?" McCain said. "Anything goes?"

"You're on," I said.

There was a third candidate at the table: Alan Keyes sat between them. He pleaded with them to focus on the moral lapses in society, but Bush and McCain couldn't wait to go at it. Some candidates get into arguments. But I felt that these guys really didn't like each other. I almost didn't have to ask any questions. At one point, when McCain said that he'd stopped authorizing any negative ads, Bush pulled one out and waved it in McCain's face.

It was wild. Whenever I mentioned the debate to either one of them afterward, they would recount vivid memories. I was always amazed that they could hug each other years later. The one statement that stands out from that debate, that seems even larger now than it did then, was Bush's comment that a president "could bring certainty into an uncertain world."

Little did he know how much uncertainty he was about to face when he became president.

Nothing could be compared to 9/11. I was eight years old

when Pearl Harbor was attacked. We didn't even know where Pearl Harbor was. But this was New York! And this time we didn't even know who was responsible. It was one of those moments in life that everybody remembers. For years, I asked nearly every guest on my show where he or she was when the hijacked planes struck the World Trade Center.

It was about ten after six in the morning when I heard the news. I stepped on the treadmill, clicked on the television, and saw the burning tower. I thought it was a commercial for Arnold Schwarzenegger's new movie. When I realized what had happened, I jumped off the treadmill and woke up Shawn. Chance was two years old. Cannon was a year old.

Everything became a blur of images. People jumping from the tops of the towers. Finding out that Barbara Olson, the CNN commentator, was on the plane that crashed into the Pentagon. I knew her husband, Ted. The windows in the apartment building where I had once lived in Washington were blown out by the speed of that plane as it came down. How did we know if the nightmare was over? Would the hijackers hit LAX? There were incredible stories—the blind man who walked down seventy-nine flights of steps with his dog. My producer, Greg, was working so hard he didn't even have time to absorb what he was watching. We had Mayor Giuliani on that night. There were no commercials. Who was going to sell foot cream next to 9/11? As soon as the show ended, Greg burst into tears.

I think we worked for fifty-three consecutive days. I went to New York. The fire commissioner took me around Ground Zero two weeks after the attack. I remember how they had me put Vicks VapoRub under my nose. The acrid smell was still in the air. I'll never forget talking to the firemen. Firemen are exceptional in that they run toward what

the rest of us run away from. One of the firemen said he had a
choice to be a fireman or a cop, and he chose to be a fireman
because people are always happy to see a fireman. I had never
thought of it that way. But he was right—a cop, you're not always happy to see. We visited a firehouse that lost its whole crew.

I remember talking to a derrick operator lifting debris out
of the site. He said, "This is not what I'm supposed to do." He
said he was supposed to build, not take away. Then I went to
the same hospital where I'd had bypass surgery and talked with
people who'd been burned. One guy couldn't be touched because
the pain was so intense. They couldn't even put a sheet on him.
When I look back on the death and damage inflicted by Al
Qaeda, I can't help but wonder about the two Saudi Arabian
students who spent hours in a Boeing flight simulator practicing mid-air turns, but not showing much interest in takeoffs
and landings. Why didn't we have a clue of what was coming?

Bush looked totally lost when he found out about the attacks while reading to schoolkids. But he seemed to grow before our eyes after the attack. His response was terrific. He
went to New York, put on a hard hat, and picked up a mega-
phone to talk to the recovery crews. He rallied the country. Democrats stood and cheered for him when he addressed the
nation. His approval ratings skyrocketed.

He had come in as a guy who was hands-off internation-
ally. Events forced him to be hands-on. He had an opening.
America had the world's sympathy, and Americans were nervous. Envelopes filled with anthrax powder were being sent
through the postal service. There wasn't much dissent in Congress when Bush set his sights on Saddam Hussein. Saddam
had used poison gas to kill the Kurds.

I believed Colin Powell when he went before the United
Nations to warn the world about Iraq's weapons of mass de-

struction. Why would he lie? It all looked believable, and who was going to stand up for Saddam Hussein? We invaded Iraq and toppled Saddam's statue. Bush showed up dressed like a fighter pilot and stood in front of a banner that read MISSION ACCOMPLISHED. But the Iraqis never greeted us in the streets the way Dick Cheney said they would. The aftermath was badly planned for. General Shinseki, who wanted more men, was pushed out. We disbanded the Iraqi Army. The people who didn't like us just disappeared and waited to attack when we weren't looking.

I couldn't understand John Kerry's campaign to unseat Bush in 2004. Kerry had won a Silver Star in Vietnam, but the members of the Swift Boat Veterans for Truth questioned his heroism. Kerry should have answered the accusations, even if he simply acknowledged a difference of opinion. All he had to do to take the matter off the table was say three words to Bush during a presidential debate: "Where were you?"

That would have been a slam dunk. Bush never served in Vietnam. Dick Cheney never served. Neither did Limbaugh, nor Buchanan. But they all came off strong and patriotic. I'd seen the same thing that happened to Kerry happen to George McGovern in 1972. McGovern was a war hero. He'd run thirty-five bombing missions over Germany during World War II. Of all the people in the Senate, nobody had a better war record than George McGovern. He was a dramatic, tough guy. Yet he was painted as a wimp by the Republicans, and the public bought it. Not many people know this, but it was McGovern who put through the bill for the Vietnam Memorial. It bothers me when we don't see the full picture.

When Kerry didn't say those three words, it made him

seem weak. You can't say, "No comment." No comment says, "I'm guilty." Kerry lost the state of Ohio and, with it, the general election in 2004.

After the 2004 election I went to see Colin Powell. We've been friends for a long time. I spent a couple of hours with him. It was clear he'd been given bad information about weapons of mass destruction to sell to the world at the United Nations. His chief aide was furious. "They screwed my man," he said.

I said to Colin, "Where's this all going?"

He said, "I don't know, but I'm out of here."

A week later, he quit.

There was no one moment that turned the American public against the war in Iraq. But the administration was shaken by the failure of the government in the wake of Hurricane Katrina. I'd lived through many hurricanes before. I even broadcasted through one on the radio in Miami. To see people in distress because of mismanagement was much different.

New Orleans is like no other city. I can remember riding on a float and throwing doubloons to the crowd during Mardi Gras. The thing about New Orleans is that no matter where you're from, you feel at home there. Which is why it was so painful to see so many people pushed out of their homes.

The guy who really called it was Anderson Cooper. I would have him on every night by satellite, and he'd point out how buses had not been used to evacuate people and that the federal government was just not responding to the magnitude of the disaster. We talked to people who'd lost their homes, people stuck in the Superdome. The government was late to help in every area. It was a total failure.

We began to look at the war in Iraq differently.

No weapons of mass destruction were ever found. The American body count passed a thousand, then fifteen hundred. It seemed like roadside bombings were becoming a daily tragedy, our soldiers didn't have the right protective armor, and the administration wouldn't allow journalists to photograph the caskets coming home. Meanwhile the cost of being there put us into a major deficit. I sometimes wondered, What if George Bush asked for some television time and said, "You know, I tried my best. I was working with the information I was given. I thought I was right. But I was working off wrong information. I don't want to lose another soldier over in Iraq. It's time for them to come home." What would that have done?

He could never do it. He'd have lost the whole right wing. Then again, it's so rare to hear *any* politician—good or bad—say, "I was wrong." Ask Jimmy Carter. Did he ever do anything wrong? Lyndon Johnson? He never came out and said he was wrong on Vietnam. But Johnson was paralyzed by it, almost suicidal. He went back to smoking and died of a heart attack. George W. Bush will never end up like Johnson at the end of his life, because he has tunnel vision and doesn't waver from his decisions. I just would have loved to see him be a little more open-minded and humble.

It seemed like Tuesday the war in Iraq was OK, then Wednesday it wasn't. Our standing in the world fell, and then so did the economy. Back in the beginning of 2007, my brother observed that Americans investing in the stock market had a more favorable view of the relatively small pharmaceutical company he worked for than they did of General Motors. How, he wondered, could that happen? Lehman Brothers collapsed as the 2008 presidential election approached.

It was a finance company with a history dating back to 1850. Night after night I had pundits on my show trying to explain the mess. I came away believing there was no real expert, no genius, in this situation. Warren Buffett was losing money. Kirk Kerkorian lost billions of dollars in a single day. I got taken for $2.8 million in the Ponzi scheme run by Bernard Madoff. We were all in the forest trying to get past the trees and find a clearing.

George Bush started to express some self-doubt at the end of his term. A 28 percent approval rating will probably do that to you. I always try to look at my guests sympathetically. But he wouldn't want my sympathy. It may be more interesting to talk to him about all this in two years. If anyone came to know how uncertain the world could be, it was George Bush. Few presidencies were hit on so many fronts. None of us can know how difficult his job was. There are things he knows that the rest of us don't. Yet for seven years after 9/11, we were not attacked on American soil.

It would be wise to wait a while before we make judgments on Bush 43. Here's why. Harry Truman was one of the most unpopular presidents when he left office in 1953. He fired an American hero, General Douglas MacArthur. MacArthur came home to a ticker-tape parade. Truman was seen as soft on Communism while he was president. When Truman set up the Marshall Plan to help Europe after World War II, I can remember people complaining. Why are we spending all this money on Greece and Turkey? What about our own people? But it was the Marshall Plan that prevented the spread of Communism in Europe. And more than fifty years later, we can see that Truman was totally right to fire MacArthur. We look back and see that it was Truman who integrated the armed forces. Now Truman is revered. *Give 'em hell, Harry!* So history has a way of turning things around.

In fifty years, it's quite possible that people will see George Bush 43 in a different light.

One of the best days I've ever spent was with Bush in the White House talking baseball. He asked me if I wanted a lift on Air Force One to talk some more. I couldn't go with him then. But I hope we can pick up the conversation.

Chapter 20

Your Questions, Please

I'M IN THE Q&A BUSINESS. So I like questions. Not only do I like asking questions. I like answering them. I especially get a kick out of having the tables turned on me during speaking engagements.

People want to know who my most difficult interview has been, what it's like to sit down with Vladimir Putin, and how the suspenders got started.

One response you'll never hear from me is, "I'm glad you asked me that question." I've come to learn that whenever a politician says those words, it really means, "I'm *not* glad you asked me that question. I'm just using a few extra seconds to think how I want to answer that question."

I'll be as honest as I can be. And when I'm not, I'll be as funny as I can be.

Who was your most difficult interview?
Without a doubt, Robert Mitchum. I admired Mitchum as an actor and I was really looking forward to talking with him. He was amazing in the original *Cape Fear*. That movie is beyond scary.

As we sat down to start, I said, "Can I call you Bob?"

He looked at me and said, "Can I call you Lar?"

There were fifty-nine minutes and fifty seconds to go. He one-worded me every step of the way. I remember asking him about the great director John Huston. "What was it like to work with John Huston?"

"You go in, do your job, go home."

"Are you saying there's no difference between directors?"

"Seen one, seen 'em all."

"What do you think of Al Pacino?"

"Don't know him."

If you don't want to talk, why come on the show? I was using every technique I'd learned over the years to get through the hour. One of the things I always try to do is ask questions that begin with the word *why*. A why question can't be answered in one word. Unless you're Robert Mitchum. Once, he replied, "Because."

It was a great example of mixed emotions, the feeling you get when someone you admire disappoints you.

I wasn't getting anything out of him. So I did something I never do. I started to fill time by elaborating. I said, "I was asking the actor David Dukes about other actors. He said the most underrated actor is Robert Mitchum. He said that in *Winds of War*, there could be six actors in the scene with lines. The scene might not necessarily have been written for Mitchum. But somehow Mitchum made it *his* scene." I summed up Dukes's compliment by saying, "It became your scene, just by your presence."

Mitchum's response was, "No kidding."

It got even stranger after the interview. As he got up to leave, he asked, "How'd I do?"

Years later, I interviewed his son Jim. I told Jim what had happened. He said, "Not surprising. My dad was putting you on. He was just having fun."

You can imagine how I felt when the producers told me they wanted to have Mitchum on again.

I couldn't believe it.

They said, "He got good ratings."

When did you start to wear the suspenders?
At one point in the '80s, I lost some weight. My ex-wife, Sharon, said, "Ever try suspenders?"

I said, "No, I've never worn them."

"Why don't you try them?" she asked.

I bought a pair, put the buttons on the pants, and wore them. That night, three or four people called in after the show and said, "Those suspenders look good!"

That was all I had to hear.

Who do you hate?
I can't hear that question without being reminded of a very particular moment in my life.

I was working in Miami when the phone rang. I picked it up.

"King. This is Boom Boom Giorno."

I didn't know any Boom Boom Giorno.

"You got a pencil? Write this down. November 14. War Memorial Auditorium. Boys Town of Italy. Sergio Franchi is the singer. You are the emcee. Black tie."

The guy hung up.

Something told me it would be in my very best interest to attend.

I got there, and everybody was telling me how glad they were to see me. I went over to Sergio Franchi. I said, "How'd they get you?"

He said, "A guy named Boom Boom Giorno called."

There was a twenty-piece orchestra. A Catholic high school marching band. A cardinal from Italy. I did jokes. Sergio sang.

They raised four hundred thousand dollars. It was a great night. Everybody was happy.

Afterward, Boom Boom walked me to my car.

He said, "We are very pleased."

I said, "My pleasure, Boom Boom."

Then came one of those moments when you remember what the moon looked like overhead.

Boom Boom said, "We owe you a favor."

"Thanks, Boom Boom," I said. "I was happy to do it. But I don't need any favors."

Boom Boom said, "We don't like to owe favors."

"Well, what do you have in mind?"

He said six words. As he said them, I could feel the sweat coming down my forehead.

"You got anybody you don't like?"

I thought I would faint. But when I didn't, the first person I thought of was the general manager of the television station. But I said, "I couldn't do that."

Boom Boom was disappointed. He said, "Do you like horse racing?"

"Yeah."

He said, "We'll be in touch."

About a week later, I got a call. Appletree in the third at Hialeah today.

I went out to Hialeah. I bet everything I could on Appletree. Appletree won. When I tell the story for large groups I always add a little joke, that I knew I had the winner when five jockeys jumped off their horses.

But think of the power in those six words.

"You got anybody you don't like?"

But, really, who don't you like?
It's not *who* I don't like. It's *what* I don't like. Bigotry is what I don't like. Hypocrisy is what I don't like.

I don't dislike Eliot Spitzer. I'm mad that Spitzer prosecuted hookers while he was seeing hookers. It's the hypocrisy that offends me.

I'm mad at the Republican congressman who wants to ban gay materials when he's gay himself. How can you get up and make flailing speeches against a group of people and be one of them yourself?

I don't know Clarence Thomas well enough to dislike him. But I'd feel better about him if I saw some compassion in his decisions. How can you be opposed to affirmative action after you've benefited from its premise?

What's it like to interview a genius?
I interviewed a German guy who won the Nobel Prize in chemistry. His prize was for something he discovered about reproduction.

I said to him, "What's the mystery of life?"

"I'll tell you the mystery." He put it as succinctly as possible. He said, "I could take every person in the world and do a hundred-page book on each of them. In this book, I could write about chromosomes, genes, hair, and blood type." He had a small jar with him and he held it up. Then he said, "And yet all the sperm that made the whole world wouldn't fill this jar."

So there's what we know. And there's what we don't know.

What did you learn from your friendship with Marlon Brando?
Marlon and I were having dinner and he pointed out a couple nearby. "They're not happy," he said.

"How do you know?" I asked.

"Look at the way the guy crosses his leg, and how he looks over her shoulder, not at her face."

His genius came from observing people.

Who have you gotten to know who would surprise us if we knew them better?

Al Gore. He's not a cardboard guy. Gore can be very funny. At a radio and TV correspondents' dinner, Gore got up with Bill and Hillary Clinton seated nearby. He said, "The question I'm most asked is, What's it like to be a heartbeat away from the president of the United States? And I always give the same answer: What's it like, Hillary?"

I had a good time with Al Gore when he came on my Mutual radio show. He lived nearby, and some nights he'd drive over by himself. Gore, Herbie, Art Buchwald, and I were having lunch at the Palm around the time Gore's book *Earth in the Balance* came out. Al asked if he could come talk about his book on the TV show. I said, "We'll have to ask the producer," and I gave him Tammy's number.

When I spoke with her about it, she said, "The environment is boring. He's boring. People are going to tune out."

Al called her personally.

She said, "I'll look into it."

A while later, Al called me back and said, "You know, your producer blew me off."

Not long after, Bill Clinton announced his vice presidential pick—and it was Al Gore!

Suddenly, Tammy was saying, "We've got to get him on!"

I called him. He was kind enough to put the past behind us. He came on the show before the convention wearing suspenders.

Gore won the popular vote against Bush in the 2000 election by something like six hundred thousand votes. It wasn't even close. What would the world be like had Gore become president? We can only guess. One thing is sure: we wouldn't have gone to war in Iraq.

Gore isn't a wild liberal. He's a moderate Democrat who

served in Vietnam. And he's a great father. How about that time his son got hit by a car while leaving a baseball game? Gore stayed in the hospital for something like thirty-three days straight. He didn't go home, and the kid pulled through. Gore never talked about it much. But that said a lot.

One of the wildest, most pulsating nights on my CNN show involved Gore. NAFTA was coming up for a vote in the Senate. It was going to be beaten. It had no chance. Gore called me early in the morning. I was lying in bed. He said, "How would you like to host a debate?"

"Between who?"

"I'll debate Ross Perot on NAFTA. Nobody in the White House is in favor of this except the president. Will you call Perot?"

I called Perot, and Ross said sure. We were on five days later. Gore showed up with every staffer in the White House. This was huge for them. Perot came in with one guy.

Ross made a big mistake. Ross knew the subject, he'd debated it before, and he took it for granted. What he didn't understand was that Gore was a champion debater at Harvard. As prepared as Perot was, Gore was superprepared. Plus, Gore had a great emotional need. It was Clinton's bill. To Perot, it was a policy he disagreed with.

Before they went on, we made certain rules. Handlers couldn't talk to the participants during breaks. There was no helping. Right before we started, Gore went over to the camera and leaned against it. Afterward, I said, "What were you doing?"

He said, "I said a prayer."

Gore started by pulling out pictures of Reed Smoot and Willis Hawley, congressmen who passed a protection bill in 1930 that raised tariffs on more than 20,000 imported goods. Gore said that many economists believed that this tariff was the principal cause of the Great Depression. It wasn't hard to get what he was implying. Hey, Ross, see these two guys, they ruined America. Want your picture next to them?

Perot got angry. But Gore was relentless. He was driven. You could see it. Ross never got off the defensive. There was one funny moment when Perot called Gore a liar. I said, "We'll be right back."

So we had two and a half minutes of commercials. No handlers were allowed to come over during that time. It was just me and the two of them. This was the first debate ever between a citizen and the vice president, and the citizen had just called the vice president a liar. Gore was very good, though. He said something like, "I understand how emotions can get carried away."

Perot wasn't going to apologize. But Gore said there was no need to apologize.

When we finished and everybody was walking out, one of Clinton's staffers said to me, "I told the president that this was a mistake. I was wrong."

We had the biggest cable audience ever at that time, a record that held for fifteen years. NAFTA passed. Not bad for a guy made of cardboard.

What makes the perfect guest?
The quality of the guest has nothing to do with his profession. A plumber can be a great guest and a statesman can be a bad one. You want someone who can explain what he or she does very well, has a passion for it, a sense of humor about it, and a little chip on his shoulder. That's why Sinatra was so great. If a person has those four things, viewers will stay tuned.

Who was the most extraordinary person you've ever met?
Nelson Mandela was easily the most extraordinary figure of the twentieth century. I went to South Africa to meet him. It still amazes me how he invited his prison guards to his inauguration. Any other man in that situation, and there would have been war. It's incredible to be that forgiving. It's a higher calling.

Do you like doing shows on UFOs?
They can be fun. They do well because most of the population
wants to believe in extraterrestrials.

There was one incredible night back in the '80s. A guest
was booked at the last minute. I didn't even know he was coming on. Tammy told me that we had the author of a book called
Communion. That's all she said.

I had no idea what the book was about. But I like it like
that. This very nice man came out. He was dressed in a tie.
Whitley Strieber was his name.

Now, communion can mean a lot of things. So I said,
"What's the book about, Whitley?"

He said something like, "Well, I was sleeping one night
and I heard a sound in my backyard. I looked out and there
was this obvious spaceship. Before I could get to the door, the
door opened and hundreds of little people came into the room.
I started to panic. Then, these little people entered every open
orifice of my body."

How do you respond to that? I couldn't help it. My hand
slammed the table and I started to laugh.

The control room was in my ear, saying, "Get a grip."

But I couldn't help it.

"I understand you're seeing the humor in all this," Whitley said. "But, Mr. King, it wasn't very funny."

So I said, "Then what happened?"

"Then they took me out to the spaceship. The spaceship
went up."

I just couldn't hold back the laughter.

"And then what happened, Whitley?"

"Again, they proceeded to enter every open orifice."

I was just sitting there picturing these little people going
up his ass. How could you not crack up?

"What do you think they were studying?"

He kept saying, "I take no offense, Mr. King. I understand how hard this is to believe."

After the show, I said, "Tammy, did you set me up?"

I was shocked to learn that the book later became a best seller and was made into a movie.

Jimmy Carter says he has seen UFOs. The governor of Arizona didn't believe in them. Then he saw one. I've had pilots tell me they've seen things in the night. UFOs dumbfound people. I don't think people feel threatened by them. We'd like to know there's life on other planets. The theory that the government doesn't release information about UFOs because they think people would panic—that doesn't wash. People would be fascinated. They'd hope it was true.

What would you like to understand?
I'd like to know why people go to see Nascar. Do they wake up and say, "Let's go watch left turns?"

Who would you like to interview?
I always used to say God. And my first question would be, "Do you have a son? Because there's a lot riding on the answer."

Seriously, I'd like to sit down with the pope. All popes interest me. Why would you want to be the pope? How do you keep your faith? I find religious leaders fascinating. They challenge me.

The most amazing thing to me is that there's a possibility that the pope knows me. That he walks by a television, sees me on it, and stops to watch.

We got a "maybe" once from Pope John Paul II. That wasn't bad.

The staff would love to get Prince Charles.

Americans are fascinated with royalty. I'm not as fascinated as my viewers. Maybe it's because all the shows about royalty have been done with panels and experts. What did the Queen

Mother think of this or that? But actually having Prince Charles on would be interesting to me. What's it like to wait to be king? What are the burdens of royalty? I would never want to be him. But I'd like to know how he handles the burdens.

The guy I'd really like to meet is the writer J. D. Salinger. He's ninety now. I was nothing like Holden Caulfield, the kid in *Catcher in the Rye*, but I understood him. Even though I had no association, I felt for him. J. D. Salinger became a recluse when he was at the top of his game. Why would you disappear from the known world? Did he stop writing? Or did he keep writing, but not publish his work?

I know a guy who likes to do impossible things for friends. When he heard my impossible thing was to interview J. D. Salinger, he found out where Salinger lived, drove four hundred miles, knocked on the door, and met Salinger's wife. He asked what would be the best way to get to J. D. She said J. D. didn't do any interviews. But the best way to get in touch was to write a letter. So I wrote him a letter a little while ago. I'd just like to talk to him.

Where's the most interesting place you've ever been?
A nuclear submarine. One thing about going on a submarine is there's always great food. These guys are underwater for six months at a time. If they didn't have great food, there'd be a mutiny.

Will there ever be peace in the Middle East?
Whenever I do Israeli-Palestinian debates, I can't help but think they're both right. The violence is wrong. But the principle of both sides is right: This is our home.

"This land was ordained to us by God."

"But we lived there."

The arguments go on and on and there's no end to them. We should remember that people didn't think there would ever be peace in Northern Ireland—and that was accomplished. I spoke with Senator George Mitchell, who helped pull that off. Even he thought that the Israeli-Palestinian situation was more difficult. It's deeply embedded in the soul.

I was with Yitzhak Rabin when he campaigned for prime minister of Israel in '92. He said, "No one hates war more than the warrior." He got tired of death. He said there's no place to go other than peace.

My eyes were opened when I went to see the Palestinian legislator Hanan Ashrawi on the West Bank. She's been on my show many times. The funny part of the visit was, it showed me how close the Palestinians and Jews really are. There's no illiteracy. We have illiteracy in the United States. But Israeli Jews are well educated. And Palestinians are well educated. Some of the most prominent poets in the world are Palestinian. The culture is similar. The food is similar. They're cousins. That they have violent thoughts toward each other is incredible.

I was with my brother, Marty, and my agent, Bob Woolf, when I went to Hanan's house. We planned to spend an hour.

Hanan said, "You're not staying for dinner? We cooked all day!" It could have been my Aunt Dora. "There's no question you're staying."

She took me around the house just like my Aunt Dora would have. "Come here, we just wallpapered, let me show you. Let me show you the kitchen."

We had a great meal. When we got in the car to go back, Marty, Bob, and I looked at each other. The first thing I said was, "How can these people be enemies?"

It may be an unsolvable problem. But amid all the recent strife, perhaps there's reason for optimism. George Mitchell was recently appointed special envoy to the Middle East. He's definitely got the right attitude. "You can have 900 bad days," he once told me. "But all you need is one good one."

Did you officially change your name to Larry King?
I changed my name in 1959, two years after I started in radio. I did it because of AFTRA—the American Federation of
Television and Radio Artists. No two artists in that union can
have the same name. Let's say someone else was born with the
name Larry King. He'd have to register as Larry King Esq.,
or something else like that. It's easy. You go to court and you
tell the judge that the reason you changed your name is that
you're on the air. If you know someone who wants to change
his name and is a little nervous about it, here's a good story to
tell him. Tell him about the judge in New York named Judge
Schmuck. If you want to change your name and you go before
him, you'd better have a good reason.

Who was your most enlightened guest?
There have been so many, but I really liked what Swami
Satchidananda told me on the Mutual show. He made a lot of
sense. There was a wonderful peace about him. I think he was
silent for a long time at one point in his life. He was fascinating to listen to.

He said, "Why worry? Why get excited about anything?
You wake up in the morning and it may be cloudy or it may be
raining. Did you deserve it? Did it come from you? No. So it was
a gift. Just thank yourself for the gift and have a wonderful day.

"Let's say you go to a restaurant and the toast you've ordered comes to you burnt. What's the best way to get good toast?
Would you scream at the waitress, 'Lady! This toast is burnt!
Get this out of here and bring me some new toast!' Or, would it
be better to say, 'Miss, I hate to bother you. The toast is a little
burnt for my taste. When you get a chance, if you could please
have the toast done a little lighter, I'd really appreciate it.'"

So I gave him a couple of challenges. I said, "OK, Swami.
Let's say I tell you that I'm going to take you to the airport tomorrow. You tell me the time of your flight and we agree on a

time to meet. 'Don't worry,' I say. 'I'll be there.' But I don't show up. You miss your flight. Then, I call you up to apologize. You're fuming—"

"No," the Swami said. "I'm not fuming."

"Why aren't you fuming?"

"Because I'm worried about my friend Larry. How is my friend Larry? He didn't come at the appointed time. So as soon as the phone rings and I can hear your voice, before you can even say I'm sorry, I'm going to say, 'How are you, my friend? Is everything OK?' There will always be another airplane. But I am happy that my friend Larry is OK. Who owns that moment, then?"

So I said, "OK, Swami. I'm going to give you the ultimate swami question. You come home from work a little early. You go upstairs and find your wife in bed with another man. What do you do?"

He said, "What would you do?"

I said, "I would go nuts."

He said, "That's fine. But what is the one thing you want when you enter that room and see that scene?"

"I don't know. What do I want?"

He said, "Information. You want to know who the man in your bed is. You want to know how it happened. What's the best way to get that information? You say, 'I'm going to go downstairs and make some tea. Why don't the two of you come down and the three of us will have tea together and talk about this.' Now, who owns that moment? You own the moment. You're not acting crazy. So the guy who is with your wife can't say you're a nut. You own the moment because it's the best way you have of learning something. That's not saying the moment is not sad to you. That's not saying the moment is not painful to you. But the thing you want in that moment is information."

Then he said, "Think about it, Larry. How do you get information? You ask good questions. You care about the person you're asking questions of. You listen respectfully to their answers. What if you screamed at them? Would you get the same answers?"

I never forgot that. Could I live the way the Swami suggested? No.

What have you learned about money from your guests?
I've done so many interviews about money—with Suze Orman, with Treasury secretaries. I do know that money makes money, and that the only rich people are the ones who don't have to go to work. That means, even if you're a retired bus driver, you're rich.

Is there anything you'd like to see more of on your show?
One of the things that I miss is talking about sports on the air. I used to be able to do it on my Mutual radio show a lot. We don't do it much on CNN. It's so fun. The Yankees stink. The Dodgers are good. Tampa Bay is lucky. Doesn't matter what you think about sports. Because sports are play and you can have any opinion on a player. "I think Rafael Furcal has a better arm than Derek Jeter! Pete Rose belongs in the Hall of Fame!" Screw it, what can they do to me?

There's that great story about when the columnist Dick Young wrote a column about a player and really blasted him. He called him the worst example of a human being that's ever walked the earth. Then he ran into him the next night and said, "Don't take it personally."

Are you bothered by people who ask you for autographs?
Tommy Lasorda of the Dodgers told me a story. He was twelve years old. He was waiting outside the Polo Grounds with his father.

A player came out.

"Can I have your autograph?" Lasorda asked.

"Screw you, kid."

Eight years later, Lasorda was pitching in the minor leagues and this same guy was on the way down.

First time up, Lasorda hit him in the shoulder.

Next time up, he hit him in the leg.

Next time the guy came to the plate, the guy yelled, "Hey, kid!"

Lasorda yelled, "Duck!"

Lasorda met him afterward and said, "Give autographs."

You've spoken at every kind of event. Is there any advice you can give about speaking at a funeral?
The day Bob Woolf died was one of the saddest days of my life. His daughter called, and I was feeling frisky when I picked up the phone.

"Hey, how are you?"

She said, "Daddy died." And I just slumped on my bed.

Wendy, my producer, knew how upset I was and wanted to send some people over from CNN. I'm really not a funeral person, but I was going to be delivering one of the eulogies. I was looking for a way to get some humor into my speech. Self-deprecating humor is always welcome.

It was a great funeral. Bob was so popular that they had speakers outside the synagogue so people could listen out in the street. Bob was Larry Bird's agent. But Larry was too shy to speak. I was the last speaker.

I got up and said, "When the phone rang in Bob's office and Larry Bird was on one line and I was on the other, who do you think got put on hold?"

Of course, it's easier to be funny when you *don't* like the person being buried.

"Wow, what a crowd," someone remarked at the funeral of the entertainer Al Jolson. I think it was the commedian George Jessel who responded: "Yeah, they came to make sure."

And when a massive throng showed up at the funeral of Hollywood impresario Harry Cohen, it might have been Jessel who said: "Give the people what they want and they'll turn out every time."

But my favorite joke about laughter and funerals is the one in which the rabbi finishes his eulogy and asks if anyone would like to come forward to say a few kind words.

Nobody in the crowd stands.

"Doesn't *anyone* want to say something?" the rabbi asks.

Nobody even stirs.

"Isn't there *something* nice," the rabbi says, "that can be said about the deceased?"

One guy stands up and says, "His brother was worse!"

Has anyone ever gotten angry with you and walked off the show?

After more than twenty years of doing the show on CNN, we had a guest walk off in 2007. It was the doctor who performed plastic surgery on Kanye West's mother the day before she died. Dr. Jan Adams. Adams agreed to do the interview. But the West family wrote him a letter asking him not to go on. When the surgeon arrived in the studio, his attorney advised him not to speak.

So he came on and said he would honor the family's wishes and not say anything. Then he removed his microphone and walked off. I didn't get upset. I go nuts if someone in my family is late for dinner. But a situation like that doesn't faze me even though it's live on national television. I just said, Okay, we'll take a commercial break.

When we came back, we had a panel assembled and we went on with the show.

The other time someone walked off was during radio days. I'll never forget the woman's name. Micki Dahne. She's a psychic. Before we went on the air, I said to her, "Explain something to me. You say you can tap into the mind of Jackie Kennedy. We're in Miami. She's in Hyannis Port. There are about forty million women along the way. How do you get to Jackie without bumping into the other forty million?"

She wouldn't answer me when I asked her, "How do you do what you do?"

Finally, she walked out.

What's it like interviewing Vladimir Putin?
I found Putin very genial. I was most surprised when the subject turned to his favorite place to visit. He was in New York. I asked him if he liked New York. He said it was all right, but not his favorite place.

So I said, "What is your favorite place?"

He said, "Jerusalem." That shocked me. He used to go there when he was with the KGB.

He surprised me more than once. Remember when that Russian submarine went down? "What's happened with the submarine?" I asked.

I expected a long, detailed answer. He could be an elaborative guy.

He said, "It sank."

That was it. It sank.

"OK, it sank."

What's it like having breakfast at your table at Nate 'n Al?
They've got the Larry King matzo brie on page eight of the menu. But when I walk into Nate 'n Al I never get the feeling that I'm "Larry King." When I sit down, I'm just a regular guy with my friends.

There's Sid. Sid has more friends than anyone I've ever met. He worries about me. If I've got a problem, he loses sleep. Sid's the guy who says no for me, because I can't. The thing about Sid is, he can lose every bet on football Sunday—except one. The one to me. And you should see the smile on his face when I pay up. As if all those other losses didn't matter.

Sid has known Asher since they were in kindergarten. Even now that he's got arthritis, Asher looks at the good side. He's glad that he can tell us when it's going to rain two days in advance. Asher's got a bad back now, too, so he doesn't come every day. When he came in on Election Day, he got an ovation.

The conversation is a potpourri. Within a half hour we might discuss asthma inhalers, the origin of the Goose Step, Sarah Palin, Bill Maher's new movie, the sexual benefits of vitamin E, Willie Sutton's bank robberies, who's pitching for the Dodgers, the steaks at Dan Tana's, gun laws, and how girls in Las Vegas can steal your chips. Between all of us, we have an answer to any problem. It may be wrong, but it'll be an answer.

We're also on the lookout for Irwinisms. Irwinisms are things that nobody else in the world but Irwin would ever say. Irwin is an incredibly successful businessman who started out in pharmacy, but he'll say things like, "Hey, Larry, is CNN going to cover the inauguration?" After Rod Blagojevich, the Illinois governor, got caught trying to auction off Barack Obama's vacant Senate seat, Irwin said, "Do you think this will harm the governor's political career?"

Which always gives George the opening to joke, "And they let *you* fill prescriptions?"

George used to produce the show *Laugh In*. He's a Democrat who watches Fox. I can't believe it. "Just because I watch a traffic accident," he'll say, "doesn't mean I like it."

It's good to have Dwight, a solid Republican, nearby for balance. Dwight bought a house in move-in condition. After "a little" touch-up work, twelve months later, he's still waiting to move in.

Then you've got Budd. Budd never says anything. He keeps his hand on his chin. Never eats.

One thing's for sure. If Gloria the waitress brought burnt toast, Budd would never yell. If we get Vicki, the great thing is she tells us what not to eat.

Sometimes Sam comes by. Sam has taken the Dale Carnegie class ten times, watched *Tuesdays with Morrie* fifty times, and seen *Dances with Wolves* sixty times. Sam sits by Bruce, the music promoter. Bruce met a beautiful Brazilian pentathlete about a foot taller than him and thirty years younger. Bruce had a huge beard and hair sprouting all over the place when he took her to the judge to get married. The judge looked at her, at him, at her, at him, then asked her, "Are you doing this of your own free will or are you drugged?" They're going on twenty-five years of marriage.

Meanwhile, Michael Viner is eating two breakfasts every morning. Turkey sandwiches with baked beans? That's a bit of an exaggeration. But who ever heard of chicken soup for breakfast?

Sometimes Michael brings his daughter in. Taylor Rose. Once, Taylor Rose ordered the chicken soup just like her dad, then she said she wouldn't eat it.

"Haven't you heard of Methuselah?" I asked her. "He lived nine hundred years. That's because every day for nine hundred years, he had the chicken soup. The first day he didn't, he dropped dead."

"Did you know Methuselah?" she asked.

"Of course!" I said. "He used to sit at this table and have breakfast every morning."

What's it like to be a father of an eight-year-old and a nine-year-old at age seventy-five?
That's a chapter.

Chapter 21

Kvelling

WAS I REALLY SEVENTY when I went to see my son Chance's first T-ball game? Nobody on either team knew how to play. Chance came up to the plate and whacked the ball to center field. Then he ran after the ball. Not to first base—straight to center field. All the kids playing the field ran after Chance. All the kids on Chance's team ran after all the kids playing the field. Everybody jumped into a pile trying to get the ball. I was laughing my head off.

I started taking Chance and Cannon to Dodgers games. First game, they didn't know what was going on, and they fell asleep by the fourth inning. The next game, they stayed awake until the fifth. After a while, I noticed them starting to ask, "Why four balls and three strikes?"

Fred Wilpon offered to have Chance throw out the first pitch at a Mets-Dodgers game. Fred is the owner of the Mets and we go back to high school together. Shawn told Chance it was a big honor and that he had to wear a Mets shirt when he went to the mound.

Chance said, "I will not wear a Mets shirt. I'm a Dodger through and through."

She said, "You have to."

"I won't."

"You must."

"I *won't*."

Finally, Shawn got him into the shirt. Chance immediately marched over to the Dodgers dugout and told every Dodger, "My mother made me wear this."

Then he went out to the mound. I stood behind him and watched him throw a perfect strike. The entire Dodgers dugout applauded. The Dodgers second baseman Jeff Kent got him a packet of sunflower seeds so he could spit like the ballplayers.

The next thing I knew, Cannon was hitting three home runs over the fence in a single game. A guy watching said he'd never seen it before in coach-pitch. I watched that little body run around the bases. Where did that come from? I never had any power as a hitter.

I gave them the gift of baseball, and they gave me the gift of youth. Never could I have guessed that some of the biggest thrills of my life were ahead of me. Taking them through the Hall of Fame in Cooperstown, seeing them hold Jackie Robinson's first uniform—they had to wear white gloves. Going to spring training at Dodgers camp. In spring training, you can sit in the cafeteria with the ballplayers. You can mingle. There was once a day when I couldn't afford a ticket into Ebbets Field. Now I was watching Tommy Lasorda carry out a birthday cake to Chance and his brother and their friends. There's only one way I know to describe the feeling. It's a Jewish idiom—*kvelling*. You get a kick out of someone else's thrill. It's for them, but it's an extension of you.

It's the best kind of accomplishment. As Brad Pitt told me during a recent show, there's nothing better than being a father. Whatever's in second place is way behind.

I'm such a better father now that I'm a great-grandfather.

There's no comparison. But the great joy my children bring me also brings me pain. I feel it when they trip. And I feel it when I trip. That's because I know that Chance is just the age I was when my father died, and Cannon is only a year younger.

I once took Chance back to Brooklyn, to show him the apartment I grew up in. We stopped where Ebbets Field used to be. The neighborhood had become housing projects. A drugstore across the street had bars over its windows. We sat on the curb and I sang him my favorite song.

There Used to Be a Ballpark Right Here

And there used to be a ballpark
Where the field was warm and green
And the people played their crazy game
With a joy I'd never seen
And the air was such a wonder
From the hot dogs and the beer
Yes, there used to be a ballpark, right here.

And there used to be rock candy
And a great big Fourth of July
With the fireworks exploding
All across the summer sky
And the people watched in wonder
How they'd laugh and how they'd cheer
And there used to be a ballpark, right here.

Now the children try to find it
And they can't believe their eyes
'Cause the old team just isn't playing
And the new team hardly tries

And the sky has got so cloudy
When it used to be so clear
And the summer went so quickly this year.

Yes, there used to be a ballpark, right here.

I told Chance how when Frank Sinatra chose that song, he said it was about more than just a ballpark. It's about life, and changing and growing up.

And the summer went so quickly this year.

Chance looked around and said, "Can we move back here?"

When I told him that would be impossible, he said, "Can we move this to Beverly Hills?"

Would I have gone back to Ebbets Field, sat on the curb, and sang that song if not for Chance? No. It's mystifying what he and Cannon have given me. My passion for baseball had been diminished by the time I moved out to Los Angeles. I stopped rooting for the Dodgers when they left Brooklyn back in the '50s and then I picked up with the Orioles when they trained in Miami. But I was only a casual fan by the time I met Shawn. I'd turn on a game. But that was it.

The more the kids grew to like it, the more I got into it. Two years ago, I bought season tickets. Now I'm back where I started: crazed. It was the kids who did it to me. They brought me back.

So much has come back to me in the last few years. I wasn't there to have breakfast with Larry Jr. when he was a boy. But when he comes to visit, Chance and Cannon run to hug him and they have pancakes together. He's their big brother, that's all. They don't know life any differently.

When Larry Jr. came back into my life and I had to tell Chaia, I didn't know how she'd feel. She could have been mad. She could have wondered where she stood. You never know how people will react. When Herbie and I sat with her and told her, she opened her arms and said, "When can I meet him?" Now Larry Jr. and Andy go to University of Miami versus Florida football games. And when Andy drives his motorcycle across country to visit, Chance and Cannon hop on for rides. It's natural to all of them, and that makes it natural to me.

I once announced a high school football game that Shawn's first child, Danny, played. After he threw a touchdown I said over the PA system, "Danny, you can stay out late tonight! Your mother says it's OK!"

Now Danny is diagramming plays for Chance and Cannon's flag football team. Chance is throwing long to Cannon. Their nanny, Lib Lib, is filming, and is as much a part of the family as Auntie Bella was to me when I was a kid.

Larry Jr. has given me three grandchildren. Andy has given me two grandchildren and they have given me two great-grandchildren. I like to joke that it makes Shawn the world's youngest great-grandmother. The great-grandchildren are infants and they can't speak yet. What do you call a great-grandpa? I guess I'll find out.

I'm not Solomon. But I've had so many experiences as a father. There's a son that I adopted, a daughter that I lost, a son that I found, a daughter, two stepdaughters from my marriage to Sharon who I'm happy to help out whenever I can, a stepson who came aboard with Shawn, plus Chance and Cannon.

It's hard to describe. But maybe it's kind of like Chance's first hit in T-ball. In their own way, everybody who wanted to was able to jump into the pile out in center field.

ANOTHER POINT OF VIEW

Shawn Southwick-King

Seeing Larry with the kids is awesome—in the literal sense of the word. It makes your heart expand.

Chaia King

We all get battered around by life and circumstances. Who knows what healing is going on with him and those kids right now?

Larry King Jr.

The evolution started when Chance and Cannon were born. He was not there for a lot of the kids in their early years in a traditional sense. But Chance and Cannon have allowed him to pour all those things he didn't do with us into them.

Lib Lib

THE NANNY

People never believe me. But it's the truth. I've never worked with a father so involved. He knows all the kids' friends. He knows everything. If the kids get a certificate in school, he's there. It's not that he has to do it. He wants to do it. He takes them to school in the morning and he picks them up. He sits at what we call the housewife bench and waits. It's one of his favorite places. I think it calms him. It's almost as if he's nesting for the first time.

A little while ago we went to see *The Curious Case of Benjamin Button*. Larry loved that movie. At first I thought it was slow. But Larry couldn't stop talking about it. The more he talked, the more it made so much sense to me. Brad Pitt kept getting younger and younger. That's what Larry wants. I think this is his best time right now, with Chance and Cannon, and he doesn't want it to end.

I said, "Larry, if for Christmas I could buy you a clock that goes backward, I would."

Larry King Jr.

We went to Busch Gardens in Florida when Chance and Cannon were younger. I got on one of those spinning rides with them. You know, one of those coasters. My dad was watching. Every time I went by, I was screaming: "Dad, dad, look at me." I was forty-five, but I was laughing and screaming, "Dad! Dad!"

I told him afterward, I didn't get to do that when I was five. So I had to do it now.

Some kids in my position would be upset over what was missed. But I don't look at it like that because of my mom's teachings. I just cherish every moment that I have with my dad.

Chaia King

My dad's like a father and a grandfather. Maybe I'm like a sister and an aunt. In the old days, sisters would help out like an aunt would. Our culture now is different. But I feel like that kind of sister to Chance and Cannon. Not that I'm there to guide them every day—I live on the other side of the country. But families pull together all the time.

When I try to describe what it's like, I have to hesitate because what your family is to you is what it is. What you know is normal. And *normal* might be the wrong word here because my dad's life has never been normal. But it ain't dull. I have never been bored.

Danny Southwick

SON

Having Larry King show up to announce your high school football game is bizarre—and that's an understatement. He wasn't doing it like a normal PA announcer. He was announcing the game. I would take the snap and hear in that one-and-only voice: "Southwick drops back to pass . . ."

He's not afraid to go out and have fun. Did you see him in the bathtub with Jim Carrey on the David Letterman show? If you haven't, you should YouTube it.

Cannon King

SON

Have you ever heard my dad sing rap songs? It's pretty funny.

Chance King

SON

In real life, he's a lot more goofy than he is on the show.

Danny Southwick

But he's also taught me a great deal about being successful. He knows exactly what he wants. He said all successful people he knows have that quality: being decisive.

Once you know what you want to do, you've got to do it to the fullest.

Larry Jr. has also taken an interest in me. Andy and Chaia live in Florida, but it's very friendly when we're together. Coaching Chance and Cannon has been some of the most fun I've had in football—and I've played a lot.

My entire family has been affected by Larry. Coming from a divorced household can be tough. To have all these other people in your life is an experience that I wouldn't trade.

Larry King Jr.

When I visit my father, I'm able to do the same things I do for my kids. I can make pancakes in the shape of animals or L.A. for the Dodgers. So I'm able to engage my brothers the way I'm able to engage my own children. But my dad's sitting at the breakfast table with them. I'm the kid serving the kids. It's almost an out-of-body experience. But it's natural.

We harass each other. They're for the Dodgers. I'm for the Rays. It's like when my brother Andy and I get together. When I was a kid sitting up in the stands at the Dolphins games, watching my dad through the binoculars and listening to him on a radio, I didn't know my brother Andy was on the sidelines. Now Andy and I harass each other because he's for the Gators and I'm for the Hurricanes.

Andy King

My dad is one of those gifted people who can focus and dedicate his life to doing what he wants to do. Early on, he wanted to be Arthur Godfrey. He's accomplished that.

He's exceeded that. Now he's getting near the end of his career and he's turned that focus toward family.

Chaia King

His life has come full circle.

Chance King

Did you know that when Chaia was little she thought that Pepto-Bismol was a drink?

Cannon King

When I was little, my dad left the house. Then my mom turned on the TV and my dad was inside. I said: "How'd you get in there, Dad?"

Chance King

Did my dad ever tell you how he got thrown out of my Little League game? I was pitching. He was arguing a call. The umpire said, "Go back to CNN!" The umpire wasn't joking. The umpire said, "If you don't go to the parking lot, this game is going to be forfeited." So my dad went to the parking lot. He said he just can't stop from arguing a bad call. It's the Leo Durocher in him.

Cannon King

My dad is just crazy about baseball. When we watch ESPN, he's screaming. I told him, "Dad, the players can't hear you."

Chance King

Sometimes he starts screaming the Brooklyn stuff. "You bums!" It's much more fun to hear him talk the Brooklyn way.

Cannon King

Young is for playing. Old is caring for other people.

I just feel like my dad's with me forever. It's really good to have that feeling in your heart when you think of your dad.

Chapter 22

Healing the Wounds

IGHT YEARS AGO, if you had told me that a black guy from Hawaii, raised by a white grandmother, who went on to become an egghead lawyer from Harvard and a Democratic politician with the most liberal voting record in the Senate, would win the presidency by beating a white American war hero, I would have said one thing: "Are you nuts?"

But four years ago, there was a sign. One evening, Barack Obama stormed the Democratic convention with a speech. I was with the Republican senator Bob Dole at the time. Dole leaned over to me and said, "You've just seen the first black president of the United States of America."

Obama's election is the most historic of our lifetime. The biggest blight on our record as a great nation has been slavery. It's something we've never lived down. Its wounds are still there because grandchildren of slaves are still among us. Think of the unbelievable nature of that. Grandchildren of slaves witnessed this election. We'll never see anything like it again.

Obama's victory is a testament to the power of eloquence. There's a lot to be said for eloquence. There's a calmness in eloquence. People will turn to an eloquent person in a crisis.

Obama ran on change and we certainly need it. Yes, it would have been a change if Hillary Clinton had been elected. But a Clinton following a Bush following a Clinton following a Bush wasn't enough change. Obama represented hope. He's black, but he's also white. He's balanced.

There was some filth thrown at him. He was called anti-American. He was called a terrorist. He was called a socialist. None of it stuck because of his composure. It made me convinced that there is less and less of our terrible history embedded in us. And I think we will keep on healing.

I was at Jackie Robinson's first game, and I interviewed him just before he died. He was blind from diabetes, and a guy who gave him a book to sign had to turn it right-side up to show him where to write his name. Jackie said, "Don't put me in a grave with promises. I don't need promises. I've heard promises all my life. Give it to me now. Then, when I die, I know it's OK."

I watched how Martin Luther King Jr. advanced the entire nation while the FBI spied on him. I listened to Harry Belafonte tell me about the ceremony at the White House when the Civil Rights Act passed. As he was going forward to shake hands with Lyndon Johnson, he said, "Thank you," to the president. Then he said to himself, *Wait a minute. I'm thanking him for my birthright. Why do I have to thank someone for my birthright?*

Now we have a black president, and an election that brought out the best in us. My wife, who voted for John McCain, was moved. McCain's concession speech, my brother Marty pointed out, was hailed in Europe as the way a democracy should function. And George W. Bush was as eloquent in speaking about the historic nature of Obama's victory as I'd ever heard him.

It will not be easy for Obama. I'll always remember being in the White House with Bill Clinton as we looked out a window at the people walking on Pennsylvania Avenue. "I envy those people," Clinton said. "They can walk on the street. This is a lonely place. A lonely place."

But we all want the healing so badly that we're going to make it work. I'll always remember my kids on election night, cheering the results. Yesterday, the boys went over to their friend's house. Dante's parents had dinner for them. My kids don't know black or white.

Maybe it's our children who'll bring about the healing.

Chapter 23

One a Day

I T's AWKWARD for me to talk about the Larry King Cardiac
Foundation even though it gives me some of my biggest
thrills. That's because people come up to me and say
things like, "I was at your foundation's gala. You do so much
good. You really ought to feel proud of yourself." It's not that
these sorts of comments make me feel embarrassed. It's just
that I don't feel deserving.

What did I do? The Cardiac Foundation came about because of a single question—and I wasn't even the one who
asked it.

The question came up at a table at Duke Zeibert's about
six months after my bypass surgery. This was 1988. Someone
asked how my heart was doing, and when I told him it was OK,
he asked, "Hey, what did the surgery cost you?"

"I don't know," I said. "Insurance paid."

It got me to thinking. How much *did* the surgery cost—
and what about people who don't have insurance? The thing
about a bypass is that it's an elective surgery. You may have
severe blockage, but your insurance company isn't necessarily going to pay for you to get it fixed. You're not forced to go

onto the operating table. You can eat healthier, exercise. The only way you can get the surgery paid for is to have a heart attack. When you show up at the emergency room in an ambulance, that's when you're covered.

The first time I went on the radio to talk about this, I said the absolute tragedy is that there should be something like a Larry King Cardiac Foundation. There'd be no need for this in Israel or Sweden or England. We're the only industrialized nation in the world that doesn't have national health insurance. Christ would be for it, there's no doubt in my mind. I absolutely believe health is a right, like speech.

So I got a few people together and we held a little fundraiser at a high school in Baltimore. Johnny Unitas, the great quarterback, came. So did Tommy Lasorda. A department store put on a fashion show. I got up and spoke. We had some laughs. Tommy made an impassioned speech. We raised about a hundred thousand dollars.

The first thing we did was set up a transplant for a coach at a Catholic school. His problem was that he was not a full-time teacher. He only went to the school to coach. So he was paid, but not insured. The beauty of the story is that he recovered and had a child. He named the kid Larry.

We brought the coach to our second fund-raiser—which we held in Washington. It's hard for someone who's had his life saved to not want to get up and thank you from the bottom of his heart. It's the most natural thing in the world. But what did I do to help him? All I did was not know how much my heart surgery cost, then stand up in a high school gym and do a little shtick. So you can see why I feel undeserving.

Really, let's look at this. What did I do? I had a heart attack in an emergency room and was saved by Dr. Richard Katz. I needed bypass surgery and was operated on by Dr. Wayne Isom. I started a foundation. Katz came on the board and hooked us up with the George Washington University hospitals. Isom and New York Presbyterian joined in. So we got great doctors and great hospitals, and all I did to get them was smoke three packs of cigarettes a day for almost forty years, eat fatty lamb chops, and then walk into an emergency room with chest pain.

Early on, most of the foundation's money came in through our annual gala. We got Marvin Hamlisch to play the piano, Vic Damone to sing, and Don Rickles to do one of his bits. Then I really felt undeserving. I certainly didn't deserve the abuse Rickles heaped on me.

He introduced me once, "Don't stand up all the way, you're not that big."

Rickles has been busting my chops for fifty years now. I can remember taking my mother to see him in Miami. Sidney Poitier was seated at our table. My mother was whispering, "What a nice-looking man!" Rickles came on and said, "Jeez, Larry, you'll hang around with anybody."

Then, "Sidney, nice to have you here. Hate to break it to you, we're out of fried chicken."

Then, like always, he turned to the band and said in mock terror, "Is he coming up to the stage?"

We had the guy who runs Morton's Steakhouse at one gala. He weighs about three hundred pounds. Rickles said, "I'd have you stand up and be introduced, but our crane operator is off tonight."

At another gala, we had Sinbad. He did a number on Jonathan Tisch of Loews hotels. Sinbad said to him, "You've got a nice hotel. Rooms for five hundred dollars a night. Good sheets. Nice pillows. But five dollars for a Snickers bar? Come on! Give it away!"

Dick Cheney hosted one of our galas. I remember when he found out he needed heart surgery. He sat down with me in a stairwell in the New Orleans Superdome at the 1988 Republican Convention. "Tell me what's going to happen," he said, "and don't leave out a thing."

George C. Scott called me before he went in for bypass surgery. Scott played General Patton. In that movie, holy shit, was he tough. Let me tell you, the heart surgery scared him to death. Anthony Quinn called, wanting to know what to expect. Pretty soon, I became synonymous with heart surgery. Talk about *What am I doing here?* moments. What was little Larry Zeiger doing at a heart foundation gala singing "Ebony and Ivory" with Stevie Wonder? My son Chance danced with James Brown. The list of people who've volunteered to perform over the years is phenomenal. Celine Dion. Gladys Knight. Rod Stewart. Ricky Martin. Seal. Tim McGraw. Lewis Black. Marc Anthony. Tony Bennett. Shania Twain. Dana Carvey. Colby Caillet. Michael Bolton.

At one gala, the magician Joe Ramano made an ornament, blew into it, and snow started to fall from the ceiling all over the ballroom. It wasn't rigged. There was nothing in the ceiling. He created snow out of nowhere over the whole ballroom. Nobody had ever seen anything like it.

As the foundation grew, I was able to make six or eight phone calls a year to tell people who didn't have insurance and couldn't afford the surgery that the foundation would cover them. There's no better feeling in the world—hearing the thrill in a voice that has just gotten good news.

I figured if we could get it up to twenty surgeries a year, what could be better? Then Larry Jr. came into my life. He had been running businesses for Intuit. We put him on our board.

Larry King Jr.

I was kind of like a fireman at Intuit. I'd go into different operations, straighten them out, and move them forward. Then I'd move to another unit. I was constantly on the move. My wife and I had moved seven times in eleven years. We were in Tampa when I came to a career crossroads. In order to stay with Intuit, I was either going to have to go back to California or consider another move.

We'd just had twins. Now Shannon and I had three kids. My wife liked living in Florida. Shannon and I had never had a home. We had houses, but not a home. We lived with boxes in rooms; some never got unpacked. They were just shuttled from one house to the next. As much as I liked working for Intuit, I wanted a home. I wanted to stay in Florida.

So I talked with my dad about it. He said, "Look, the president of the foundation is moving on. Do you want to help out as president for six months while you figure out what you want to do?"

I'd had great opportunities being around icons in Silicon Valley and observing how to build businesses. My dad was the classic example of a founder who has a great idea and starts a business, but is not necessarily the person to make it really grow. I felt like I could provide the information the foundation needed to see where it could go.

I would be taking a huge pay cut to do it. But it was only six months. The lower salary wasn't the obstacle. The number one obstacle for me was that I would have to sacrifice my identity. Now I wouldn't be able to hold off until someone asked me directly, "Are you Larry King's son?" It would be out there.

I've always wanted to be in my own skin. Now I would have to hold out a Larry King Cardiac Foundation business card and say, "I'm Larry King Jr." It was something I knew I wasn't going to be comfortable with at first. But I was going to help save lives, so I did it.

At the start, it was a struggle to be Larry King Jr. I'd meet with CEOs, and I could sense that some thought I'd gotten the job as a handout from my dad. Then the conversation would get going and I'd start talking about strategic planning and business-driven metrics. All of a sudden, I could see their eyes open.

Larry King

One day Larry came to me and said, "We've got to run a gap analysis."

I said, "A *what?*"

He tells me a gap analysis is when you see where your business is today, then you compare it to where you want to be tomorrow. Then you can see the gap between those two points.

He said, "Dad, you can give heart surgery to someone who needs it every day."

A surgery every single day? At first, I thought Larry Jr. was nuts. You'd have to raise huge sums of money to save a life a day.

Larry King Jr.

About six months in, when I started to see the possibilities of what the foundation could do, it really became exciting.

In order to save a life a day, we needed to come up with fifteen million dollars a year in donations. But the experience I received working in Fortune 500 companies came in handy. We were able to reduce the cost of each patient served by 60 percent. We were able to do that by getting doctors to donate their time, companies to donate free products, and hospitals to work with us on containing costs.

Then something really opened my eyes. There was this eleven-year-old boy whose father had died of cardiac arrest at the age of forty-three. Matt, the boy's name was. A few days after his father died, Matt made up wristbands that said BE SMART SAVE A HEART. They look just like those yellow bands that Lance Armstrong uses to fight cancer. Matt sold more than two thousand dollars worth of them at school. He sent us the money and wrote us a letter saying something like, "Mr. King, please use this to save the life of a father so that this doesn't happen to another son like me."

We brought Matt to a gala. He gave a speech. And then he was introduced onstage to a father whose life he'd saved. It was an unbelievable moment.

Matt Markel

FRIEND

I was really nervous when I got onstage. When I hugged Everett, who'd been saved by the operation, it was one of the most moving moments of my life. I can't describe it. The best that I can do is say that it felt like my life had a purpose. And I felt like my dad was there watching.

I still to this day do not believe my dad died. He was jumping on a trampoline with us only hours before. We thought he was healthy as a horse. Then I woke up in the middle of the night to a bunch of noise, and came out of my room to see the medics.

My mom told me about the Larry King Cardiac Foundation. I didn't know much about how things worked with celebrities. I raised the money and sent a letter and thought that somebody would read it. The next thing I knew, I got a phone call from Larry King.

We talked about what happened. He told me how his dad had died of a heart attack when he was a kid. Then I got to meet him at the gala.

What I'd done didn't hit me until I was on that stage. When I came off, all these people started coming up to me and telling me that what I'd done was amazing. I just wanted to do more.

Larry King Jr.

It was unbelievable for anyone sitting in that room. I can't begin to describe what it was like for me. There was my father. He'd lost his father to a heart attack at age nine. And because of the foundation he'd started, an eleven-year-old kid was able to give life to another kid's father. And there I was. I'd never been around my father when I grew up. Now I was getting a chance to work to make a moment like that and then watch my father have it.

I'd love to know what my father was thinking when he saw that father hug that kid.

Larry King

It was surreal. Watching it was almost like an out-of-body experience. Look what this kid has done!

I wasn't thinking about my father's death. I don't dwell on my father's death. I no longer believe that my father abandoned me. I know it wasn't his fault. He didn't want to leave. Instead, I just move forward and have this crazy life that puts me in the position to be in these situations. The only way I can explain it to you is that my life is hard for me to believe.

Larry King Jr.

After a moment like that, how could I leave for another job to sell software or a credit card? Matt raised thirty thousand dollars more, and saved ten other fathers.

In my first year as president, the foundation funded twenty-two surgeries.

The second year, we did about a hundred.

The next year, we did about a hundred and fifty.

In 2008, we did three hundred.

We're going to get to one a day. We're going to get to one a day because the more people hear these stories, the more people want to help. One hundred and ten people in Los Angeles are alive today because of Larry King. Not only that, he's touching people all over the world. The stories are amazing.

Larry King

One of the most memorable stories to me was this boy in Afghanistan. The Pentagon flew him in, and we did the surgery at Washington Children's Hospital. I went and visited the boy and his father. They didn't speak English. But I didn't have to understand what they were saying because I could see it on their faces.

Larry King, Jr.

There was a young woman who couldn't walk up a flight of stairs. Her sister wrote us an amazing letter asking for help. We got her the surgery. Afterward she got a job, re-married, and gave birth to her first child on Christmas day. She's now chipping in to help others. A guy named Chris, who runs a little photography business, didn't have insurance and was in need of heart valve surgery. Now he comes to our gala every year and photographs the event for free. I can go on all day.

My goal for my dad is not something he wants for himself. It's something I want to do for him. My dad already has a legacy in journalism. But this is something else. Thirty or forty years from now, you're not going to see Larry King on CNN. Maybe there will be some odd video clip every now and then. But every day, he will be responsible for saving somebody's life. My father's name will be mentioned well into his grandchildren's lifetime. It's like Anthony Robbins said at our recent gala, "The greatest use of life is to spend it on something that will outlast it."

Larry King

They say I've interviewed more than forty thousand people. I really don't have any idea. Nobody would deny that I've met a lot of people. I haven't met many who've impressed me like Larry Jr.

Larry King, Jr.

It has not only come full circle with me. It's gone beyond. Chance and Cannon will be involved with this foundation. My kids, Asher, Max, and Stella, will be involved many years down the road. The family will have a touch on this foundation as long as it is needed.

Not long ago, my children were selling cupcakes at school to raise money for the foundation. I went inside and saw all these kids walking around with little red bands on their wrists, the ones Matt made three years ago. All I can say is that this burns within me. It tells me who I am.

My oldest son wrote a letter to my father saying how proud he is to be connected to the foundation. He's seamlessly connected with his grandfather. He'll never understand I was never close with his grandfather growing up. He'll only see what's true today.

We just sent a team of doctors to Uganda to help save people and train local doctors to save more in the future. My son sees me writing a thank-you note to someone in Germany who's donated a dollar. Here's a person in Germany who's connected to my dad, who's connected to me, who's connected to my son.

Chapter 24

Sleeper

O NE NIGHT, when I was young and just getting started in Miami, I came home feeling a little tired. It was a Friday night, and I'd done my radio show, my television show, and announced at the dog track. I had the next couple of days off. So I didn't set my alarm clock. Whenever I get up, I figured, I get up. I had a date the next evening. Even better, if I got up early enough, I could fit in an afternoon at the track before my big Saturday night.

So I went to sleep. When I woke up, I felt great. I looked at the clock. It said ten. Wonderful! That gave me plenty of time to get breakfast, have a nice afternoon at the track, come home, shower, and then go on my date.

I lived in an apartment building at the time, and I walked to the lobby to get my newspaper. It was a beautiful day. I picked up the paper and blinked. It said that it was Sunday.

Was I out of my mind? I couldn't have slept through a whole day. I stood there and thought about it. I must have woken up and gone to the bathroom—but I couldn't remember. That woman who was waiting for me to pick her up on Saturday night? She never went out with me again.

I was reminded of that day last November 19. That's because I woke up on that morning and found out that I was seventy-five years old. Seventy-five! How could that be? Yesterday, I was just a kid. I absolutely refused to accept seventy-five. It was bad enough when I turned fifty. I remember getting in the car, flipping on the radio and hearing a commercial, "Over fifty? You're eligible to join AARP—"

I hit the switch to change the station and heard, "Fifty or over, get twenty percent off on your Metro ticket—"

But seventy-five? When my friends and I were kids and we met somebody who was seventy-five, we thought, "Oh my God!" Back then, there weren't that many people who lived to be that old. Suddenly, I'm seventy-five? "It's impossible!" I said, slamming my fist on the table over breakfast at Nate 'n Al.

"Look at the bright side," someone said. "You may be seventy-five today. But you're still slamming your fist on the table."

"Yeah," I said. "But now my hand hurts."

When I look back, there are a few regrets. I certainly wouldn't have gotten married eight times. But I don't dwell on regrets. When I think of regrets, I think of something I witnessed when I was married to Sharon. Sharon's father was an amateur baseball player, and he was pretty good. But he went into the Marines, and afterward his father made him take a job in the post office. One time, I took him to an Orioles game. We were on the field during batting practice, standing behind the cage, watching the players hit. It was a typical scene that you see game after game, year after year. But as I turned toward Sharon's father, I saw tears running down his face.

I said, "What's the matter?"

He said, "I should have tried."

I'll never forget that. I may have regrets. But one thing I'll never have to say is, I wish I had taken the risk.

A lot of what I do is about still being that curious kid who showed up at the radio station looking for a job in Miami. Yogi Berra once said, "I don't want to get the kid out of me." I agree 100 percent. But I've got to be realistic. While there are times I don't feel seventy-five, there are other moments when I get up from the table at Nate 'n Al and hear myself utter that other great Jewish idiom, "*Oy, abrucht . . .*" I love Jewish idioms. These little expressions that sound exactly like what they mean. Nothing sums up seventy-five better than "*Oy, abrucht.*" My mother used to say it. Now I know what it means. In 2011, when my contract with CNN is up, I'll be seventy-eight. Seventy-eight-year-olds usually don't get offered three- or four-year contracts.

People forget, retirement used to be at sixty-five. Walter Cronkite was retired by CBS. It was company policy. But maybe today's seventy-eight is yesterday's sixty. I still get good ratings. And if I went off the air, what would it do to the ninety-nine-year-old woman who credits her longevity to watching my show every night? I just called her up to wish her a happy birthday.

I got a wonderful letter from Peter Jennings right before he died of cancer. He said something like, "I never had much time in the past to watch you. But since this illness, I've seen you frequently. I must say how good you are."

A note like that makes it hard to imagine getting up in the morning and not having a show to do. Artie Shaw, one of the great clarinet players of all time, just died, in his nineties. He was a brilliant guy, had an IQ of 190. When I interviewed him, he told me he stopped playing the clarinet when he was in his fifties.

I asked, "Why?"

He said, "Nothing more to learn. Nothing more to play."

I feel just the opposite. One of the reasons I felt so sorry for Tim Russert is because of what he missed after his sudden death. He loved politics, breathed it. For him to not be around to witness the hubbub around Sarah Palin's nomination was incredibly sad to me. If he did witness it from above—as those who believe assure me he could—he must have been dying to be here. Of course, he was already dead. But he had to be dying.

One of the hardest parts of aging, as Kirk Kerkorian told me, is that your friends die. I remember Sinatra saying near the end, "Everyone I know is dead." What would kill me is if Herbie, Sid, or Asher went before me. I don't want to experience that pain. I'd rather go before—even as much as I fear death.

But I can't go. I can't go because of my kids. The two youngest are so much a part of my life that it scares me. I know that one day I'm not going to be around. I doubt I'm going to make ninety. Let's say I get to eighty-five. That means I see Chance and Cannon graduate from high school. Sometimes, I see athletes talk about their fathers. I'd love to see Chance and Cannon talk about how their dad took them to play when they were kids.

Not long ago, I went in to do some estate planning. When you go to sign your will, you can't help but think about death. All I could think of were jokes. There's the old Henny Youngman line at the reading of his will. "To my brother Henry, who said that he would not be mentioned in my will, 'Hello, Henry!'"

So I told them to write in my will: "If I'm ever hooked up on life support, and I'm still breathing and not in pain, if there's any chance, *don't* pull the plug. Even if we have to go broke. Let the kids sell lemonade on the corner. Just don't pull the plug!"

I agree with Woody Allen. I'm not that afraid of death. I just don't want to be there when it happens.

And if I do go, freeze me! Being frozen is a good way to go because maybe it's a good way to not go.

I don't like the thought of being in the ground. And cremation, I don't like that either. My hope is to stay around. Freeze me—just on the chance they can bring me back.

It reminds me of that Woody Allen movie—*Sleeper*. This guy goes in for surgery for a peptic ulcer and wakes up two hundred years later after being submerged in a liquid nitrogen tank. The beauty of the scene where he wakes up is the angle at which it was shot. You don't hear the doctors and nurses telling him. It's shot from outside the window. So you only see the doctors and nurses telling him, and him jumping up and down and going crazy.

What would I say if they woke me up two hundred years from now? "Did the Cubs ever win the World Series?" I'm sure I'd get around to "What am I doing here?" Which would make it very much like the rest of my life.

But I really don't have time to dwell on these things. I barely have time to stop and look at the scrapbook of my seventieth birthday party or the picture of me and Sandy Koufax on the street corner with a bunch of kids when we were teenagers. I really don't look back. You know why?

My cell phone is ringing, and it will keep on ringing about twenty times every hour.

Wendy will be on the line to tell me who we've got lined up for tonight.

Patty, my assistant, will have twenty things for me to do.

Irwin is waiting for me to get my bets in with him for the track.

Larry Jr. will have some phone calls for me to make to tell people we're going to pay for their heart operation. Can you believe it? Shawn and Larry arranged with the Cubs for me and the boys to sing "Take Me Out to the Ball Game" during the seventh-inning stretch. How'd he know? All these years and I'd never been to Wrigley Field.

I need to go to the bank. Chance and Cannon just found

out about savings accounts. Chance gave me six dollars to deposit, and when Cannon heard about the wonders of interest he gave me fifty-eight cents to put in his account.

There are so many things to do before I pick up the kids from school.

Then I've got to get to the studio. There's a show to do. Gotta go.

Acknowledgments

There are so many people I would have to acknowledge for helping me along my remarkable journey that a simple list would fill another book.

And I've got to be honest. I've never read an acknowledgments page in my life. So I really don't see the sense in writing one.

But a few people must be singled out.

I must salute Harvey Weinstein, for his enthusiasm, encouragement, and support.

Then there's Michael Viner of Phoenix Books, and the agent David Vigliano, for their wisdom and guidance in setting *My Remarkable Journey* on just the right track.

And publisher Judy Hottensen, Kristin Powers, and everyone else at Weinstein Books, for the great spirit and execution in bringing the book home.

Herb Cohen, Sid Young, and Asher Dan have been friends of Larry Zeiger for life.

While the writer, Cal Fussman, showed me that even at the age of seventy-five you can make a new friend.

And I can't leave out all the fathers who hang out with me at Nate 'n Al Deli. They don't need this book to know the story of my life.

Of course, I have to thank the staff at *Larry King Live*—who I always depend upon. Occasionally, someone will call me boss. That makes me cringe. I just happen to be the host. We all work together.

To everyone else, I will definitely acknowledge you when I see you on the street. If I don't, well, then you wouldn't have been on this page anyway.